FUTURE
English for Results

4

Jane Curtis
with Jeanne Lambert
and Julie Schmidt

Series Consultants
Beatriz B. Díaz
Ronna Magy
Federico Salas-Isnardi

PEARSON
Longman

Future Student Book 4
English for Results

Pearson Education, 10 Bank Street, White Plains, NY 10606

Staff credits: The people who made up the **Future 4** team, representing editorial,
production, design, and manufacturing, are Rhea Banker, Elizabeth Carlson,
Aerin Csigay, Karen Davy, Dave Dickey, Nancy Flaggman, Irene Frankel, Mike Kemper,
Katie Keyes, Linda Moser, Liza Pleva, Sherry Preiss, Barbara Sabella, Loretta Steeves,
Kim Steiner and Marian Wassner.

Cover design: Rhea Banker
Cover art: Si Huynh/Illustration Works/Getty Images
Text design: Elizabeth Carlson
Text composition: Word & Image Design Studio Inc.
Text font: Minion Pro

Library of Congress Cataloging-in-Publication Data

Nishio, Yvonne Wong.
    Future: English for results / Yvonne Wong Nishio ... [et al.].
        p. cm.
    ISBN 978-0-13-240876-9 (student bk. intro)—ISBN 978-0-13-199144-6 (student
bk. 1)—ISBN 978-0-13-199148-4 (student bk. 2)—ISBN 978-0-13-199152-1
(student bk. 3)—ISBN 978-0-13-199156-9 (student bk. 4)—ISBN 978-0-13-240875-2
(student bk. 5)
    1. English language—Textbooks for foreign speakers. I. Title.
    PE1128.N56 2009
    428.0076--dc22

                                                                    2008021069

ISBN-13: 978-0-13199156-9
ISBN 10: 0-13-199156-6

1 2 3 4 5 6 7 8 9 10 – WC – 14 13 12 11 10 09

Contents

Acknowledgments

The author and publisher would like to extend special thanks to our Series Consultants
whose insights, experience, and expertise shaped the course and guided us throughout its development.
Beatriz B. Díaz Miami-Dade County Public Schools, Miami, FL
Ronna Magy Los Angeles Unified School District, Los Angeles, CA
Federico Salas-Isnardi Texas LEARNS, Houston, TX

We would also like to express our gratitude to the following individuals. Their kind assistance was indispensable
to the creation of this program.

Consultants

Wendy J. Allison Seminole Community College, Sanford, FL
Claudia Carco Westchester Community College, Valhalla, NY
Maria J. Cesnik Ysleta Community Learning Center, El Paso, TX
Edwidge Crevecoeur-Bryant University of Florida, Gainesville, FL
Ann Marie Holzknecht Damrau San Diego Community College, San Diego, CA
Peggy Datz Berkeley Adult School, Berkeley, CA
MaryAnn Florez D.C. Learns, Washington, D.C.
Portia LaFerla Torrance Adult School, Torrance, CA
Eileen McKee Westchester Community College, Valhalla, NY
Julie Meuret Downey Adult School, Downey, CA
Sue Pace Santa Ana College School of Continuing Education, Santa Ana, CA
Howard Pomann Union County College, Elizabeth, NJ
Mary Ray Fairfax County Public Schools, Falls Church, VA
Gema Santos Miami-Dade County Public Schools, Miami, FL
Edith Uber Santa Clara Adult Education, Santa Clara, CA
Theresa Warren East Side Adult Education, San Jose, CA

Piloters

MariCarmen Acosta American High School, Adult ESOL, Hialeah, FL
Resurrección Ángeles Metropolitan Skills Center, Los Angeles, CA
Linda Bolognesi Fairfax County Public Schools, Adult and Community Education, Falls Church, VA
Patricia Boquiren Metropolitan Skills Center, Los Angeles, CA
Paul Buczko Pacoima Skills Center, Pacoima, CA
Matthew Horowitz Metropolitan Skills Center, Los Angeles, CA
Gabriel de la Hoz The English Center, Miami, FL
Cam-Tu Huynh Los Angeles Unified School District, Los Angeles, CA
Jorge Islas Whitewater Unified School District, Adult Education, Whitewater, WI
Lisa Johnson City College of San Francisco, San Francisco, CA
Loreto Kaplan Collier County Public Schools Adult ESOL Program, Naples, FL
Teressa Kitchen Collier County Public Schools Adult ESOL Program, Naples, FL
Anjie Martin Whitewater Unified School District, Adult Education, Whitewater, WI
Elida Matthews College of the Mainland, Texas City, TX
Penny Negron College of the Mainland, Texas City, TX
Manuel Pando Coral Park High School, Miami, FL
Susan Ritter Evans Community Adult School, Los Angeles, CA
Susan Ross Torrance Adult School, Torrance, CA
Beatrice Shields Fairfax County Public Schools, Adult and Community Education, Falls Church, VA
Oscar Solís Coral Park High School, Miami, FL
Wanda W. Weaver Literacy Council of Prince George's County, Hyattsville, MD

Reviewers

Lisa Agao Fresno Adult School, Fresno, CA
Carol Antuñano The English Center, Miami, FL
Euphronia Awakuni Evans Community Adult School, Los Angeles, CA
Jack Bailey Santa Barbara Adult Education, Santa Barbara, CA
Robert Breitbard District School Board of Collier County, Naples, FL
Diane Burke Evans Community Adult School, Los Angeles, CA
José A. Carmona Embry-Riddle Aeronautical University, Daytona Beach, FL
Donna Case Bell Community Adult School, Huntington Park, CA
Veronique Colas Los Angeles Technology Center, Los Angles, CA
Carolyn Corrie Metropolitan Skills Center, Los Angeles, CA
Marti Estrin Santa Rosa Junior College, Sebastopol, CA
Sheila Friedman Metropolitan Skills Center, Los Angeles, CA
José Gonzalez Spanish Education Development Center, Washington, D.C.
Allene G. Grognet Vice President (Emeritus), Center for Applied Linguistics
J. Quinn Harmon-Kelley Venice Community Adult School, Los Angeles, CA
Edwina Hoffman Miami-Dade County Public Schools, Coral Gables, FL
Eduardo Honold Far West Project GREAT, El Paso, TX
Leigh Jacoby Los Angeles Community Adult School, Los Angeles, CA
Fayne Johnson Broward County Public Schools, Ft. Lauderdale, FL
Loreto Kaplan, Collier County Public Schools Adult ESOL Program, Naples, FL
Synthia LaFontaine Collier County Public Schools, Naples, FL
Gretchen Lammers-Ghereben Martinez Adult Education, Martinez, CA
Susan Lanzano Editorial Consultant, Briarcliff Manor, NY
Karen Mauer ESL Express, Euless, TX
Rita McSorley North East Independent School District, San Antonio, TX
Alice-Ann Menjivar Carlos Rosario International Public Charter School, Washington, D.C.
Sue Pace Santa Ana College School of Continuing Education, Santa Ana, CA
Isabel Perez American High School, Hialeah, FL
Howard Pomann Union County College, Elizabeth, NJ
Lesly Prudent Miami-Dade County Public Schools, Miami, FL
Valentina Purtell North Orange County Community College District, Anaheim, CA
Barbara Raifsnider San Diego Community College, San Diego, CA
Mary Ray Fairfax County Adult ESOL, Falls Church, VA
Laurie Shapero Miami-Dade Community College, Miami, FL
Felissa Taylor Nause Austin, TX
Meintje Westerbeek Baltimore City Community College, Baltimore, MD

Thanks also to the following contributing authors for the
Persistence Activities and Team Projects.

MaryAnn Florez D.C. Learns, Washington, D.C.
Lisa Johnson City College of San Francisco, San Francisco, CA

About the Series Consultants and Author

SERIES CONSULTANTS

Dr. Beatriz B. Díaz has taught ESL for more than three decades in Miami. She has a master's degree in TESOL and a doctorate in education from Nova Southeastern University. She has given trainings and numerous presentations at international, national, state, and local conferences throughout the United States, the Caribbean, and South America. Dr. Díaz is the district supervisor for the Miami-Dade County Public Schools Adult ESOL Program, one of the largest in the United States.

Ronna Magy has worked as an ESL classroom teacher and teacher-trainer for nearly three decades. Most recently, she has worked as the ESL Teacher Adviser in charge of site-based professional development for the Division of Adult and Career Education of the Los Angeles Unified School District. She has trained teachers of adult English language learners in many areas, including lesson planning, learner persistence and goal setting, and cooperative learning. A frequent presenter at local, state and national, and international conferences, Ms. Magy is the author of adult ESL publications on life skills and test preparation, U.S. citizenship, reading and writing, and workplace English. She holds a master's degree in social welfare from the University of California at Berkeley.

Federico Salas-Isnardi has worked for 20 years in the field of adult education as an ESL and GED instructor, professional development specialist, curriculum writer, and program administrator. He has trained teachers of adult English language learners for over 15 years on topics ranging from language acquisition and communicative competence to classroom management and individualized professional development planning. Mr. Salas-Isnardi has been a contributing writer or consultant for a number of ESL publications, and he has co-authored curriculum for site-based workforce ESL and Spanish classes. He holds a master's degree in applied linguistics from the University of Houston and has completed a number of certificates in educational leadership.

AUTHOR

Jane Curtis began teaching ESOL in Barcelona, Spain. She has been a classroom teacher, materials writer, and teacher trainer for nearly thirty years. Jane currently teaches in the English Language Program at Roosevelt University, where she also serves as special programs coordinator.

Scope and Sequence

UNIT	LISTENING	SPEAKING AND PRONUNCIATION	GRAMMAR	
Pre-Unit **Getting Started** *page 2*	• Listen for personal information	• Give personal information	• Verb tense review	
1 **Catching Up** *page 5*	• Listen to two acquaintances catching up • Listen to a conversation about goals • Listen to a radio show about entrepreneurs	• Talk about yourself and your family • Describe changes in routines • Describe a successful person • Discuss short-term and long-term goals • Talk about people's past experiences • Pronunciation of stressed words in sentences • Reduced pronunciation of *did you*	• Simple present and present continuous • Future with *will, be going to*, and present continuous • Simple past and *used to*	
2 **Tell Me about Yourself** *page 25*	• Listen to a conversation between an employment specialist and a jobseeker • Listen to advice on finding a job • Listen to a job interview	• Talk about work-related goals • Discuss job-related skills and abilities • Talk about your experiences with job-hunting • Talk about job-interview questions • Respond to common interview questions • Describe previous work experience and duties • Pronunciation of silent syllables • Pronunciation of stressed syllables in words	• Infinitives and gerunds • Gerunds as objects of prepositions • Simple past and perfect present	
3 **Community Life** *page 45*	• Listen to a conversation about a festival • Listen to a conversation about community problems • Listen to a conversation about ways to improve a community	• Talk about cultural festivals and traditions • Describe your feelings about your neighborhood • Describe community issues • Talk about community services • Talk about making changes in a community • Discuss ways to improve a community • Pronunciation of unreleased final stop consonants • Weak and blended pronunciation of *to*	• Participial adjectives • *Wish* in the present and future • Verb + Object + Infinitive	
4 **On the Job** *page 65*	• Listen to an on-the-job training session • Listen to medical personnel discussing patients • Listen to an employee's performance review	• Talk about your experiences at a new job • Communicate with supervisors and co-workers • Check your understanding of a situation at work • Ask and answer questions about performance reviews • Give and follow work-related instructions • Stress in phrasal verbs • Pronunciation of auxiliary verbs	• Phrasal verbs • Negative *Yes/No* questions • Indirect instructions, commands, and requests	

LIFE SKILLS	READING	WRITING	PROBLEM SOLVING	PERSISTENCE
	• Scanning for specific information	• Write about classmates		• Orientation to book

• Interpret and complete a school application	• Read about a successful immigrant
	• *Reading Skills:*
	  ◦ Skim for the main idea
	  ◦ Scan for specific information
		• Write sentences about your short-term goals
		• Write a biographical paragraph
		• *Writing Tip:* Put information in chronological order
			• Make suggestions to a friend for how to meet his goal of buying a house	• Community building
				• *Team Project:* Make a Venn diagram about your routines

• Interpret and write a résumé	• Read about some methods of finding a job • Read about job-interview questions • *Reading Skill:* Use details to understand important ideas	• Write sentences about your work-related goals • Write a cover letter • *Writing Tip:* Don't include unnecessary information	• Discuss ways to avoid being late for a job interview	• Planning for learning • *Team Project:* Make a brochure of job-search resources
• Listen for and give information and directions	• Read about a community garden • *Reading Skill:* Make inferences	• Write sentences describing your feelings about your neighborhood • Write a paragraph about your neighborhood • *Writing Tip*: Include details such as examples	• Discuss things a family can do to continue living in a changing community	• Community building • *Team Project:* Make a poster for a community service in your area
• Read an employee handbook	• Read about common workplace injuries • *Reading Skill:* Recognize restatements	• Write instructions for a simple procedure • Write a memo to a supervisor • *Writing Tip*: Use language that is direct and clear in a memo.	• Discuss solutions to problems caused by work schedules	• Planning for learning • *Team Project:* Make an outline for a presentation on how to be a successful team player

Text in red = Civics and American culture

UNIT	LISTENING	SPEAKING AND PRONUNCIATION	GRAMMAR	
5 **Safe and Sound** *page 85*	• Listen to a fire-safety class • Listen to a radio interview with a meteorologist • Listen to a public-service announcement about making a 911 call	• Identify ways to improve fire safety in your home • Discuss what to do in case of fire • Talk about natural disasters • Talk about dangerous weather • Discuss weather reports • Communicate in a 911 emergency • Talk about emergencies • Intonation in sentences with two clauses • Pronunciation of the vowels /i/ and /ɪ/	• Present real conditionals • Adverb clauses of time • Expressing degrees of certainty	
6 **Moving In** *page 105*	• Listen to a conversation about a new apartment • Listen to an expert discuss tenants' rights on a radio talk show • Listen to a conversation about bothersome neighbors	• Identify tenant responsibilities • Talk about landlord responsibilities • Discuss problems with neighbors • Intonation in tag questions • Intonation in exclamations	• Expressing expectation and permission • Tag questions with *be* • Reported speech	
7 **Behind the Wheel** *page 125*	• Listen to a conversation about buying a car • Listen to a radio show host talk about ways to keep vehicles in good working order • Listen to a conversation about a car accident	• Talk about things to consider when buying a car • Describe preferences in cars • Discuss car maintenance and repairs • Describe a car accident • Stress and intonation used to highlight information. • Pronunciation of a pronoun + *'d*	• *Would rather* and *Would prefer* to express preferences • Embedded *Wh-* questions • Embedded *Yes/No* questions • Past perfect	
8 **How Are You Feeling?** *page 145*	• Listen to a conversation between a patient and a doctor • Listen to two 911 calls about medical emergencies • Listen to a public service announcement about children's immunizations	• Communicate with medical personnel • Describe symptoms • Report a medical emergency • Describe ways to reduce health risks • Discuss ways to stay healthy • Beginning consonant clusters • Stress in words ending in *-cal, -ity, -tion, -ize,* and *-ate*	• Present perfect continuous • *Such . . . that* and *So . . . that* • *Should, Ought to, Had better,* and *Must*	

LIFE SKILLS	READING	WRITING	PROBLEM SOLVING	PERSISTENCE
• Read an evacuation map • Understand ways to prepare for a hurricane	• Read about preparing for natural disasters • *Reading Skill:* Identify an author's purpose	• Write suggestions for what to do after a 911 call • Write a plan for an emergency situation • *Writing Tip:* Put the steps of a process in a logical order	• Determine which emergency supplies should be bought first	• Planning for learning • *Team Project:* Make a disaster-readiness poster
• Interpret a lease	• Read about moving trends in the U.S. • *Reading Skill:* Distinguish an author's main ideas from details	• Write a letter of complaint to a landlord • *Writing Tip:* Clearly state the problem and ask for a solution in a complaint letter	Suggest how a person might get to know his or her neighbors better.	• Self-evaluation • *Team Project:* Design a website page for newcomers about renting an apartment
• Read a car insurance renewal notice • Interpret information about buying car insurance	• Read about consumer-protection laws • *Reading Skill:* Use visuals	• Write car-care tips • Write about a good or bad purchase • *Writing Tip:* Use time words and phrases to signal the steps in a process	• Discuss solutions to a problem a driver is having with her car	• Planning for learning • *Team Project:* Design an Internet ad for a used car
• Interpret and complete a medical history form • Interpret and complete a health insurance form	• Read about preventive health practices • *Reading Skill:* Scan a list for details	• Write sentences about advice, suggestions, recommendations, or requirements for good health • Describe a personal experience with health care • *Writing Tip:* Use sensory details to help the reader see, hear, feel, smell, or taste what you are describing	• Give advice for changes that can be made to have a healthier diet	• Community building • *Team Project:* Make a booklet about ways to reduce stress

Text in red = Civics and American culture

UNIT	LISTENING	SPEAKING AND PRONUNCIATION	GRAMMAR	
9 **Partners in Education** *page 165*	• Listen to a conversation between a parent and a guidance counselor • Listen to a parent talking to a secretary about enrolling a child in school • Listen to a school principal talking to a group of parents, teachers, and community leaders	• Communicate with school personnel about a student's progess • Ask about enrolling a child in school • Talk about parents' rights and responsibilities • Talk about after-school programs • Talk about improving schools • Talk about school safety • Contrastive stress • Pronunciation of past modals	• Adverb clauses of reason • Infinitives and adverb clauses of purpose • Adjective clauses • Past modals	
10 **Safety First** *page 185*	• Listen to a conversation between a contractor and a subcontractor • Listen to two co-workers discussing safety on the job • Listen to a manager telling an employee she has been promoted	• Give a progress report • Talk about work requirements • Discuss ways to prevent accidents at work • Make requests, suggestions, and offers at work • Linking a final consonant to a beginning vowel • Pronunciation of the letter *o*	• *Make/let/have/get* + verb • Reflexive pronouns • *Could you / I . . . ? / Why don't I . . . ? / Would you mind . . . ?*	
11 **Know the Law!** *page 205*	• Listen to a conversation about a misdemeanor • Listen to a couple discussing courtroom TV shows • Listen to a talk show about traffic violations	• Identify and discuss misdemeanors • Talk about legal problems • Describe what goes on in a courtroom • Talk about DNA evidence • Discuss traffic laws • Weak pronunciation of *be* • Weak words in sentences	• Past continuous for interrupted action • Passives: present and simple past • Adverb clauses of condition and contrast	
12 **Saving and Spending** *page 225*	• Listen to a conversation between a customer service officer and a bank customer • Listen to a financial expert giving a caller advice on a radio show • Listen to two friends talking about what they would do with a lot of money	• Describe bank services • Talk about opening a business • Talk about your monthly budget • Talk about your dreams for the future • Stress in compound nouns • Pronunciation of *would you*	• Indefinite and definite articles • Future real conditionals • Present unreal conditionals	

LIFE SKILLS	READING	WRITING	PROBLEM SOLVING	PERSISTENCE
• Interpret a report card • Correspond with a teacher	• Read an opinion about after-school programs • *Reading Skill:* Distinguish fact from opinion	• Write a note to a teacher • Write a letter to the editor • *Writing Tip:* Put similar information together in each paragraph	• Discuss ways to improve communication between school and parents	• **Self-efficacy** • *Team Project:* Make a booklet about after-school programs
• Interpret and complete an employee accident report	• Read about workplace safety • *Reading Skill:* Look for words that show chronological order	• Write an e-mail to a supervisor suggesting a solution to a problem • *Writing Tip:* When writing about a problem, identify the problem, explain the cause, and suggest a solution	• Discuss ways for restaurant workers to prevent accidents	• Self-evaluation • *Team Project:* Write a work-related letter and response to an advice column
• Identify people in a courtroom	• Read about DNA evidence • *Reading Skill:* Understand long sentences	• Write a paragraph comparing and contrasting legal rights of accused people in your country and the U.S. • *Writing Tip:* When comparing and contrasting, use words that signal similarities and differences	• Discuss what someone should do when she thinks her car was towed away unfairly	• Self-evaluation • *Team Project:* Make a poster about citizens' rights and responsibilities in the U.S.
• Create a budget • Interpret an income tax form	• Read about someone whose dream of opening a restaurant came true • *Reading Skill:* Write a summary that includes the main idea and the most important information in a text to show that you understand it. • Read about income tax in the U.S.	• Write about a charity that you would support • *Writing Tip:* Focus a paragraph by asking a question and answering it	• Discuss ways a couple can save to buy a house	• Self-efficacy • *Team Project:* Make a poster about a business

Text in red = Civics and American culture

Correlations

UNIT	CASAS Reading Basic Skill Content Standards	CASAS Listening Basic Skill Content Standards	
1	**U1:** 3.2; 3.6; **L2:** 3.3; **L4:** 3.5; 6.1; 6.4; 7.2; **L4:** 3.4; **L5:** 3.3; **L6:** 3.4; **L8:** 3.3; **L9:** 3.3; 4.3; 4.9; **SWYK Review and Expand:** 3.3	**U1:** 2.7; 4.2; **L1:** 4.6; 6.4; **L2:** 3.2; **L3:** 5.8; **L4:** 4.6; **L5:** 3.1; **L7:** 1.5; 4.6; 4.11; **L8:** 3.9; **SWYK Review and Expand:** 4.6; 4.7	
2	**U2:** 3.2; 3.6; **L2:** 3.5; **L3:** 4.7; 4.8; **L4:** 3.2; 3.4; **L5:** 3.3; **L6:** 2.12; 3.5; 6.1; 7.2; 7.2; **L7:** 2.10; 3.3; **L8:** 3.3; **L9:** 3.4; 4.1; 4.3; 4.8; **SWYK Review and Expand:** 3.3	**U2:** 2.7; 4.2; **L1:** 4.2; 4.6; 6.4; **L4:** 4.6; **L7:** 1.6; 4.6; **L8:** 3.9; 3.13; **SWYK Review and Expand:** 4.6; 4.7	
3	**U3:** 3.2; 3.6; **L3:** 3.5; 4.8; 4.9; **L6:** 6.1; 7.2; 7.9; 7.12; **L7:** 7.13; **L8:** 3.3; **L9:** 3.5; 7.12; **SWYK Review and Expand:** 3.3	**U3:** 2.7; 4.2; **L1:** 4.6; 4.7; **L3:** 4.6; 5.5; **L4:** 4.7; **L5:** 3.1; **L7:** 1.5; 4.6; 5.8; **SWYK Review and Expand:** 4.6	
4	**U4:** 3.2; 3.6; **L3:** 3.7; **L5:** 3.5; 3.6; **L6:** 3.5; 7.2; 7.3; **L8:** 3.7; **L9:** 3.4; **SWYK Review and Expand:** 3.3	**U4:** 2.7; 4.2; **L1:** 1.4; 2.8; 4.6; **L2:** 2.3; 3.13; 4.6; **L4:** 1.4; 4.6; **L5:** 3.5; 3.6; **L6:** 2.7; 5.6; 6.8; **L7:** 4.6; 5.6; **L8:** 3.13; **SWYK Review and Expand:** 4.6	
5	**U5:** 3.2; 3.6; **L1:** 3.12; **L2:** 3.4; **L3:** 3.5; 6.1; 6.5; 7.2; 7.11; **L4:** 3.4; **L5:** 3.4; 7.5; **L6:** 4.9; **L9:** 3.5; 7.5; **SWYK Review and Expand:** 3.3	**U5:** 2.7; 4.2; **L1:** 1.7; 4.6; 5.9; **L2:** 3.13; **L4:** 4.6; 4.11; **L7:** 1.1; 4.11; **SWYK Review and Expand:** 4.6; 5.5	
6	**U6:** 3.2; 3.6; **L2:** 3.6; 4.10; **L3:** 4.7; **L6:** 2.12; 3.5; 3.13; 7.2; 7.3; **L8:** 3.5; **L9:** 3.5; 4.3; **SWYK Review and Expand:** 3.3	**U6:** 2.7; 4.2; **L4:** 1.4; 3.14; 4.11; **L5:** 3.5; 3.14; **L7:** 1.7; 4.6; **L8:** 3.8; 3.13; **SWYK Review and Expand:** 4.6	
7	**U7:** 3.2; 3.6; **L2:** 3.5; **L3:** 4.7; **L4:** 3.5; **L6:** 3.5; 3.13; 4.8; 4.9; 4.10; 6.1; **L8:** 7.4; **L9:** 3.3; **SWYK Review and Expand:** 3.3	**U7:** 2.7; 4.2; **L1:** 4.6; **L3:** 4.6; 6.5; **L4:** 1.7; 4.6; 4.11; **L5:** 3.6; 3.14; **L6:** 5.9; **L7:** 2.4; 3.3; 4.6; **L8:** 3.13; **SWYK Review and Expand:** 4.6	
8	**U8:** 3.2; 3.6; **L1:** 3.3; 4.6; 5.5; **L2:** 3.3; **L3:** 4.7; **L5:** 3.4; **L6:** 3.5; 4.10; 6.3; 6.5; 6.6; **L8:** 3.3; 3.5; **L9:** 3.5; 7.1; **SWYK Review and Expand:** 3.3	**U8:** 2.7; 4.2; **L1:** 2.4; 4.6; **L2:** 3.13; 3.64; 4.6; **L4:** 4.11; **L5:** 3.7; **L6:** 5.8; **L7:** 1.6; 4.6; 4.11; **SWYK Review and Expand:** 4.6	
9	**U9:** 3.2; 3.6; **L2:** 3.4; **L3:** 4.5; 4.7; **L4:** 4.6; **L6:** 3.5; 6.1; 7.10; **L8:** 3.3; **L9:** 3.5; **SWYK Review and Expand:** 3.3	**U9:** 2.7; 4.2; **L1:** 1.4; 4.6; **L4:** 4.6; **L6:** 5.9; **L7:** 3.9; 4.6; 5.8; **L8:** 3.9; 4.6; **SWYK Review and Expand:** 4.6	
10	**U10:** 3.2; 3.6; **L2:** 3.1; 3.8; **L3:** 2.12; 3.5; 3.12; 7.5; **L5:** 3.3; **L6:** 4.7; **L8:** 3.3; **L9:** 3.5; **SWYK Review and Expand:** 3.3	**U10:** 2.7; 4.2; **L1:** 4.6; **L2:** 3.1; 3.8; **L3:** 3.11; 5.9; **L4:** 4.6; **L5:** 3.2; **L7:** 4.6; **SWYK Review and Expand:** 4.6	
11	**U11:** 3.2; 3.6; **L1:** 2.1; **L2:** 3.3; **L3:** 3.3; **L5:** 3.3; **L6:** 3.5; 3.9; **L7:** 2.1; **L9:** 3.5; **SWYK Review and Expand:** 3.3	**U11:** 2.7; 4.2; **L1:** 4.6; **L2:** 3.9; 3.13; **L4:** 1.7; 4.6; **L5:** 3.1; 3.9; **L6:** 5.8; **L7:** 1.7; 2.4; 4.6; 4.11; **SWYK Review and Expand:** 4.6	
12	**U12:** 3.2; 3.6; **L1:** 3.3; **L2:** 3.3; **L3:** 3.13; 7.7; **L4:** 4.4; 4.5; 4.8; **L5:** 4.4; **L6:** 3.3; 4.4; 4.7; **L7:** 1.5; **L8:** 3.3; **L9:** 3.4; 4.4; **SWYK Review and Expand:** 4.8	**U12:** 2.7; 4.2; **L1:** 1.4; 2.9; 4.6; **L3:** 5.8; **L4:** 4.11; **L5:** 3.13; 4.6; **L7:** 1.5; 4.6; **L8:** 3.13; **SWYK Review and Expand:** 4.6	

CASAS Competencies	LAUSD ESL High Intermediate Competencies	Florida Adult ESOL Curriculum Standards
U1: 0.1.2; 0.1.5; 0.1.7; 0.2.1; 0.2.4; **L1:** 0.1.8; 0.2.4; **L4:** 7.1.1; 7.1.2; **L5:** 7.1.1; 7.1.2; **L6:** 0.2.2; 4.1.2; **SWYK Review and Expand:** 7.1.1; 7.2.2	**A Course:** 2; 3; 5a; 5b; 7a; 7b; 7c; 7d; 8b; 11b; 42; 44 **B Course:** 1a; 3; 5; 6a; 8a; 8d; 9a; 10b; 35; 37; 40	5.03.02; 5.03.05; 5.03.13
U2: 0.1.2; 0.1.5; 0.1.7; 0.2.1; 0.2.4; **L1:** 4.1.3; 7.1.1; **L2:** 7.1.1; **L3:** 4.1.2; **L4:** 4.13; **L5:** 4.1.2; 4.1.8; **L6:** 4.1.5; **L7:** 4.1.5; 4.1.7; **L8:** 4.1.5; **L9:** 4.1.2; **SWYK Review and Expand:** 4.1.3; 4.1.5	**A Course:** 1b; 4b; 5a; 5b; 7a; 7b; 7c; 7d; 8b; 34, 36, 37, 42, 44 **B Course:** 4; 5; 6a; 6c; 8a; 8d; 29; 30; 31a; 31b; 31c; 37; 40	5.03.02; 5.03.03; 5.03.04
U3: 0.1.2; 0.1.5; 0.1.7; 0.2.1; 0.2.4; **L1:** 2.7.9; **L2:** 0.1.8; **L3:** 2.2.1; 2.2.5; 2.5.9; **L4:** 2.5.8; 2.8.9; **L5:** 2.8.9; **L6:** 2.6.1; 2.8.9; **L7:** 2.8.9; 5.1.6; 5.1.7; **L8:** 5.1.6; 5.1.7; **SWYK Review and Expand:** 2.6.3	**A Course:** 5a; 5b; 6; 7a; 7b; 7c; 7d; 8b; 8c; 16a; 42; 44; 45 **B Course:** 5; 6a; 6c; 7; 8a; 8d; 9b; 12; 37; 40; 41b	5.02.02; 5.02.03
U4: 0.1.2; 0.1.5; 0.1.7; 0.2.1; 0.2.4; **L1:** 0.1.6; 4.6.1; 4.8.1; 4.8.2; **L2:** 4.6.1; 4.8.1; 4.8.2; **L3:** 4.2.4; 4.2.5; **L4:** 4.8.1; 4.8.2; **L5:** 4.8.1; 4.8.2; **L6:** 4.3.2; **L7:** 4.4.1; 4.4.4; **L8:** 4.6.1; 4.6.5; **L9:** 4.6.2; 4.6.5; **SWYK Review and Expand:** 4.2.4; 4.6.1; 4.8.1; 4.8.2	**A Course:** 5a; 5b; 7a; 7b; 7c; 7d; 8b; 38a; 38b; 38c; 39c; 40b; 41; 42; 44 **B Course:** 4; 5; 6a; 6c; 8a; 8d; 32; 33a; 33b; 34a; 37; 40	5.03.06; 5.03.07; 5.03.11
U5: 0.1.2; 0.1.5; 0.1.7; 0.2.1; 0.2.4; **L1:** 0.1.3; 3.4.2; **L2:** 2.5.1; **L3:** 3.4.8; **L4:** 2.3.3; 3.4.8; **L5:** 2.3.3; **L6:** 3.4.8; **L7:** 2.5.1; **L8:** 2.5.1; **L9:** 3.4.8; **SWYK Review and Expand:** 2.5.1; 3.4.8	**A Course:** 5a; 5b; 7a; 7b; 7c; 7d; 8b; 12; 32; 42; 44 **B Course:** 5; 6a; 6c; 8c; 8d; 28; 37; 40	5.02.05
U6: 0.1.2; 0.1.5; 0.1.7; 0.2.1; 0.2.4; **L1:** 1.4.6; 1.4.7; **L2:** 1.4.5; **L3:** 1.4.3; **L4:** 1.4.5; **L5:** 1.4.5; **L7:** 0.1.3; 0.1.8; 7.3.1; 7.3.2; **L8:** 0.1.3; 0.1.8; 7.3.1; 7.3.2; **L9:** 1.4.7; **SWYK Review and Expand:** 1.4.7	**A Course:** 5a; 5b; 7a; 7b; 7c;7d; 23; 24; 42; 44 **B Course:** 5; 6a; 6c; 8a; 8d; 20; 37; 40; 41b	5.04.04; 5.04.05
U7: 0.1.2; 0.1.5; 0.1.7; 0.2.1; 0.2.4; **L1:** 1.9.5; **L2:** 1.9.5; **L3:** 1.9.5; 1.9.8; **L4:** 1.9.6; **L5:** 1.9.6; **L6:** 1.6.3; **L7:** 1.9.7; 1.9.9; **L8:** 1.9.7; **SWYK Review and Expand:** 0.1.8; 1.9.6; 1.9.7	**A Course:** 5a; 5b; 7a; 7b; 7c; 7d; 8b; 25b; 42; 44; 45 **B Course:** 5; 6a; 8a; 8d; 14; 15; 16; 24a; 37; 40	5.06.04
U8: 0.1.2; 0.1.5; 0.1.7; 0.2.1; 0.2.4; **L1:** 0.18; 3.1.3; 3.2.1; 3.3.1; 3.6.4; **L3:** 3.1.6; **L4:** 2.1.2; 2.5.1; **L5:** 3.5.9; **L6:** 3.5.9; **L7:** 3.1.3; 3.4.6; **L8:** 3.5.2; 3.5.9; **L9:** 2.7.9; **SWYK Review and Expand:** 3.5.2	**A Course:** 3; 5a; 5b; 7a; 7b; 7c; 7d; 28; 30a; 30b; 30c; 44; 45 **B Course:** 3;5; 6a; 6c; 8a; 8d; 26; 27; 37; 38b; 40	5.05.01; 5.05.03
U9: 0.1.2; 0.1.5; 0.1.7; 0.2.1; 0.2.4; **L1:** 2.8.6; **L2:** 2.8.9; **L3:** 0.2.3; 2.8.4; 2.8.6; 2.8.8; **L4:** 2.8.3; 2.8.6; **L5:** 2.8.8; 2.8.9; **L6:** 2.5.9; 2.8.3; **L7:** 2.8.6; **L8:** 2.8.6; **L9:** 2.8.6; 2.8.8; **SWYK Review and Expand:** 2.8.6; 2.8.8; 2.8.9	**A Course:** 5a; 5b; 7a; 7b; 7c; 7d; 8a; 8b; 10b; 11a; 44 **B Course:** 4; 5; 6a; 6b; 6c; 8a; 8d; 10a; 11; 37; 40	5.02.07; 5.02.08
U10: 0.1.2; 0.1.5; 0.1.7; 0.2.1; 0.2.4; **L1:** 4.6.1; 4.6.4; 4.6.5; **L2:** 4.4.6; 4.6.1; **L3:** 4.3.1; 4.3.2; **L4:** 4.3.3; 4.5.1; 4.5.7; **L5:** 4.3.2; 4.3.3; 4.3.4; **L6:** 4.3.4; **L7:** 4.4.2; **L8:** 0.1.3; 4.6.1; 4.6.5; **L9:** 4.6.2; **SWYK Review and Expand:** 4.3; 4.4	**A Course:** 3; 5a; 5b; 7a; 7b; 7c; 7d; 8b; 32; 33; 38a; 38b; 38c; 39a; 39b; 40c; 44 **B Course:** 3; 5; 6a; 6b; 6c; 8a; 8d; 32; 33a; 34b; 37; 40	5.03.05; 5.03.06; 5.03.07; 5.03.08; 5.03.14; 5.03.15
U11: 0.1.2; 0.1.5; 0.1.7; 0.2.1; 0.2.4; **L1:** 5.3.1; 5.3.7; **L2:** 5.3.1; 5.3.2; **L3:** 5.3.3; **L4:** 5.3.3; **L5:** 5.3.3; **L6:** 5.73; **L7:** 1.9.1; 1.9.2; 5.3.1; **L8:** 1.9.2; 5.3.1; 5.3.7; **L9:** 2.7.9; 5.3.2; **SWYK Review and Expand:** 5.3.1; 5.3.2; 5.3.7	**A Course:** 5a; 5b; 7a; 7b; 7c; 7d; 8b; 25b; 44 **B Course:** 5; 6a; 6b; 6c; 7; 8a; 8d; 23a; 37; 40	05.02.04; 05.07.02
U12: 0.1.2; 0.1.5; 0.1.7; 0.2.1; 0.2.4; **L1:** 1.8.1; 1.8.3; **L2:** 1.8.1; 1.8.3; 1.8.4; **L3:** 5.4.5; **L4:** 1.5.1; 1.5.2; **L5:** 1.5.1; **L6:** 5.4.1; **L8:** 7.1.2; **L9:** 5.7.6; **SWYK Review and Expand:** 1.5.1; 7.3.1	**A Course:** 5a; 5b; 7a; 8b; 7c **B Course:** 5; 6a; 6c; 8a; 8d; 9b; 19	5.04.07; 5.04.08

All units of *Future* meet most of the EFF **Content Standards**. For details, as well as for correlations to other state standards, go to www.pearsonlongman.com/future.

To the Teacher

Welcome to *Future*
English for Results

Future is a six-level, four-skills course for adults and young adults correlated to state and national standards. It incorporates research-based teaching strategies, corpus-informed language, and the best of modern technology.

KEY FEATURES

Future provides everything your students need in one integrated program.

In developing the course, we listened to what teachers asked for and we responded, providing six levels, more meaningful content, a thorough treatment of grammar, explicit skills development, abundant practice, multiple options for state-of-the-art assessment, and innovative components.

Future serves students' real-life needs.

We began constructing the instructional syllabus for *Future* by identifying what is most critical to students' success in their personal and family lives, in the workplace, as members of a community, and in their academic pursuits. *Future* provides outstanding coverage of life skills competencies, basing language teaching on actual situations that students are likely to encounter and equipping them with the skills they need to achieve their goals. The grammar and other language elements taught in each lesson grow out of these situations and are thus practiced in realistic contexts, enabling students to use language meaningfully, from the beginning.

Future grows with your students.

Future takes students from absolute beginner level through low-advanced proficiency in English, addressing students' abilities and learning priorities at each level. As the levels progress, the curricular content and unit structure change accordingly, with the upper levels incorporating more academic skills, more advanced content standards, and more content-rich texts.

Level	Description	CASAS Scale Scores
Intro	True Beginning	Below 180
1	Low Beginning	181–190
2	High Beginning	191–200
3	Low Intermediate	201–210
4	High Intermediate	211–220
5	Low Advanced	221–235

Future is fun!

Many of the conversations and other listenings texts are designed to be amusing or interesting—something to anticipate with pleasure and to then take great satisfaction in once it is understood. In addition, many activities have students interacting in pairs and groups. Not only does this make classroom time more enjoyable, it also creates an atmosphere conducive to learning in which learners are relaxed, highly motivated, and at their most receptive.

Future puts the best of 21st-century technology in the hands of students and teachers.

In addition to its expertly developed print materials and audio components, *Future* goes a step further.

- Every **Student Book comes with a Practice Plus CD-ROM** for use at home, in the lab, or wherever students have access to a computer. The Practice Plus CD-ROM can be used both by students who wish to extend their practice beyond the classroom and by those who need to "make up" what they missed in class.
- The **CD-ROM** also includes the entire class audio program as MP3 files so students can get extra listening practice at their convenience.
- The **Tests and Test Prep** book comes with the *Future Exam View® Assessment Suite*, enabling teachers to print ready-made tests, customize these tests, or create their own tests for life skills, grammar, listening, and reading.
- The **Teacher Training DVD** provides demo lessons of real teachers using *Future* with their classes. Teachers can select from the menu and watch a specific type of lesson, such as a grammar presentation, or a specific type of activity, such as a role-play activity, at their own convenience.
- The **Companion Website** provides a variety of teaching support, including a pdf of the Teacher's Edition and Lesson Planner notes for each unit in the Student Book.

Future provides all the assessment tools you need.

- The **Placement Test** evaluates students' proficiency in all skill areas, allowing teachers and program administrators to easily assign students to the right classes.
- The **Tests and Test Prep** book for each level provides:
  - **Printed unit tests** with accompanying audio CD. These unit tests use standardized testing formats, giving students practice "bubbling-in" responses as required for CASAS and other standardized tests. In addition, reproducible test prep worksheets and practice tests provide invaluable help to students unfamiliar with such test formats.

- The *Future* **Exam**View® *Assessment Suite* is a powerful program that allows teachers to create their own unique tests or to print or customize already prepared tests.
- **Performance-based assessment:** Lessons in the Student Book end with a "practical assessment" activity such as Role Play, Make It Personal, or Show What You Know. Each unit culminates with both a role-play activity and a problem-solving activity, which require students to demonstrate their oral competence in a holistic way. The **Teacher's Edition and Lesson Planner** provides speaking rubrics to make it easy for teachers to evaluate students' oral proficiency.
- **Self-assessment:** For optimal learning to take place, students need to be involved in setting goals and in monitoring their own progress. *Future* has addressed this in numerous ways. In the Student Book, checkboxes at the end of lessons invite students to evaluate their mastery of the material. End-of-unit reviews allow students to see their progress in grammar. And after completing each unit, students go back to the goals for the unit and reflect on their achievement. In addition, the CD-ROM provides students with continuous feedback (and opportunities for self-correction) as they work through each lesson, and the Workbook contains the answer keys, so students can check their own work outside of class.

Future addresses multilevel classes and diverse learning styles.

Using research-based teaching strategies, *Future* provides teachers with creative solutions for all stages of lesson planning and implementation, allowing them to meet the needs of all their students.

- The **Teacher's Edition and Lesson Planner** offers pre-level and above-level variations for every lesson plan as well as numerous optional and extension activities designed to reach students at all levels.
- The **Practice Plus CD-ROM** included with the Student Book is an extraordinary tool for individualizing instruction. It allows students to direct their own learning, working on precisely what they need and practicing what they choose to work on as many times as they like. In addition, the CD-ROM provides all the audio files for the book, enabling students to listen as they wish to any of the material that accompanies the text.
- The **Workbook**, similarly, allows students to devote their time to the lessons and specific skill areas that they need to work on most.
- The **Tests and Test Prep** book, as noted on page xiv, includes *Future* **Exam**View® *Assessment Suite*, which allows teachers to customize existing tests or create their own tests using the databank.

Future's persistence curriculum motivates students to continue their education.

Recent research about persistence has given us insights into how to keep students coming to class and how to keep them learning when they can't attend. Recognizing that there are many forces operating in students' lives—family, jobs, childcare, health—that may make it difficult for them to come to class, programs need to help students:

- Identify their educational goals
- Believe that they can successfully achieve them
- Develop a commitment to their own education
- Identify forces that can interfere with school attendance
- Develop strategies that will help them try to stay in school in spite of obstacles
- Find ways to continue learning even during "stopping out" periods

Future addresses all of these areas with its persistence curriculum. Activities found throughout the book and specific persistence activities in the back of the book help students build community, set goals, develop better study skills, and feel a sense of achievement. In addition, the Practice Plus CD-ROM is unique in its ability to ensure that even those students unable to attend class are able to make up what they missed and thus persist in their studies.

Future supports busy teachers by providing all the materials teachers need, plus teacher support.

The **Student Book** and **Workbook** were designed to provide teachers with everything they need in the way of ready-to-use classroom materials so they can concentrate on responding to their students' needs. The **Future Teacher Training DVD** gives teachers tips and models for conducting various activity types in their classroom.

Future provides ample practice, with flexible options to best fit the needs of each class.

The Student Book provides 60–100 hours of instruction. It can be supplemented in class by using:

- Teacher's Edition and Lesson Planner expansion ideas
- Workbook exercises
- Tests
- CD-ROM activities
- Activities on the Companion Website (longmanusa.com/Future)

TEACHING MULTILEVEL CLASSES

Teaching tips for pair and group work

Using pair and group work in an ESL classroom has many proven benefits. It creates an atmosphere of liveliness, builds community, and allows students to practice speaking in a low-risk environment. Many of the activities in *Future* are pair and small-group activities. Here are some tips for managing these activities:

- Limit small groups to three or four students per group (unless an activity specifically calls for larger groups). This maximizes student participation.
- Change partners for different activities. This gives students a chance to work with many others in the class and keeps them from feeling "stuck."
- If possible, give students a place to put their coats when they enter the classroom. This allows them to move around freely without worrying about returning to their own seats.
- Move around the classroom as students are working to make sure they are on task and to monitor their work.
- As you walk around, try to remain unobtrusive, so students continue to participate actively, without feeling they are being evaluated.
- Keep track of language points students are having difficulty with. After the activity, teach a mini-lesson to the entire class addressing those issues. This helps students who are having trouble without singling them out.

Pairs and groups in the multilevel classroom

Adult education ESL classrooms are by nature multilevel. This is true even if students have been given a placement test. Many factors—including a student's age, educational background, and literacy level—contribute to his or her ability level. Also, the same student may be at level in one skill, but pre-level or above-level in another.

When grouping students for a task, keep the following points in mind:

- *Like-ability* groups (in which students have the same ability level) help ensure that all students participate equally, without one student dominating the activity.
- *Cross-ability* groups (in which students have different ability levels) are beneficial to pre-level students who need the support of their at- or above-level classmates. The higher-level students benefit from "teaching" their lower-level classmates.

For example, when students are practicing a straightforward conversation substitution exercise, like-ability pairings are helpful. The activity can be tailored to different ability levels, and both students can participate equally. When students are completing the more complex task of creating their own conversations, cross-ability pairings are helpful. The higher-level student can support and give ideas to the lower-level student.

The *Future* Teacher's Edition and Lesson Planner provide specific suggestions for when to put students in like-ability versus cross-ability groups, and how to tailor activities to different ability levels.

Unit Tour

Unit Opener

Each unit starts with a full-page photo that introduces the themes and vocabulary of the unit.

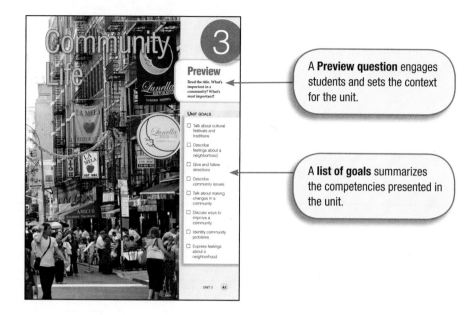

A **Preview question** engages students and sets the context for the unit.

A **list of goals** summarizes the competencies presented in the unit.

Listening and Speaking

Three listening lessons present the core competencies and language of the unit.

Before You Listen activities introduce new language and cultural concepts.

Listening comprehension questions focus first on topic or main idea and then on specific information.

The **Pronunciation Watch** and pronunciation exercises focus on the sound patterns, stress, and intonation of English.

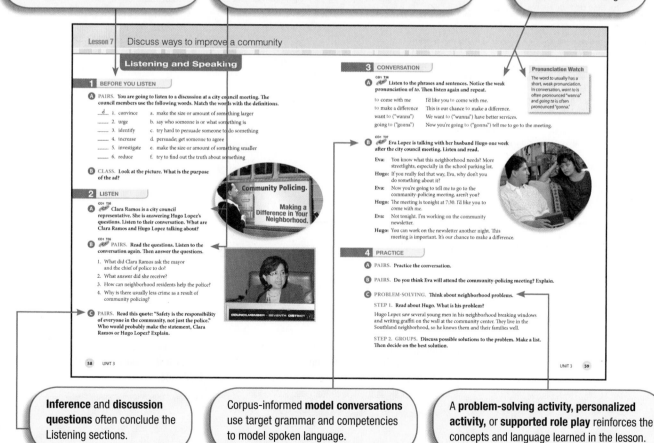

Inference and **discussion questions** often conclude the Listening sections.

Corpus-informed **model conversations** use target grammar and competencies to model spoken language.

A **problem-solving activity, personalized activity,** or **supported role play** reinforces the concepts and language learned in the lesson.

Grammar

Each unit presents three grammar points in a logical, systematic grammar syllabus.

Grammar charts clearly present the target grammar.

Grammar Watch notes call attention to specific aspects of the grammar point.

Contextualized **grammar practice** progresses from controlled to open-ended exercises.

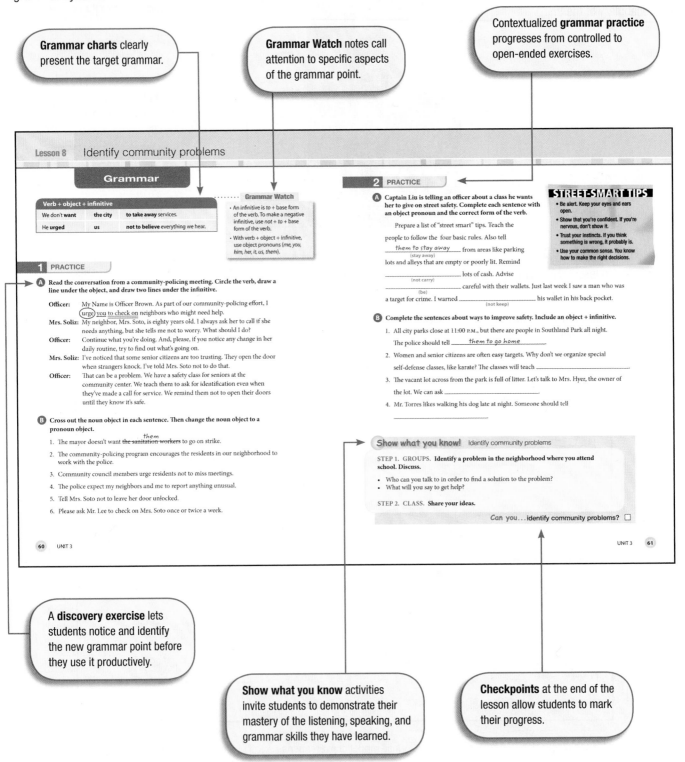

Lesson 8 Identify community problems

Grammar

Verb + object + infinitive

| We don't **want** | **the city** | **to take away** services. |
| We **urged** | **us** | **not to believe** everything we hear. |

Grammar Watch
- An infinitive is *to* + base form of the verb. To make a negative infinitive, use *not* + *to* + base form of the verb.
- With verb + object + infinitive, use object pronouns (*me, you, him, her, it, us, them*).

1 PRACTICE

A Read the conversation from a community-policing meeting. Circle the verb, draw a line under the object, and draw two lines under the infinitive.

Officer: My Name is Officer Brown. As part of our community-policing effort, I urge you to check on neighbors who might need help.

Mrs. Soliz: My neighbor, Mrs. Soto, is eighty years old. I always ask her to call if she needs anything, but she tells me not to worry. What should I do?

Officer: Continue what you're doing. And, please, if you notice any change in her daily routine, try to find out what's going on.

Mrs. Soliz: I've noticed that some senior citizens are too trusting. They open the door when strangers knock. I've told Mrs. Soto not to do that.

Officer: That can be a problem. We have a safety class for seniors at the community center. We teach them to ask for identification even when they've made a call for service. We remind them not to open their doors until they know it's safe.

B Cross out the noun object in each sentence. Then change the noun object to a pronoun object.

1. The mayor doesn't want the sanitation workers to go on strike. *them*
2. The community-policing program encourages the residents in our neighborhood to work with the police.
3. Community council members urge residents not to miss meetings.
4. The police expect my neighbors and me to report anything unusual.
5. Tell Mrs. Soto not to leave her door unlocked.
6. Please ask Mr. Lee to check on Mrs. Soto once or twice a week.

60 UNIT 3

2 PRACTICE

A Captain Liu is telling an officer about a class he wants her to give on street safety. Complete each sentence with an object pronoun and the correct form of the verb.

Prepare a list of "street smart" tips. Teach the people to follow the four basic rules. Also tell ____them to stay away____ from areas like parking (stay away) lots and alleys that are empty or poorly lit. Remind _____ lots of cash. Advise (not carry) _____ careful with their wallets. Just last week I saw a man who was (be) a target for crime. I warned _____ his wallet in his back pocket. (not keep)

STREET-SMART TIPS
- Be alert. Keep your eyes and ears open.
- Show that you're confident. If you're nervous, don't show it.
- Trust your instincts. If you think something is wrong, it probably is.
- Use your common sense. You know how to make the right decisions.

B Complete the sentences about ways to improve safety. Include an object + infinitive.

1. All city parks close at 11:00 P.M., but there are people in Southland Park all night. The police should tell ____them to go home____
2. Women and senior citizens are often easy targets. Why don't we organize special self-defense classes, like karate? The classes will teach _____
3. The vacant lot across from the park is full of litter. Let's talk to Mrs. Hyer, the owner of the lot. We can ask _____
4. Mr. Torres likes walking his dog late at night. Someone should tell _____

Show what you know! Identify community problems

STEP 1. GROUPS. **Identify a problem in the neighborhood where you attend school. Discuss.**

- Who can you talk to in order to find a solution to the problem?
- What will you say to get help?

STEP 2. CLASS. **Share your ideas.**

Can you... identify community problems? ☐

UNIT 3 61

A **discovery exercise** lets students notice and identify the new grammar point before they use it productively.

Show what you know activities invite students to demonstrate their mastery of the listening, speaking, and grammar skills they have learned.

Checkpoints at the end of the lesson allow students to mark their progress.

Reading

High-interest articles introduce students to cultural concepts and useful, topical information. Students read to learn while learning to read in English.

Before You Read exercises activate students' background knowledge and build other pre-reading skills.

Comprehension questions check understanding of the article and build reading skills.

Essential **reading skills**, such as making inferences, are explicitly taught and practiced.

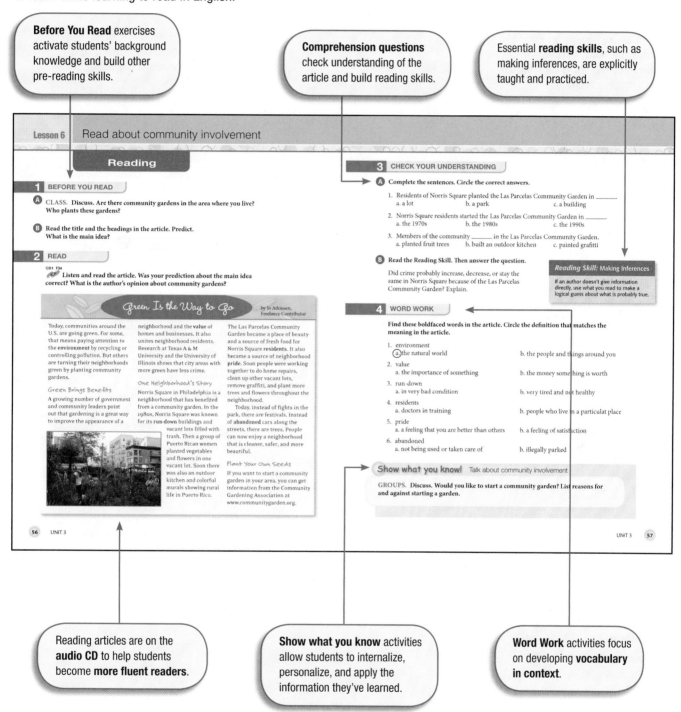

Reading articles are on the **audio CD** to help students become **more fluent readers**.

Show what you know activities allow students to internalize, personalize, and apply the information they've learned.

Word Work activities focus on developing **vocabulary in context**.

Life Skills

The Life Skills lesson in each unit focuses on functional language, practical skills, and authentic printed materials, such as schedules, maps, labels, and signs.

> **Civics, life skills,** and **cultural information** related to life in the U.S. are introduced in context.

> **Study skills,** such as map-reading skills, are introduced and practiced in real-life contexts.

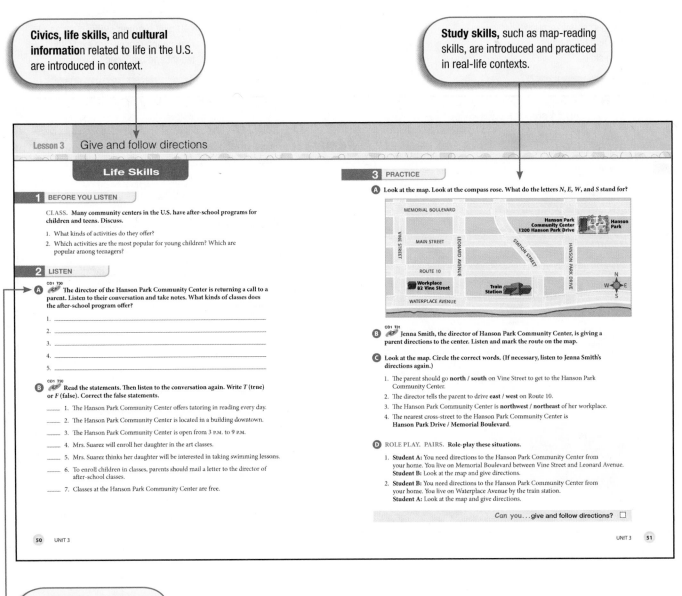

Lesson 3   Give and follow directions

Life Skills

1 BEFORE YOU LISTEN

CLASS. Many community centers in the U.S. have after-school programs for children and teens. Discuss.

1. What kinds of activities do they offer?
2. Which activities are the most popular for young children? Which are popular among teenagers?

2 LISTEN

A CD1 T30 The director of the Hanson Park Community Center is returning a call to a parent. Listen to their conversation and take notes. What kinds of classes does the after-school program offer?

1. _____
2. _____
3. _____
4. _____
5. _____

B CD1 T30 Read the statements. Then listen to the conversation again. Write *T* (true) or *F* (false). Correct the false statements.

_____ 1. The Hanson Park Community Center offers tutoring in reading every day.

_____ 2. The Hanson Park Community Center is located in a building downtown.

_____ 3. The Hanson Park Community Center is open from 3 P.M. to 9 P.M.

_____ 4. Mrs. Suarez will enroll her daughter in the art classes.

_____ 5. Mrs. Suarez thinks her daughter will be interested in taking swimming lessons.

_____ 6. To enroll children in classes, parents should mail a letter to the director of after-school classes.

_____ 7. Classes at the Hanson Park Community Center are free.

3 PRACTICE

A Look at the map. Look at the compass rose. What do the letters *N, E, W,* and *S* stand for?

B CD1 T31 Jenna Smith, the director of Hanson Park Community Center, is giving a parent directions to the center. Listen and mark the route on the map.

C Look at the map. Circle the correct words. (If necessary, listen to Jenna Smith's directions again.)

1. The parent should go **north / south** on Vine Street to get to the Hanson Park Community Center.
2. The director tells the parent to drive **east / west** on Route 10.
3. The Hanson Park Community Center is **northwest / northeast** of her workplace.
4. The nearest cross-street to the Hanson Park Community Center is **Hanson Park Drive / Memorial Boulevard**.

D ROLE PLAY. PAIRS. Role-play these situations.

1. **Student A:** You need directions to the Hanson Park Community Center from your home. You live on Memorial Boulevard between Vine Street and Leonard Avenue. **Student B:** Look at the map and give directions.
2. **Student B:** You need directions to the Hanson Park Community Center from your home. You live on Waterplace Avenue by the train station. **Student A:** Look at the map and give directions.

Can you...give and follow directions? ☐

> Meaningful practice mirrors **real-life tasks**.

Writing

Writing instruction is process-based, leading students to write well-organized paragraphs about familiar topics.

Before You Write activities **stimulate thinking** about the topic and provide a student **model paragraph** for the assignment.

Thinking on Paper presents pre-writing strategies and graphic organizers that students can use to plan their writing.

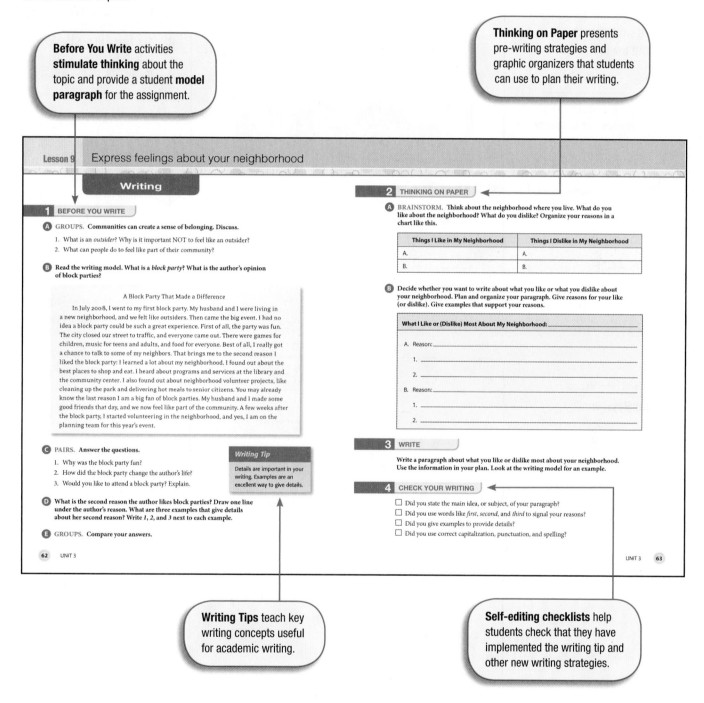

Lesson 9 Express feelings about your neighborhood

Writing

1 BEFORE YOU WRITE

A GROUPS. Communities can create a sense of belonging. Discuss.

1. What is an *outsider*? Why is it important NOT to feel like an outsider?
2. What can people do to feel like part of their community?

B Read the writing model. What is a *block party*? What is the author's opinion of block parties?

> A Block Party That Made a Difference
>
> In July 2008, I went to my first block party. My husband and I were living in a new neighborhood, and we felt like outsiders. Then came the big event. I had no idea a block party could be such a great experience. First of all, the party was fun. The city closed our street to traffic, and everyone came out. There were games for children, music for teens and adults, and food for everyone. Best of all, I really got a chance to talk to some of my neighbors. That brings me to the second reason I liked the block party: I learned a lot about my neighborhood. I found out about the best places to shop and eat. I heard about programs and services at the library and the community center. I also found out about neighborhood volunteer projects, like cleaning up the park and delivering hot meals to senior citizens. You may already know the last reason I am a big fan of block parties. My husband and I made some good friends that day, and we now feel like part of the community. A few weeks after the block party, I started volunteering in the neighborhood, and yes, I am on the planning team for this year's event.

C PAIRS. Answer the questions.

1. Why was the block party fun?
2. How did the block party change the author's life?
3. Would you like to attend a block party? Explain.

Writing Tip

Details are important in your writing. Examples are an excellent way to give details.

D What is the second reason the author likes block parties? Draw one line under the author's reason. What are three examples that give details about her second reason? Write *1*, *2*, and *3* next to each example.

E GROUPS. Compare your answers.

62 UNIT 3

2 THINKING ON PAPER

A BRAINSTORM. Think about the neighborhood where you live. What do you like about the neighborhood? What do you dislike? Organize your reasons in a chart like this.

Things I Like in My Neighborhood	Things I Dislike in My Neighborhood
A.	A.
B.	B.

B Decide whether you want to write about what you like or what you dislike about your neighborhood. Plan and organize your paragraph. Give reasons for your like (or dislike). Give examples that support your reasons.

What I Like or (Dislike) Most About My Neighborhood: _____
A. Reason: _____   1. _____   2. _____   B. Reason: _____   1. _____   2. _____

3 WRITE

Write a paragraph about what you like or dislike most about your neighborhood. Use the information in your plan. Look at the writing model for an example.

4 CHECK YOUR WRITING

- [ ] Did you state the main idea, or subject, of your paragraph?
- [ ] Did you use words like *first*, *second*, and *third* to signal your reasons?
- [ ] Did you give examples to provide details?
- [ ] Did you use correct capitalization, punctuation, and spelling?

UNIT 3 63

Writing Tips teach key writing concepts useful for academic writing.

Self-editing checklists help students check that they have implemented the writing tip and other new writing strategies.

Review & Expand

The final page of the unit allows students to review and expand on the language, themes, and competencies they have worked with throughout the unit.

> Cross-references direct students to the **Grammar Review, Persistence Activity,** and **Team Project** for that unit.

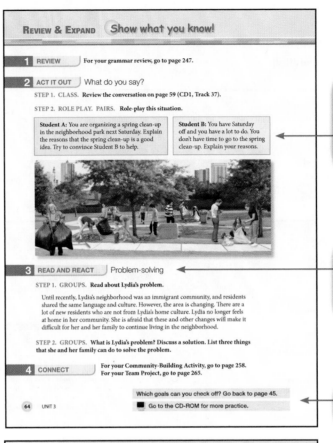

REVIEW & EXPAND Show what you know!

1 REVIEW For your grammar review, go to page 247.

2 ACT IT OUT What do you say?

STEP 1. CLASS. Review the conversation on page 59 (CD1, Track 37).

STEP 2. ROLE PLAY. PAIRS. Role-play this situation.

Student A: You are organizing a spring clean-up in the neighborhood park next Saturday. Explain the reasons that the spring clean-up is a good idea. Try to convince Student B to help.

Student B: You have Saturday off and you have a lot to do. You don't have time to go to the spring clean-up. Explain your reasons.

3 READ AND REACT Problem-solving

STEP 1. GROUPS. Read about Lydia's problem.

Until recently, Lydia's neighborhood was an immigrant community, and residents shared the same language and culture. However, the area is changing. There are a lot of new residents who are not from Lydia's home culture. Lydia no longer feels at home in her community. She is afraid that these and other changes will make it difficult for her and her family to continue living in the neighborhood.

STEP 2. GROUPS. What is Lydia's problem? Discuss a solution. List three things that she and her family can do to solve the problem.

4 CONNECT For your Community-Building Activity, go to page 258.
For your Team Project, go to page 265.

Which goals can you check off? Go back to page 45.
Go to the CD-ROM for more practice.

64 UNIT 3

> Lively **Role-Play** activities motivate students, allowing them to feel successful. Teachers can use these activities to assess students' mastery of the material.

> **Problem-solving** tasks encourage critical thinking and allow students to demonstrate understanding of topics.

> **Checkpoints** allow students to see the unit goals they have accomplished.

Grammar Review

Grammar Review allows students to check their mastery of the unit grammar.

UNIT 5

A Combine the two clauses to make a conditional sentence. Keep the clauses in the same order and add *if* to one clause. Include a comma if necessary.

1. a person is badly injured / don't move him or her
   If a person is badly injured, don't move him or her.

2. you don't have a smoke detector / you need to get one
   _____

3. get under a piece of furniture / there's an earthquake
   _____

4. you are prepared for a fire / you have a better chance of surviving it
   _____

5. call 911 / there's an emergency
   _____

B Complete the sentences. Circle the correct adverb.

1. You should check the weather frequently **until / when** there's a severe weather watch.
2. **Until / As soon as** we felt the earth shake, we got under the table.
3. They didn't know about the hurricane **as soon as / before** they saw the weather report.
4. **After / Before** the storm started, everyone stayed inside.
5. Stay on the phone with the 911 operator **until / after** he tells you to hang up.

C Complete the sentences. Circle the correct answer.

1. I see smoke. There _____ be a fire somewhere.
   a. may   b. must   c. can't
2. In an emergency, some people _____ be very nervous.
   a. couldn't   b. might   c. must not
3. It _____ rain today. I didn't see the weather report, so I'm not sure.
   a. could   b. must   c. couldn't
4. Jane is allergic to milk, but she didn't have an allergic reaction after she ate that cookie. The cookie _____ have milk in it.
   a. may not   b. might not   c. must not
5. There's a hurricane watch for this area. The storm _____ affect us.
   a. may   b. must not   c. couldn't

GRAMMAR REVIEW **249**

Persistence Activities

Persistence activities build community in the classroom, help students set personal and language goals, and encourage students to develop good study skills and habits.

> Controlled activities provide scaffolding for the **real-life application activities** that follow.

Unit 9   Then and Now

A Think about how a pre-school child learns to speak a language, whether it is English or a native language. Then think of how you, as an adult, are learning English. Complete the chart below.

	Learning as a child	Learning as an adult
What strategies do children or adults use to learn a language? By imitating? By listening to an audio? By reading?		
Where do children or adults learn a language? At home? At school? In the playground?		
What do children or adults learn when learning a language? Vocabulary? Conversation? Grammar?		
From your observation, who is the faster learner, a child or an adult?		
In your opinion, what is the best way for children or adults to learn a language?		

B PAIRS. Share your answers to Exercise A. How do you feel about learning English as an adult?

Unit 10   How Students Learn Best

A Think of how you've been learning English. Check (✓) five types of activities you liked best.

- ☐ working alone
- ☐ working in pairs
- ☐ working in groups
- ☐ reading activities
- ☐ conversations
- ☐ grammar activities
- ☐ listening activities
- ☐ writing activities
- ☐ vocabulary activities
- ☐ using life skills materials (maps, graphs, forms, etc.)
- ☐ Other: _____

B Look at the activities you checked. What did you like about them? How did they help you learn English?

C PAIRS. Talk about other activities in the book. Which activities didn't you like? Why?

D GROUPS. Compare your answers to Exercises A, B, and C. What are some similarities in the ways you prefer to learn English? Make a list of activities that help students learn effectively.

E CLASS. Present your list to the class. Explain why these activities help students learn. Also discuss the activities that you didn't include. Why do you think those activities aren't as effective?

SELF-EFFICACY/SELF-EVALUATION   **261**

Team Projects

Each unit includes a collaborative project that integrates all of the unit themes, language, and competencies in a community-building activity.

> A **graphic organizer** helps students collect the information they need for the project.

> Students work in teams to create a **poster**, **chart**, **graph**, or **booklet** that relates to the unit theme.

Unit 7   Used Car for Sale   DESIGN AN INTERNET AD

Materials
- large paper
- markers
- magazine or Internet car advertisements (optional)

TEAMS OF 4 Captain, Co-captain, Assistant, Spokesperson

GET READY
Team: Imagine you have a used car that you want to sell.
Captain: Ask your teammates to describe the car you're selling.
Co-captain: Keep time. You have ten minutes.
Assistant: Take notes in the chart.

Make and model	
Year	
Mileage	
Options	
Other information	

CREATE
Co-captain: Get the materials. Then keep time. You have fifteen minutes.
Team: Create an Internet ad for your car. Use the information from your chart. Add art if you want.

REPORT
Spokesperson: Share your ad with the class. Describe the car you want to sell.

> Teams give **oral presentations** to share their project with the class.

TEAM PROJECTS   **269**

UNIT TOUR   **xxiii**

Getting Started

Welcome to Class

1 LEARN ABOUT YOUR BOOK

A CLASS. **Turn to page iii. Answer the questions.**

1. What information is on this page?
2. How many units are in this book?
3. Which unit is about health?
4. Which unit is about money?
5. Which unit is about work?

B CLASS. **Where is the Practice Plus CD-ROM? What kind of practice does it provide?**

C CLASS. **Sometimes you will need to go to the back of the book to do activities. Where will you find the following? Find each section. Write the page number.**

Grammar Review _____   Persistence Activities _____   Team Projects _____

D PAIRS. **There is additional information for you at the back of the book. Find each section. Write the page number.**

Grammar Reference _____   Audio Script _____   Index _____

2 LEARN ABOUT YOURSELF

A **Take the Learning Styles Survey on page 3.**

B **Count the number of *a*, *b*, and *c* answers. Write the numbers.**

_____ a answers   _____ b answers   _____ c answers

C GROUPS. **Discuss your learning styles.**

- If you scored mostly *a*'s, you may have a visual learning style. You learn by seeing and looking.
- If you scored mostly *b*'s, you may have an auditory learning style. You learn by hearing and listening.
- If you scored mostly *c*'s, you may have a kinesthetic learning style. You learn by touching and doing.

Knowing your learning style can help you understand why some things are easier for you than other things.

1. Are you surprised by the results you got? Explain.
2. Do you think knowing your learning style will help you in your class? In what ways?

What's Your Learning Style?

Choose the first answer that you think of.
Circle *a*, *b*, or *c*.

1 When I study, I like to _____.
   a. read notes or read diagrams and illustrations
   b. repeat information silently to myself
   c. write notes on cards or make diagrams

2 When I listen to music, I _____.
   a. picture things that go with the music
   b. sing along
   c. tap my feet

3 When I solve a problem, I _____.
   a. make a list of things to do and check them off as I do them
   b. talk about the problem with experts or friends
   c. make a diagram of the problem

4 When I read for pleasure, I prefer _____.
   a. a travel book with a lot of pictures
   b. a novel with a lot of conversation
   c. a crime story where you have to solve a mystery

5 When I'm learning to use a computer or new equipment, I prefer _____.
   a. watching a DVD about it
   b. listening to someone explain it
   c. using the equipment and figuring it out for myself

6 When I'm at a party, the next day I will remember _____.
   a. the faces of the people I met there, but not their names
   b. the names of the people there, but not their faces
   c. what I did and said there

7 When I tell a story, I'd rather _____.
   a. write it
   b. tell it out loud
   c. act it out

8 When I'm trying to concentrate, the thing I find most distracting is _____.
   a. things I see, like people moving around
   b. things I hear, like other people's conversations
   c. things I feel, like hunger, worry, or neck pain

9 When I don't know how to spell a word, I will usually _____.
   a. write it out to see if it looks right
   b. sound it out
   c. write it out to see if it feels right

10 When I'm standing in a long line, I'll usually _____.
   a. read a newspaper
   b. talk to the person in line in front of me
   c. tap my foot and move around

3 MEET YOUR CLASSMATES

CD1 T2

A 🔲 **Read and listen to the conversation.**

Ivan: Hi. My name is Ivan.

Ruth: Hi. My name is Ruth. Nice to meet you.

Ivan: Nice to meet you, too. Where are you from, Ruth?

Ruth: Colombia. What about you?

Ivan: I'm from Ukraine.

Ruth: Oh! How long have you been here?

Ivan: Three years. I came here when I finished school.

Ruth: Wow! You speak English very well.

Ivan: Thank you, but I need to study more.

Ruth: Well, I've been a student here for a year now.
It's an excellent school. You'll learn a lot here.

Ivan: Great! I think you speak well, too. Why are you studying English?

Ruth: I'm planning to go to college. I'm going to apply next year.

Ivan: That's terrific. I'm hoping to get a better job.

B PAIRS. Practice the conversation.

C PAIRS. Make similar conversations. Use your own names and information.

4 REVIEW VERB TENSES

GROUPS. Look at the conversation between Ivan and Ruth. Find one example of each of the following verb tenses and write the sentence on the line. There may be more than one correct answer.

Simple present   _____

Simple past   _____

Future   _____

Present perfect   _____

Present continuous   _____

Catching Up

Preview

Read the title. Who are the people? What are they saying to each other?

UNIT GOALS

- ☐ Talk about yourself and your family
- ☐ Describe routines
- ☐ Discuss goals
- ☐ Interpret and complete a school application
- ☐ Discuss ways to succeed
- ☐ Discuss people's past experiences
- ☐ Write about a role model

Listening and Speaking

1   **BEFORE YOU LISTEN**

CLASS. Look at the picture. Arturo Pérez and Brenda Kraig work at the Café Royale, a restaurant in a large hotel. What do you think they're talking about?

2   **LISTEN**

CD1 T3

A   Listen to the first part of the conversation between Arturo and Brenda. Then complete the sentences.

1. Brenda is ordering _____
   _____.

2. Arturo is surprised at the customer's order

   because _____.

B   **PAIRS.** Arturo knows Brenda's name. Predict. How do Arturo and Brenda know each other?

CD1 T4

C   Read the questions. Then listen to the whole conversation. Circle the correct answers.

1. How do Arturo and Brenda know each other?
   a. Their families lived next door to each other.
   b. They dated in high school.
   c. They worked together at another restaurant.

2. When did Arturo begin working at the Café Royale?
   a. a week ago   b. a month ago   c. a year ago

3. What time of day does Arturo usually work?
   a. in the morning   b. in the afternoon   c. in the evening

4. What is Manny, the regular cook, doing today?
   a. looking for a new job   b. taking care of personal things   c. enjoying his vacation

D   **PAIRS.** Discuss. What do you think Arturo and Brenda are going to talk about during their break?

3 CONVERSATION

CD1 T5

A 🔘 **Listen to the sentences. Notice the stressed words. Then listen again and repeat.**

Where are you **liv**ing?

We **have** an a**part**ment on **Fifth** Street.

It's a **lit**tle **nois**y, but we **like** it.

Pronunciation Watch

The important words in a sentence are *stressed*. They sound louder and longer than the other words. Stressed words usually have a clear meaning, such as nouns, verbs, adjectives, adverbs, and question words.

CD1 T6

B 🔘 **Listen to the sentences. Which words are important? Put a dot (•) over the stressed words.**

1. How's your family?
2. My wife is working at a restaurant.
3. She usually works at night.
4. She's planning to go to school.
5. What does she want to study?
6. She wants to study nursing or nutrition.

CD1 T7

C 🔘 **Arturo and Brenda are talking during their break at the Café Royale. Listen and read their conversation.**

Brenda: So how's everything going? Where are you living now?

Arturo: We have an apartment on Fifth Street. It's a little noisy, but we like it.

Brenda: We? So tell me about your family!

Arturo: We have three beautiful kids. Isabel is eight. Michelle is five. And Arturo Jr. is two.

Brenda: How wonderful! And your wife?

Arturo: Oh, yeah…my wife. My wife is great. She's working in a lawyer's office. She's a receptionist now, but she's planning to go to school to be a paralegal.

4 PRACTICE

A PAIRS. **Practice the conversation.**

B ROLE PLAY. PAIRS. **Role-play a conversation between two acquaintances. Both of you worked at the same company five years ago, but you haven't seen each other since then. Make up the information.**

Student A: You are standing in line at a supermarket near your home. You see Student B, an old work acquaintance, walk by. Tell about your life.

Student B: You're shopping at a supermarket near your job. You see Student A, an old work acquaintance, standing in the checkout line. Tell about your life.

Grammar

Simple present and present continuous

Simple present	Present continuous
I always **work** later in the day.	I**'m working** in the morning this week.
Manny **doesn't** usually **work** at night.	Manny **isn't working** today.
How often **do** Arturo and Brenda **work** together?	**Are** Brenda and Arturo **working** today?
Do you **work** mornings or evenings?	Where **are** you **working** these days?

Grammar Watch

- Use the simple present to talk about usual activities or general statements of fact.
- Use the present continuous to talk about things that are happening now (today, this week, this month) or things that are happening temporarily.
- Stative (non-action) verbs are commonly used in the simple present, not the present continuous: I **have** a small apartment on Fifth Street now. (See page 278 for a list of stative verbs.)

1 PRACTICE

A Read the conversation. Draw one line under the simple present verbs. Draw two lines under the present continuous verbs.

Brenda: Hi, Arturo. How come you're cooking breakfast again today?

Arturo: I'm helping Manny out. He needs some more time off this week.

Brenda: I don't understand. Why is Manny missing work? Is he sick?

Arturo: No, he's fine. He and his fiancée are preparing for their wedding this week. His family is visiting from Mexico, so it's a good time to discuss the plans.

B Complete the paragraph. Circle the correct words.

Arturo and Brenda **catch up / are catching up** during their break. They **have / are having** the same schedule because Manny **takes / is taking** some time off this week. They **talk / are talking** about Brenda's older brother, Edward. When Edward was young, he wanted to travel around the world, but he **doesn't care / isn't caring** about a life of adventure anymore. Instead, he **takes / is taking** a short two-week vacation every year and **works / is working** as a computer programmer the other fifty weeks of the year. He **thinks / is thinking** his life is wonderful.

A Complete the conversation. Use the simple present or the present continuous.

Arturo: I __'m trying__ to remember the name of your old friend from Juniper
(try)

Street. Oh, I _____. Her name was Teresa, right?
(know)

Brenda: Right. You _____ a great memory.
(have)

Arturo: How _____ she _____ these days? _____ you
(do) (see) (do)

_____ her anymore?
(see)

Brenda: Teresa and I _____ both really busy, so we _____
(be) (not talk)

very often. But she and my sister usually _____ together. They
(hang out)

_____ at the community college this semester. They both
(study)

_____ to be accountants.
(want)

B Read the conversations. Find and correct the mistakes in each conversation.

1. **Arturo:** ~~Are~~ *Do* you always work during the day?

   Brenda: Yes. I am preferring a daytime schedule. I always feel tired when I'm working
   at night.

2. **Arturo:** How you spend your evenings?

   Brenda: I usually watch TV, but sometimes my sister and I are going to a movie.

3. **Arturo:** Are you having a boyfriend now?

   Brenda: Yes, but at the moment, he visits his grandmother in Poland. I'm really
   missing him!

Show what you know! Describe routines

STEP 1. Think about three things you're doing this month. Make a list.

> 1. I'm taking courses at the community college.

STEP 2. GROUPS. Discuss the three things you're doing this month. Are they
different from what you usually do? Explain.

Can you... describe routines? ☐

Reading

1 BEFORE YOU READ

A CLASS. What is "the American dream"? Is it possible for this "dream" to come true?

B Read the Reading Skill. Then skim the article. Underline the title and the section headings. Predict. What is the main idea of the article?

> **Reading Skill:** Skimming
>
> Before you read a text for complete understanding, skim it, that is, read it quickly for a general idea. Look at the title, the heading of each section, and the illustrations or photos.

2 READ

CD1 T8

Listen and read the article. Was your prediction about the main idea correct? Who is Devorah Hernandez? Why is she an interesting person to read about?

Ready, Set, Go!

Devorah Hernandez knows how to set goals and do what's necessary to achieve them.

A Search for the American Dream

In 1988, Devorah and her husband left Mexico to find a better future for themselves and their children. However, when they first arrived in Salinas, California, they had **financial** difficulties. In Mexico, Devorah was a bank secretary. In the U.S., she got a job in a fast-food restaurant and earned additional money babysitting. When her family moved to Watsonville, California, she became a farm worker. Devorah wanted more. She decided her first step would be to learn English.

The First Difficult Steps

Devorah enrolled in classes at Watsonville/Aptos Adult Education. It wasn't easy to go to school, take care of her family, and work as a part-time housekeeper and a jewelry salesperson. In her first year of school, she learned basic English, completed her GED in Spanish, and studied office skills. And that was just the beginning.

New Goals, New Achievement

Devorah continued to work and study, taking computer and ESL classes at Cabrillo College. In addition, she fulfilled her dream of becoming a U.S. citizen. **Eventually**, she returned to the agriculture industry when Driscoll's, a California company

that grows and sells berries, offered her a job as a quality-control inspector. Devorah is now the head of the company's food-safety department.

Several years ago, Devorah Hernandez received the Latin People Succeed Award. That was a great honor, but she is still trying to **get ahead**. Her current goals are to **make the most of** what life offers, try new things, and work hard for success.

A   Look back at the article. Check (✓) each job that Devorah Hernandez has done.

☐ babysitter   ☐ fast-food worker   ☐ farm worker   ☐ factory worker

☐ teacher's aide   ☐ housekeeper   ☐ quality-control inspector   ☐ jewelry salesperson

B   Complete the sentences. Circle the correct answers.

1. Devorah Hernandez came to the U.S. _____.
   a. to work in a bank   b. to study English   c. to find a good life for her family

2. At Cabrillo College, Devorah Hernandez studied _____.
   a. office skills   b. for her GED   c. computer skills

C   GROUPS. Discuss. Why do you think Devorah Hernandez received the Latin People Succeed Award?

Find the boldfaced words in the article. Complete the sentences.
Circle the correct answers.

1. **Financial** difficulties are problems related to _____.
   a. transportation   b. health   c. money

2. If we do something **eventually**, we do it _____.
   a. quickly   b. after a long time   c. carefully

3. One way to **get ahead** is to _____.
   a. move to a cheaper apartment   b. start your own company   c. take another English class

4. When you **make the most of** something, you _____.
   a. use an opportunity well   b. waste your time   c. ask a lot of questions

Show what you know!   Describe a successful person

GROUPS. Discuss the meaning of each word below. Which word best describes Devorah Hernandez? What other words describe a successful person?

determined   disciplined   goal-oriented   hardworking   smart

Listening and Speaking

1 BEFORE YOU LISTEN

PAIRS. Arturo Pérez is an ambitious person. What does the word *ambitious* mean? Are you ambitious? Explain.

2 LISTEN

CD1 T9

A Read the list of positions at the Café Royale. Then listen to the first part of the conversation. Check (✓) the job that Arturo has now. Circle the job he wants next.

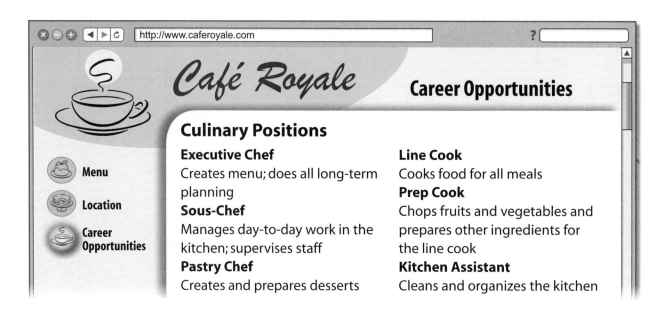

http://www.caferoyale.com   ?

Café Royale   **Career Opportunities**

Menu

Location

Career Opportunities

Culinary Positions

Executive Chef
Creates menu; does all long-term planning
Sous-Chef
Manages day-to-day work in the kitchen; supervises staff
Pastry Chef
Creates and prepares desserts

Line Cook
Cooks food for all meals
Prep Cook
Chops fruits and vegetables and prepares other ingredients for the line cook
Kitchen Assistant
Cleans and organizes the kitchen

CD1 T10

B Read the questions. Listen to the whole conversation. Then answer the questions.

1. What is Arturo going to do next month?

2. What is Arturo's long-term goal? (What does he want to do ten years from now?)

3. What will Arturo do after he finishes the program?

4. What is Arturo going to do about his job at the Café Royale?

C GROUPS. Discuss. What do you think about Arturo's plans?

3 CONVERSATION

A GROUPS. Discuss. What additional steps do you think Arturo must take to achieve his long-term goal?

CD1 T11

B Arturo and his cousin Diana are talking about her plans for the future. Diana's long-term goal is to be a store manager. Listen and read.

Diana: I don't want to be a cashier my whole life. Eventually, I want to be a manager. I think it's time for me to go to school.

Arturo: Have you decided where to study?

Diana: Not yet. First I need to do more research. I'm looking at different business programs online.

Arturo: Are you going to visit any schools?

Diana: Yes, a few. I'll start sending in my applications by the end of the month.

Arturo: It sounds like you have a plan.

4 PRACTICE

A PAIRS. Practice the conversation.

B MAKE IT PERSONAL. Think about your short-term goals.

STEP 1. Think of a long-term goal you have at work, school, or home. How are you going to achieve your goal? Take notes.

STEP 2. GROUPS. Share your ideas.

Grammar

Future with *will*, *be going to*, and present continuous

Will	*Be going to*	Present continuous
I**'ll take** daytime classes and **work** in the evening.	I**'m going to take** cooking classes in August.	I**'m starting** classes there next month.

1 PRACTICE

A Read the e-mail that Brenda Kraig wrote to her sister. Underline the examples of future with *will*, *be going to*, and present continuous.

Grammar Watch

- Use *will*, *be going to*, or present continuous to talk about the future.
- Use *will* to express a willingness or promise to do something: *I'**ll do** it tomorrow.*
- Use *be going to* or present continuous to talk about plans or things that someone intends to do.

Subject : New Plans

Hi, Kayla!

I just want to let you know that everything is fine. I'm happy, but I need to think about where I'll be five years from now.

Pawel and I aren't going to get married anytime soon—in fact, he's in Poland now and won't be back until next month. In the meantime, I'm going to make a few decisions about my life. The community college near my apartment is having an open house later this week. That will give me a chance to visit the campus and find out about classes. I'm also going to talk to a counselor at the career center to find out what's best for me.

So what will Pawel say? I'm writing to him tonight. I'll let you know how everything goes.

Brenda

B Complete the sentences with the correct future form.

1. My sister ____is getting married____ next week.
   (present continuous/get married)

2. Do you have any idea where you _____ in twenty years?
   (will/be)

3. My neighbors _____ a party on Friday night.
   (be going to/have)

4. We hope the party _____ too loud.
   (will/not/be)

5. I _____ my neighbors that I _____ a cake.
   (be going to/tell) *(will/bring)*

6. I have to leave early because I _____ a class at the community
   (present continuous/start)
   college tomorrow morning at 9 o'clock.

A Complete the sentences. Use one of the verbs in the box with the correct future form.

go   have   start

I just saw Mike Cho in the street. Remember Mike? He's doing well, but he's thinking

about getting a better job. He ____is going to go____ back to school, and he
                                    (be going to)

_____ in September. Canyon College _____ an
         (will)   (present continuous)

information session next week, and Mike _____ to it. The college
                                                (be going to)

_____ some counselors there to talk about the program—and
         (will)

Mike hopes they _____ refreshments!
                         (will)

B Look at Marta's short-term goals and activities for the next month.
Write three sentences with *be going to* and two sentences with *will*.

Goals for Next Month
1. Plan for next semester's classes
   - register for classes
   - ask for more scholarship money
2. Prepare for job after finishing school
   - attend job/search workshop
   - search for jobs online
   - continue volunteer work at community center

Show what you know!   Discuss goals

STEP 1. Write two or three short-term goals you would like to achieve in the
coming year.

STEP 2. What can you do to meet your goals for this year? Write two activities
for each of your short-term goals.

STEP 3. GROUPS. Take turns sharing your ideas and giving your opinions.

Can you...discuss goals? ☐

Interpret and complete a school application

Life Skills

1 READ AN APPLICATION

A **CLASS.** What kinds of application forms have you completed? What information do most applications ask for?

B Read the application that Arturo Pérez completed for the Helman Culinary School.

2 PRACTICE

A Find these words in the form. Match the words with the definitions.

__e__ 1. credit   a. a document that shows student classes and grades

____ 2. fee   b. money that cannot be returned to you after you pay it

____ 3. maiden name   c. not required, but something you can choose to do

____ 4. non-refundable   d. the family name a woman had before marriage

____ 5. optional   e. a unit to measure college or university work

____ 6. transcript   f. money you pay to do something

B Read the statements about Arturo. Write *T* (true) or *F* (false). Correct the false statements.

__F__ 1. He wants to start classes in ~~Fall~~ *Spring* 2010.

____ 2. His phone number at home is 858-555-1492.

____ 3. He is a U.S. citizen.

____ 4. He completed his GED in August 2007.

____ 5. He was a prep cook before he became a line cook.

____ 6. He worked as a prep cook for just under a year.

C **PAIRS.** Answer the questions.

1. How much money did Arturo pay when he submitted his application?

2. What address did Arturo send his completed application to?

3 . What languages does Arturo speak?

D Find an application for a school in your area. Use the Internet or visit a school admissions office. Bring the application to class.

E **GROUPS.** Complete your applications. Help one another with vocabulary.

Helman Culinary School
www.helman.edu • 619-555-4000

Office of Admissions | 1075 First Avenue, San Diego, CA 92101

Submit the following:
1. Application
2. $25 non-refundable application fee
3. Official transcripts of high school and college
4. Personal Statement

Applying for:
- ☐ Fall 20 _____
- ☑ Spring 20 _10_
- ☐ Summer _____

Specializing in:
- ☑ Cooking
- ☐ Event Planning
- ☐ Management

Contact Information

Pérez | Arturo | Antonio
Last Name: | Maiden Name: | First Name: | Middle Name:

2492 Jefferson St. | San Diego | CA | 92110
Street Address | City | State | Zip

858-555-3410 | 858-555-1492 | Arturo1989@gotmail.com
Home Phone | Cell Phone | E-mail

Personal

Date of Birth: 06/27/75 (MM/DD/YY) | 123-89-0000 Social Security Number

Gender:
- ☑ Male
- ☐ Female

Citizenship:
- ☑ United States
- ☐ Other

Native Language:
- ☐ English
- ☑ Other bilingual in Spanish and English

Optional: Helman Culinary School is an equal opportunity institution. This information is requested to comply with federal law and will not affect consideration of your application.

Ethnicity:
- ☐ African American, Black
- ☐ American Indian/Alaskan
- ☐ Asian or Pacific Islander
- ☐ Hispanic or Latino
- ☐ White, Non-Hispanic
- ☐ Other
- ☐ Prefer not to answer

Education

Delgado H.S., San Diego, CA
Last High School Attended

Central College, San Diego, CA
Colleges Attended

- ☐ High School Graduate: _____ (mm/yy)
- ☐ Passed GED Test: 08/07 (mm/yy)

Most Credits or Highest Degree Earned
- ☐ Associate's Degree
- ☐ Bachelor's Degree
- ☐ Some Credits: _____
- ☐ Certificate: _____

Work History (Begin with most recent employer.)

Employer: Café Royale | Job Title: Line Cook
City and State: San Diego, CA | Dates Employed: from 08/09 to present

Employer: Café Royale | Job Title: Prep Cook
City and State: San Diego, CA | Dates Employed: from 09/07 to 08/09

Employer: Mi Comida | Job Title: Kitchen Assistant
City and State: San Diego, CA | Dates Employed: from 03/06 to 09/07

Applicant signature: Arturo Pérez | Date: 12/01/10

Can you…interpret and complete a school application? ☐

Listening and Speaking

1   BEFORE YOU LISTEN

GROUPS. Check (✓) the information that you believe is true about entrepreneurs. Help one another with new vocabulary. Then discuss the qualities of entrepreneurs and give examples of entrepreneurs.

> An *entrepreneur* is a person who starts a business and takes risks to make a profit.

Entrepreneurs . . .

- ☐ have creative ideas.
- ☐ are usually happy working for big companies.
- ☐ want to be self-sufficient or independent.
- ☐ usually have a lot of self-confidence.
- ☐ are not afraid to take financial risks.
- ☐ are usually young.

2   LISTEN

CD1 T12

A   Holly Maxwell is the host of "Real-Life Entrepreneurs," a weekly radio show. Listen. What is the focus of her show this week?

CD1 T12

B   Read the questions. Listen to Holly Maxwell again. Then answer the questions.

1. What kind of business did Nadia Gorsky start?
2. What is a three-generation household?
3. Where is Nadia's grandmother from?
4. Why did Nadia's grandmother take care of her when Nadia was a child?
5. What did Nadia help her grandmother do?
6. What degrees did Nadia get?
7. What was her career goal when she was in school?
9. What did Nadia dream of doing?

C   **GROUPS.** Discuss. What did Nadia's parents use to tell her? How did that advice help Nadia to become successful?

3 CONVERSATION

A Listen to the pronunciation of *did you* and *did your*. Then listen again and repeat.

did you ("didja")   Where did you grow up?

What did you do when you came here?

Did you work in a factory?

did your ("didjer")   Where did your daughter learn to cook?

Pronunciation Watch

In conversation, words are sometimes blended together. *Did you* is often pronounced "didja" and *did your* is often pronounced "didjer." The words are joined together and pronounced as one word.

CD1 T14

B Listen to the sentences. Circle the words you hear.

1. Where **do / did** you work?

2. **Do / Did** you ever think about starting a business?

3. What **do / did** you like to do after work?

4. How many hours **does / did** your daughter work?

5. **Does / Did** your daughter always like to cook?

CD1 T15

C Before the show, Holly Maxwell talked to Nadia's mother. Listen and read.

Holly Maxwell:	Where did you grow up, Mrs. Gorsky?
Mrs. Gorsky:	I grew up in Moscow. Things were tough.
Holly Maxwell:	Did you work there?
Mrs. Gorsky:	Yes. I used to work in a factory. I was a garment worker.
Holly Maxwell:	And what about when you came to the U.S.? What did you do when you came here?
Mrs. Gorsky:	My first job here was as a cleaning woman in an office building. My husband was a baker. We both used to work nights. We didn't have much, and we worked hard. But we were happy....We've had a good life here.
Holly Maxwell:	That's terrific!
Mrs. Gorsky:	And now my daughter is a successful entrepreneur!

4 PRACTICE

A PAIRS. Practice the conversation.

B MAKE IT PERSONAL. PAIRS. Talk about where you grew up and what you did before you came to this country. Mention any successes that you and your family had before or after you came to this country.

Grammar

Simple past
Nadia **realized** that she **wasn't** satisfied.
She **began** to dream about owning her own business.
She **didn't forget** her grandmother's recipe.
Did you **work there**?

Grammar Watch

- Use the simple past to talk about actions, feelings, or situations in the past.
- *See page 279 for a list of verbs that are irregular in the simple past.*

1 PRACTICE

A Read the information about Ali Pashko. Find all of the verbs in the simple past. Write them in a chart like the one below. Then write the correct base form.

Ali Pashko had a hard life when he first arrived in the U.S. He got a job at a gas station and often worked more than eighty hours a week. Most days he started at 4:00 P.M., and he didn't finish until 9:00 or 10:00 the next morning. He didn't have a car, so he took the bus. He never got much sleep, and he often fell asleep as soon as he found a seat on the bus. Ali worked hard for several years and saved a lot of money. Last year he got a better job. And he finally bought a car.

Regular Verbs		Irregular Verbs	
Simple past	**Base**	**Simple past**	**Base**
arrived	arrive	had	have

B Complete the conversation between Holly Maxwell and her station manager. Use the simple past.

Manager: I ___enjoyed___ your show yesterday about California entrepreneurs.
(enjoy)

Holly: Thank you, sir. A lot of our listeners _____ the station
(call)

and _____ e-mails after the show to say how much they
(send)

_____ it.
(like)

Manager: I can see why you _____ to talk about Nadia Gorsky on the
(decide)

program. She _____ much money when she was a child, and
(not have)

now she's a successful entrepreneur. It's a great story.

Used to
Nadia **used to help** her grandmother around the house.
Nadia's mother **didn't use to work** during the day.
How many hours a day **did** Nadia's mother **use to work** when she first came here?

• Use **used to** + base form for repeated past actions, feelings, or situations.

• Use **used to** for contrast between the past and the present: I **didn't use to have** a car, but now I have one.

2 PRACTICE

A Complete the sentences. Use *used to* or *didn't use to* and a verb from the box.

drive	go	listen	live	take

1. Sandra Castillo ___used to live___ in New York, but now she has a home in California.

2. She _____, but now she goes everywhere by car.

3. She _____ the bus to work, but she no longer takes public transportation.

4. She _____ music on the radio, but now her car radio is always on.

5. She _____ to concerts, but now she spends most of her time working.

B Read the paragraph. Find and correct four more mistakes.

                                                      work
      Claudio Rialto used to ~~worked~~ as a cook in a big restaurant, but he always dream
of having his own business. He wanted to make the delicious pasta dishes that his
grandmother always use to prepare when Claudio was young. He worked long hours for
many years and saved a lot of money. One day he hear about a man who was looking
for a partner to start a restaurant. Claudio invited the man to lunch. When the man try
Claudio's pasta, he immediately asked Claudio to be his partner.

Show what you know! Discuss people's past experiences

STEP 1. GROUPS. Prepare five questions to find out about your classmates' lives when they first arrived in the U.S.

STEP 2. PAIRS. Choose a partner. Use your questions to interview each other.

STEP 3. CLASS. Take turns reporting what you learned about your classmates.

Can you...discuss people's past experiences? ☐

Writing

1 BEFORE YOU WRITE

A GROUPS. Discuss. What is a *role model*? Is it important to have role models in your life? Explain.

B Read the writing model. Why does the author want to be like Mrs. Popa?

Lifelong Learning

Romina Popa is my next-door neighbor and my role model. I can learn a lot from her example. Mrs. Popa came to the U.S. from Moldova in 1995. At that time, she was married and had two young children. Her family was the most important part of her life, but she wanted to do other things, too. Her first goal was to learn English, so she took classes at the local community college. Her next goal was to get an associate's degree in nursing. She began her studies in 1998 and graduated in 2001. By then, her children were in school during the day, so she got a job as an emergency room nurse and did volunteer work. Although she was very busy taking care of her family, working, and volunteering, she went back to school for a bachelor's degree in nursing in 2003 and graduated in 2005. Mrs. Popa is now fifty years old. Her children are in college, and she is, too. She's taking classes for a master's degree. I really admire Mrs. Popa. She sets goals and works hard to reach them. I want to be a lifelong learner just like her.

C PAIRS. Answer the questions.

1. How does the author know Mrs. Popa?
2. How old is Mrs. Popa?
3. What is Mrs. Popa's current goal?

> **Writing Tip**
>
> When you write a biographical paragraph, put information about the person's life in chronological (time) order.

D Add information about Mrs. Popa to the timeline.

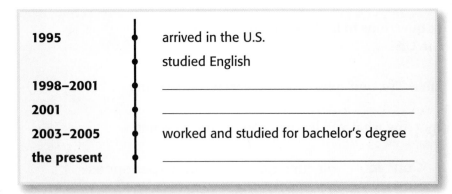

1995	arrived in the U.S.
	studied English
1998–2001	_____
2001	_____
2003–2005	worked and studied for bachelor's degree
the present	_____

A BRAINSTORM. Who are the people that you admire? Why do you admire them? Organize your ideas in a chart like this.

People I Admire	Reasons

B Plan and organize your own paragraph. Answer the questions.

1. Who do you admire most?
2. Why do you admire this person?
3. What did this person do? What is this person doing now? (Use chronological order.)
4. What important lesson can you learn from this person?

3 WRITE

Write a paragraph about the person you admire most. Give reasons to explain why you admire the person. Use the information in your chart. Look at the writing model for an example.

4 CHECK YOUR WRITING

☐ Did you describe the person's achievements?
☐ Did you put information about the person's life in chronological order?
☐ Did you give reasons to explain why you admire the person?
☐ Did you use correct capitalization, punctuation, and spelling?

1 REVIEW

For your grammar review, go to page 245.

2 ACT IT OUT What do you say?

STEP 1. Review the conversations on pages 6-7 (CD1 Tracks 4 and 7).

STEP 2. ROLE PLAY. PAIRS. Role-play this situation.

Student A: Yesterday you saw an old high school friend for the first time in almost ten years. You found out about your old friend's job, family, and life in general. Now you are at a party and talking to another high school friend.

Student B: You are talking to an old high school friend at a party. Yesterday, your friend saw another high school friend for the first time in almost ten years. You want to know everything about that person's job, family, and life in general.

3 READ AND REACT Problem-solving

STEP 1. Read about the problem.

Your good friend started talking about buying a house three years ago, but he is still renting an apartment. He hasn't taken any steps toward buying a house and needs help. He wants to know how to meet his goal.

STEP 2. GROUPS. What is the problem? Discuss a solution. Make a list of two short-term goals for your friend. Write two activities for each short-term goal.

4 CONNECT

For your Community-Building Activity, go to page 257.
For your Team Project, go to page 263.

Which goals can you check off? Go back to page 5.

 Go to the CD-ROM for more practice.

Tell Me about Yourself

Preview

Read the title. Who are the people? What are they saying to each other?

UNIT GOALS

- [ ] Talk about work-related goals

- [ ] Interpret and write a résumé

- [ ] Use job-information sources

- [ ] Discuss job-related skills and abilities

- [ ] Respond to common interview questions

- [ ] Describe previous work experiences and duties

- [ ] Write a cover letter

Listening and Speaking

1 BEFORE YOU LISTEN

A CLASS. Why do people go to career centers? What can employment specialists do for their clients?

B GROUPS. When you are *motivated*, you really want to be successful at doing something. Discuss. What are you motivated to do?

2 LISTEN

CD1 T16

A Listen to the first part of a conversation between Catherine Tote, an employment specialist, and her client, Nedim Buric. Then answer the questions.

1. What are two reasons that clients come to Sun County Career Center?

   a. _____

   b. _____

2. What does Nedim want to do?

   _____

B PAIRS. Predict. What is the first thing that Catherine and Nedim will discuss: his work experience, his skills, or his education? What other things do employment specialists ask clients about?

CD1 T17

C Read the statements. Then listen to the whole conversation. Write *T* (true) or *F* (false). Correct the false statements.

__F__ 1. Today is Nedim's ~~second~~ *first* meeting with Catherine Tote.

_____ 2. Nedim has a job but is looking for a new one.

_____ 3. Nedim has good computer skills.

_____ 4. Nedim pays attention to details.

_____ 5. Nedim graduated from a university in Bosnia.

_____ 6. Catherine has already found a job for Nedim.

3 CONVERSATION

CD1 T18

A Listen to the words. Notice that one syllable is not pronounced. Then listen again and repeat.

Pronunciation Watch

Some words have a syllable that is not usually pronounced.

cam~~e~~ra (2 syllables)   int~~e~~rested (3 syllables)

fam~~i~~ly (2 syllables)   diff~~e~~rent (2 syllables)

B GROUPS. Discuss. What is an example of an entry-level job? What are the advantages and disadvantages of this type of job?

CD1 T19

C Nedim's friend Tatiana is looking for a job in the Help Wanted section of the newspaper. Listen and read.

Nedim: What kind of job are you looking for?

Tatiana: Well, I'm interested in photography. And I'd like to find a job with some opportunity for the future.

Nedim: Here's something at a camera store. Would you consider doing this?

Tatiana: Hmm. It's a position as a salesperson. It's a good entry-level job.

Nedim: You're certainly the right kind of person for the job. You're friendly and helpful.

Tatiana: And motivated. I'll work during the day and take classes at night.

4 PRACTICE

A PAIRS. Practice the conversation.

B MAKE IT PERSONAL. Think about your work-related goals.

STEP 1. What job would you like to have? Write information about yourself.

Goal: I want to work as a(n) _____ .			
Interests: what I'm most interested in	**Personal Qualities:** kind of person I am	**Skills:** what I know how to do	**Steps:** ways to get the job I want

STEP 2. GROUPS. Discuss.

1. In what ways are you qualified for the job you would like to have?

2. What additional skills do you need? How will you get them?

3. How long will it take to achieve your goal?

Grammar

Infinitives and gerunds

Verb + Infinitive	Verb + Gerund
I **want** *to find* a job.	They **discussed** *finding* a job.
I **decided** *to come* to the U.S.	My uncle **recommended** *finishing* my degree in the U.S.
We can **start** *to look at* available positions.	We can **start** *looking at* available positions.

Grammar Watch

- Use an infinitive after verbs such as *agree, decide, need, wait, want,* and *would like.*
- Use a gerund after verbs such as *enjoy, discuss, finish,* and *recommend.*
- Use either an infinitive or a gerund after verbs such as *begin, continue, like quit, prefer* and *start.*
- *See page 280 for a list of verbs.*

1 PRACTICE

A Read the newspaper article. Underline the examples of verb + infinitive. Circle the examples of verb + gerund.

Sun County Career Center

Sun County Career Center (SCCC) began helping jobseekers thirty years ago. SCCC always planned to offer English and work-skills training to immigrants who needed to find employment, but in 2000, they decided not to limit their services and opened their doors to anyone who was looking for a job. The organization continues to offer ESL classes and job training. It recently started offering job placement and counseling services as well.

B Complete the conversation between Catherine Tote and Mi Young Park, her co-worker at SCCC. Circle the correct words.

Catherine: I met with an interesting client earlier today. When he came in, he wanted **to look / looking** at the job listings immediately. He couldn't wait **to find / finding** a job.

Mi Young: Did he finally agree **to discuss / discussing** the kind of work that might be good for him?

Catherine: Yes, after I explained why we needed **to talk / talking** about his personal qualities and his skills. He finally understood how important it is to look for a job that he can enjoy **to do / doing**.

Complete the conversation between another SCCC career specialist and his client.
Use infinitives and gerunds. Where appropriate, write two answers.

Michael: Yesterday we discussed _____*setting*_____ long-term and short-term goals.
(set)
Let's continue _*to talk/talking*_ about that today.
(talk)

Violette: I finished _____ the information you gave me about goal-
(read)
setting, and I'd really like _____ the time to think about my
(take)
goals. But I need _____ some money right now.
(earn)

Michael: OK. Then you should consider _____ a job that might lead to a
(take)
better position later.

Violette: That's a good idea. I can start _____ money while I'm planning
(make)
for the future. As I think you know, I prefer _____ in an office.
(work)

Michael: Yes. Let's see . . . You like _____ research, don't you?
(do)

Violette: Definitely. That's what I liked most about my last job. The only reason I quit
_____ there was that I moved.
(work)

Show what you know!   Talk about work-related goals

STEP 1. **Complete the sentences about your work-related goals.**

1. I really enjoy _____.

2. My friends think I should try _____.

3. I hope _____.

4. A teacher recommended _____.

5. Someday, I am going to learn _____.

STEP 2. GROUPS. **Discuss. What are the most popular answers for questions 1, 2, and 3?**

Can you. . . talk about work-related goals? ☐

Life Skills

1 INTERPRET A RÉSUMÉ

A **CLASS.** A *résumé* is typed information about your education, skills, and experience. Have you used a résumé to find a job? Do people usually give a résumé to an employer before or after a job interview?

B **GROUPS.** Skim Francis Kouadio's résumé. What kind of information is in the *Objective* section of the résumé? In the *Qualifications* section? In the *Related Experience* section?

Francis Kouadio
2038 Crabtree Court, Barrington, IL 60010
847-555-1054
frankkouadio@mymail.com

OBJECTIVE: To work as a software programmer and developer

QUALIFICATIONS
- Creative in the design of new computer software
- Skilled at analyzing and solving problems
- Proficient in computer programming languages such as C/C++, Java, and SQL
- Able to work with PC, Macintosh, and Linux platforms

RELATED EXPERIENCE

Technology Specialist
2008–present
RescueMe Computing
Barrington, IL

Started RescueMe at-home visits for computer set-up and repair. Helped clients with business and personal computer needs. Designed database software for doctors and dentists.

Sales Associate
2005–2008
Ted's Electronics
Lake Zurich, IL

Answered customer questions and assisted in purchase of computers, televisions, and other equipment. Received an award for most sales in December 2008.

Volunteer
2004–2005
District 10 Middle School

Taught an after-school program: Computer Skills for the Classroom

EDUCATION
Cutter College,
Chicago, IL

B.S., Computer Science, June 2005

References available upon request.

2 READ

A Read Francis Kouadio's résumé.

B GROUPS. Discuss.

1. Why does Francis Kouadio include his address, telephone number, and e-mail address at the top of his résumé?

2. Why does Francis include achievements such as "started RescueMe at-home visits" and "received an award for most sales in December 2008" in his work experience?

3. Why does Francis include a volunteer position along with his paid jobs?

C CLASS. *References* are people who can describe your personal qualities, skills and abilities, and experience. Discuss.

1. What kinds of people can provide references?

2. Who would you use as a reference?

3 WRITE

A BRAINSTORM. Think about your education and training, experience, and skills. Record your information in a chart like this.

Schools Attended	
Degrees or Certificates	
Places of Employment	
Titles and Responsibilities	
Achievements and Awards	
Skills and Abilities	
Personal Qualities	
Interests	

B Write an objective for a job that you would like.

C Write your own résumé. Use the information and the job objective that you wrote for Exercises A and B. Use Francis Kouadio's résumé as a model.

Can you...interpet and write a résumé?   ☐

Listening and Speaking

1 BEFORE YOU LISTEN

GROUPS. Discuss the information in the Job-Search Tips. Have you ever followed any of the tips to find a job? What happened?

2 LISTEN

CD1 T20

A Lisa Wong is talking to her niece Angela at a family party. Listen to Lisa's advice on finding a job. What are some ways Lisa suggests that Angela could find a job?

CD1 T20

B Read the questions. Then listen to Lisa again. Circle the correct answers.

1. When did Lisa get her first job in the U.S.?
   a. twelve years ago
   b. twenty years ago
   c. twenty-five years ago

2. Where was Lisa's first job in the U.S.?
   a. in a newspaper office
   b. in a flower shop
   c. in a job-placement agency

3. How did Lisa find her job?
   a. by reading a newspaper ad
   b. by going into a store with a "Help Wanted" sign
   c. by networking

4. Who did Lisa talk to before she was hired?
   a. the manager
   b. the owner
   c. the secretary

C Read the Job-Search Tips again. According to Angela's aunt, what is the best way to find a job? Circle your answer.

Job-Search Tips

Are you getting tired of looking for work? Use one of these proven methods for finding a job.

- Look at want ads in the job section of your local newspaper.
- Go online. Do research on one of today's many job-related websites.
- Look for "Help Wanted" signs in your neighborhood.
- Take advantage of the services of a job-placement agency.
- Get information about possible jobs by networking (talking with people you know and trying to meet new people to help you find work).

A GROUPS. Discuss.

1. What kinds of information might you want to learn about a job before applying?
2. Where can you get information about a job before you apply?

CD1 T21

B  Angela is talking to her neighbor Harold. Listen and read.

Harold: Hi, Angela. How's your job-hunt going?

Angela: It's going OK. I've been sending my résumé out online, but I haven't heard back from anyone yet.

Harold: Have you thought about going to an employment agency?

Angela: Yeah, but I don't want to pay to get a job.

Harold: But you don't pay! The employer usually pays!

Angela: Really? That's great. I'll definitely try that then!

Harold: Also, what about getting help at the library? I think they give job-search workshops. Maybe they can give you some ideas.

Angela: That would be a big help. I was planning on going to the library anyway to use their computers. I'll check it out.

4 PRACTICE

A PAIRS. Practice the conversation.

B ROLE PLAY. PAIRS. Role-play a conversation between a person looking for a job and a friend who is suggesting ideas for finding a job. Use the Job-Search Tips on page 32. Use the ideas below for places to get help.

> community career center   job fair   library   school

C MAKE IT PERSONAL. GROUPS. Discuss your experiences with job-hunting. What did you do to find a job? Were you successful?

Grammar

Gerunds as objects of preposition

I'm **thinking about** *applying for* a position at a hair salon.

I was **worried about** *not having* enough money to live on.

Adjective + Preposition		Verb + Preposition	
capable of	interested in	believe in	plan on
good at	excited about	choose between	think about

> **Grammar Watch**
>
> • Use a gerund (verb + *-ing*)—not an infinitive (*to* + base form of verb)—after a preposition.
>
> • *See page 281 for a list of verbs + prepositions and for a list of adjectives + prepositions.*

1 PRACTICE

A Read the conversation between friends. Underline the prepositions. Circle the gerunds.

Carmen: What's the matter? You look worried. Are you concerned <u>about</u> (getting) a job?

Min-Ji: Yes. I didn't plan on looking for work for so long. I'm beginning to wonder if I'll ever find a job! And I'm getting tired of going on interviews.

Carmen: I know. It's not much fun.

Min-Ji: I'd be excited about taking any job, even a low-paying one, as long as it's something I'd enjoy doing. My friend Ben told me about a position as a sales representative for a pharmaceutical company. I'm really interested in finding out more about it.

Carmen: That would be a good job for you. You'd be good at selling.

B Complete the conversation. Use gerunds.

Edith: Thanks for _____letting_____ me know about the teacher assistant job.
(let)

Kevin: I'm glad you're interested in _____ for it. You've been talking about
(apply)

_____ back to school to become a teacher for a long time.
(go)

Edith: I'm not looking forward to _____ the school office to get more
(call)

information about the job. I'm terrible at _____ to strangers. I'm always
(talk)

concerned about _____ a good impression.
(not make)

Kevin: You'll be fine. The first person that you'll talk to is the secretary, Mrs. Leshem.

Don't be afraid of _____ her anything you want. She's really nice.
(ask)

Complete each conversation. Use each phrase in the box once. Use gerunds.

> answer questions about benefits
> ~~apply for the teacher assistant job~~
> get your application materials
>
> not have a certificate
> send my application and résumé today
> solve problems

1. **Margaret:** Hello. I'm interested in *applying for the teacher assistant job* .

 Receptionist: OK. Please fill out this application.

2. **Antonio:** I want to apply for a job as an auto mechanic, but I'm worried about

 _____. Do I need to get training?

 Receptionist: Yes. You need a Certificate of Completion from a vocational training

 program for a job with us.

3. **Interviewer:** If you're good at _____ and have a

 desire to learn, we'll give you on-the-job training.

 Fernando: That's great. Thanks.

4. **Ibrahim:** I'd like to discuss the benefits the company offers.

 Receptionist: I'm sorry. You'll have to talk to Joan Leshem, but she's away from her

 desk. She's responsible for _____.

5. **Receptionist:** You can go to our website and get the job application there.

 Silvio: Thank you. I'm planning on _____.

 Receptionist: We look forward to _____.

Show what you know! Discuss job-related skills and abilities

STEP 1. Choose a job. Complete the sentences about the job you chose.

A/An _____
 (name of job)

- must be good at _____.
- is responsible for _____.
- is used to _____.
- sometimes worries about _____.

STEP 2. GROUPS. Discuss the jobs you choose.

Can you...discuss job-related skills and abilities? ☐

Reading

1 BEFORE YOU READ

A CLASS. Discuss. What is the meaning of the word *discrimination*? What types of discrimination might occur at work?

B GROUPS. Who decides which questions employers can and cannot ask during a job interview?

C Read the title and the headings for each section of the article. Predict. What is the main idea of the article?

2 READ

CD1 T22

Listen and read the article. Was your prediction about the main idea correct? What is a problem that sometimes happens at job interviews?

http://www.getandkeepajob.com

Get and Keep a Job   Home   Interviews   Résumés

Do I Really Have to Answer That?

Imagine this. You're at a job interview. You're nervous, but everything is going well. Then the employer asks, "I see you're not wearing a wedding ring. Are you planning to get married soon?"

For years, job applicants have complained about employers who ask for information that isn't related to work skills or experience, such as the question above about marital status. Here's what the experts say about questions that are too personal and maybe even **illegal**.

Interview Do's and Don'ts

U.S. **anti-discrimination** laws forbid some questions but allow others. For example, an interviewer cannot ask, "How long have you lived in the U.S.?" But she can ask, "What is your current address and phone number?" It's against the law to ask, "How much do you weigh?" Instead, an interviewer should explain a job's physical requirements and find out if you're capable of doing the work.

Other questions, such as "If you could be any animal, what animal would you like to be?" or "What's your favorite book?" are legal but shouldn't be part of an interview. They confuse applicants and don't relate directly to worker qualifications.

Answers to Inappropriate Questions

So what should you do if you find yourself in front of an interviewer who is asking **inappropriate** questions?

Some people answer them because they feel it's the best way to get a job. Job experts recommend that applicants respond to every question—but with information that shows they can meet the job requirements. For example, a good reply to "Do you live far from here?" is "I'm a responsible employee. I always come to work on time." Applicants who refuse to answer illegal and inappropriate questions should know that the company probably won't offer them a position, but in the end, it might not be the best place to work.

Before you decide what to do, ask yourself two questions: "How much do I want the job?" and "What kind of boss am I looking for?"

A Complete the sentences. Circle the correct answers.

1. An interviewer cannot ask about your _____.
   a. marital status   b. address   c. work skills

2. U.S. anti-discrimination laws say that an interviewer can ask _____.
   a. how long you've been in the U.S.   c. what kind of experience you have
   b. how much you weigh

3. Employment specialists suggest that applicants _____ during an interview.
   a. answer all the questions   c. ask the interviewer two questions
   b. complain about illegal questions

B Read the Reading Skill. Then circle the answer that best completes the statement.

The author of the article gives details by _____.

a. telling personal stories   c. providing numbers

b. using names of people and places   d. including examples

> *Reading Skill:* Using Details to Understand Important Ideas
>
> Look for details to help you understand an author's ideas more completely.

C GROUPS. Discuss. Why is it important for job applicants to ask themselves "How much do I want the job?" and "What kind of boss am I looking for?"

4 WORD WORK

A prefix is a group of letters added to the beginning of a word to change its meaning. Look at the boldfaced words in the article. Complete the sentences.

1. The prefixes *il-* in *illegal* and *in-* in *inappropriate* mean _____.

2. The prefix *anti-* in *anti-discrimination* means _____.

Show what you know!   Discuss job-interview questions

STEP 1. Think about job interviews in your country. List questions employers can and can't ask.

STEP 2. GROUPS. Discuss. How are the interview dos and don'ts in the U.S. similar to and different from those in your country?

Listening and Speaking

1 BEFORE YOU LISTEN

CLASS. Discuss.

1. What questions do employers ask applicants during a job interview?

2. Have you ever been on a job interview? What questions were you asked?

2 LISTEN

A CD1 T23

Kyong-Mo Lee is interviewing Steve Santos for a job at Capital Express Delivery Services. Listen. What position is Steve applying for?

B CD1 T23

Read the questions. Listen to the job interview again. Then answer the questions.

1. What is Steve's job now?
   a. truck driver
   b. supermarket manager
   c. dispatcher

2. What kind of license does he have?
   a. chauffeur's license
   b. bus driver's license
   c. commercial driver's license

3. What is one reason that Steve wants to leave his job at Trends Supermarket?
   a. He wants a job closer to home.
   b. He wants different work hours.
   c. He wants more money.

4. What is one reason that Steve wants to be a dispatcher some day?
   a. He wants to work indoors.
   b. He enjoys solving problems.
   c. He is tired of his current job.

C GROUPS. Discuss. Do you think Steve made a good impression? Why or why not?

3 CONVERSATION

CD1 T24

A Listen to the words. Notice the stressed syllable in each word. Then listen again and repeat.

Pronunciation Watch

In words with more than one syllable, one syllable is stressed. The stressed syllable sounds louder than other syllables and has a strong, clear vowel sound.

•   •   •   •

general   im**por**tant   de**li**very   **su**permarket

CD1 T25

B Listen to these words. Put a dot (•) over the stressed syllable.

1. control   2. interesting   3. experience   4. interview   5. responsible   6. absolutely

CD1 T26

C Steve Santos's job interview with Kyung-Mo Lee continues. Listen and read.

Mr. Lee: I have a general question. What's the most important thing you've learned from your work experience?

Mr. Santos: Oh, that's an interesting question! Let me think. I've learned a lot! Sometimes things happen that you don't expect; for example, when there's bad weather or something goes wrong with a delivery. I learned a long time ago that I can't control everything—especially not the weather—but I can control my response. There's no reason to get upset with things you can't control.

Mr. Lee: So, do you think you stay calm under pressure?

Mr. Santos: Yes. Absolutely. Everyone who knows me thinks I'm a really calm person.

4 PRACTICE

A PAIRS. Practice the conversation.

B PAIRS. Discuss.

1. Do you think Mr. Santos gave a good answer to Mr. Lee's question about what he's learned from his work experience? Why or why not?

2. Imagine that you are being interviewed for a job. How would you answer that question?

C ROLE PLAY. PAIRS. Role-play a job interview.

Student A: You are the interviewer. Ask, "What's the most important thing you've learned from your work experience?"

Student B: You are the job applicant. Use the answer you discussed in Exercise B.

Grammar

Simple past and present perfect

Simple past	Present perfect
Steve **learned** a long time ago that he can't control everything.	Steve **has learned** a lot from his work experience.
Steve **worked** at Grand Supermarkets from 2001 to 2006.	Steve **has worked** for Trends Supermarkets since 2006.
When **did** you **start** working there?	How long **have** you **been** a driver?

Grammar Watch

- Use the simple past for actions, feelings, or situations that occurred at a specific time in the past.
- Use the present perfect for actions, feelings, or situations that occurred at an indefinite time in the past.
- Use the present perfect with *for* or *since* to show that an action, feeling, or situation started in the past and continues up to now.

1 PRACTICE

A Read the information about Li's work history. Underline six examples of the simple past. Circle five more examples of the present perfect.

I've lived in the U.S. since 2000, and I've been lucky with finding work. I've had a few different jobs at CDS Drugtores. My first job there was as a stock clerk. Next I worked as a cashier. But then I got a job in the pharmacy department, and I really liked it. I've always liked working with people and I was good in chemistry in school, so I decided to become a pharmacist. I've just enrolled in a program at the university. I haven't started my classes yet, but I hope to get a job as a pharmacist in the future.

B Two managers are talking about an employee. Complete the sentences. Use the present perfect.

Bob: How long ___has Dan worked___ here?
            (Dan/work)

Jim: Since 2006. He _____ one of our best employees since he
                                        (be)
            started here. He won the Employee of the Month award three times in the

            last three years.

Bob: Is it true that he _____ the highest sales in the company for
                                    (have)
            the last two years?

Jim: Yes, and he's also very dependable. He _____ a day's work in
                                                                    (not miss)
            the last two years. And he's easygoing and calm. He _____
                                                                        (never/raise)
            his voice.

Unscramble the sentences. Put the words in order. Use the present perfect or the simple past. More than one order may be possible.

<u>Dan Miller</u>

1. (win / last week / Dan / his third Employee of the Month Award)

   Dan won his third Employee of the Month Award last week.

2. (since 2006 / an outstanding employee / Dan / be)

   _____

<u>Raquel Hernandez</u>

3. (her back / Raquel/ two months ago / injure)

   _____

4. (since her injury occurred / She / work / not)

   _____

5. (I / for five years / Raquel / know)

   _____

<u>Michael Shen</u>

6. (arrive late for his interview / Michael / last week)

   _____

7. (interested in the job / He / during the interview / seem/not)

   _____

8. (He / since last Tuesday / not / the interviewer's phone calls / return)

   _____

Show what you know! Describe previous work experience and duties

GROUPS. **Discuss.**

1. What is your current job? How long have you had the job?
2. What other jobs have you had?
3. Which job has been the best job for you? Why?

Can you... describe previous work experiences and duties? ☐

Write a cover letter

Writing

1 BEFORE YOU WRITE

A CLASS. Discuss. What is the purpose of a cover letter? How is a cover letter different from a résumé?

B Read the writing model.

Writing Tip

Do not include unnecessary information in a cover letter.

2038 Crabtree Court
Barrington, IL 60010
June 12, 2010 ← **Applicant's Address**

Ms. Alice Kwan
Creative Director
Avenue Technology ← **Employer's Full Name, Title, and Address**
1759 W. 48th Avenue, Suite 118
Zion, IL 60099

Dear Ms. Kwan: ← **Greeting**

    I am sending you my résumé in response to your ad for a game developer in yesterday's Daily News. I am interested in the position because it is a perfect fit with my interests, training, and experience.

    I have loved technology since childhood, and I have designed several electronic games. I completed a bachelor's degree in computer science last month. As part of my degree requirements, I worked with three other students to develop software to teach spelling to elementary-school children. Through my classes, I gained technical knowledge and problem-solving skills. I also learned the importance of teamwork. ← **Body Paragraphs**

    I am familiar with the computer games that Avenue Technology develops and would love to be a member of your team. I am available for an interview at any time that is convenient for you.

I look forward to hearing from you.
Sincerely, ← **Closing**

Francis Kouadio ← **Applicant's Name and Signature**
Francis Kouadio

Enclosure: Résumé

C PAIRS. **Answer the questions.**

1. Why does Francis think he is the best person for the game developer position?

2. An *enclosure* is something inside an envelope (or an electronic file) along with a letter. What is the enclosure with Francis Kouadio's letter?

D What kind of information is in the first body paragraph of Francis Kouadio's cover letter? the second paragraph? the third paragraph?

2 THINKING ON PAPER

A BRAINSTORM. **Read the résumé that you prepared for Exercise 3C on page 31. Then use a newspaper, the Internet, or your networking skills to find a job that you would like to apply for.**

B Plan and organize the body paragraphs of a cover letter for the job you want. Organize your ideas in a chart like this.

Qualifications

Interests and Personal Qualities

Skills

Education and Experience

3 WRITE

Write a cover letter for the job you want to apply for. Use your brainstorming ideas and the information in your chart. Look at the writing model for an example.

Writing Tip

If you don't know the name of the person you are writing to, use *To Whom It May Concern:* as a greeting.

4 CHECK YOUR WRITING

☐ Did you include the date, your address, the employer's address, and your name and signature?

☐ Did you tell how you heard about the job?

☐ Did you explain why you think you're the best person for the job?

☐ Did you use correct capitalization, punctuation, and spelling?

1 REVIEW

For your grammar review, go to page 246.

2 ACT IT OUT What do you say?

STEP 1. CLASS. Review what you learned on pages 30–31 about preparing a résumé.

STEP 2. ROLE PLAY. PAIRS. Role-play this situation. Use the résumé you wrote for Exercise 3C on page 31.

Student A: You are an employment specialist at a career center. You are meeting with a client who has visited you several times before. She brought her résumé today for you to look at. You are giving her advice on ways to improve it.

Student B: You are a jobseeker. You need help with your résumé, so you brought a copy of it to the career center. Ask the employment specialist for advice and suggestions.

3 READ AND REACT Problem-solving

STEP 1. GROUPS. Read about Usman's problem.

Usman Amir has a job interview at 9:00 this morning. It is now 8:15. It will take him at least thirty minutes to drive to the interview. Usman needs an extra copy of his résumé to take to the interview, but he just discovered that his printer isn't working.

STEP 2. GROUPS. What is Usman's problem? Discuss a solution. List three things that he can do.

4 CONNECT

For your Planning for Learning, go to page 257.
For your Team Project, go to page 264.

Which goals can you check off? Go back to page 25.

 Go to the CD-ROM for more practice.

Community Life

Preview

Read the title. What's important in a community? What's *most* important?

UNIT GOALS

- [ ] Talk about cultural festivals and traditions

- [ ] Describe feelings about a neighborhood

- [ ] Give and follow directions

- [ ] Describe community issues

- [ ] Talk about making changes in a community

- [ ] Discuss ways to improve a community

- [ ] Identify community problems

- [ ] Express feelings about a neighborhood

Listening and Speaking

1 BEFORE YOU LISTEN

CLASS. Look at the picture. What kind of festival do you think this is? Are festivals like this a tradition in your home country?

2 LISTEN

CD1 T27

A Mali Prem and Eric Torres are talking about a Thai Festival. Listen. Who is going to the festival?

CD1 T27

B Read the questions. Then listen to the conversation again. Circle the correct answers.

1. What does the festival celebrate?
   a. the first day of spring
   b. Thai Independence Day
   c. Thai New Year's Day

2. What does Mali say about the food at the festival?
   a. It's spicy.
   b. It's amazing.
   c. It's cheap.

3. What do some children do at the festival?
   a. play games
   b. drink water
   c. throw water

C GROUPS. What things are common in your culture that people from other cultures might find surprising?

3 CONVERSATION

CD1 T28

A Listen to the words. Notice the short, quiet pronunciation of the underlined consonant sounds. Then listen again and repeat.

sho<u>p</u>	grea<u>t</u>	a<u>t</u> nigh<u>t</u>	bore<u>d</u>	thin<u>k</u>
chea<u>p</u>	bes<u>t</u>	foo<u>d</u>	ba<u>ck</u>	perfe<u>ct</u>

CD1 T29

B Mali and Eric talk after the festival. Listen and read.

Mali: So what did you think of Thai Town?

Eric: It's pretty amazing. It has so many restaurants and shops. Is it always so crowded?

Mali: Mostly at night and on the weekends. A lot of people come to eat and shop.

Eric: The things in the stores looked really interesting. I'm usually bored by shopping, but I'd like to come back and check out the crafts.

Mali: Great. I'll tell you about the best restaurants where the food is cheap.

Eric: Perfect!

4 PRACTICE

A PAIRS. Practice the conversation.

B MAKE IT PERSONAL. GROUPS. Discuss.

1. What kind of neighborhood do you live in? Is it a neighborhood like Thai Town where people share a common language and culture, or is it a diverse neighborhood?

2. Which is better—a neighborhood where people share a common language and culture, or a diverse neighborhood?

3. Make two charts: one for neighborhoods where people share a common culture and one for diverse neighborhoods. List advantages and disadvantages for each.

Describe feelings about a neighborhood

Grammar

Participial adjectives	
It's pretty **amazing**.	I'm **amazed** at all the restaurants and shops.
Shopping is **boring**.	Eric is usually **bored** by shopping.

Grammar Watch

- Adjectives ending in -ing and -ed refer to feelings. Use an -ing adjective to describe the cause of a feeling. Use an -ed adjective to describe a feeling experienced by a person. *See page 281 for a list of* -ed *and* -ing *(participial) adjectives.*
- Some adjectives, like *worried* and *relieved*, have only -ed forms.
- Prepositions often follow -ed adjectives: *Eric is bored by shopping.* (*See page 281 for a list of* -ed *adjectives + prepositions*).

1 PRACTICE

A Mark the boldfaced adjectives *F* (feeling experienced by a person) or *C* (cause of the feeling).

                              C

Because life in a new country is **exciting** but difficult, immigrants often live in neighborhoods with people from their homeland. That way, when they're **worried** about food, schools, or medical care, or when they feel **confused** about something that happens at work or school, they can find help. If it becomes too **frustrating** to speak English, there's always someone who can speak their native language. Besides, at the end of a long hard day, it's simply more **relaxing** to be in a place that seems like home.

B Complete the conversation between Laila Kassim and Maria Ruiz. Use the prepositions *about, at, of,* or *with*. More than one answer is sometimes possible.

Laila: I'm worried __*about*__ my children. I can't let them play outside.

Maria: I understand. My husband and I moved to our neighborhood about a month ago. At first, I was excited _____ having American neighbors. But that changed quickly. I'm surprised _____ how busy people are all the time.

Laila: I know what you mean. But I have a happy story. When my sister first moved, she was nervous _____ bothering the American family next door. She was embarrassed _____ her English, and they didn't seem very helpful. But then the children started playing together, and everything changed. Now she's thrilled _____ the great relationship she has with her neighbors.

A Read the sentences about Maria's feelings. Circle the correct adjectives.

1. Maria didn't find what she expected when she moved to a new neighborhood. Maria was (disappointed)/ disappointing.

2. One of Maria's neighbors always says, "Hello. How are you?" but never waits for an answer. Maria is **confused / confusing** and wonders why.

3. Maria asked one of her neighbors her age. Later she found out that it's not OK to ask that question. Maria felt **embarrassed / embarrassing**.

4. Maria wanted to know more about Laila's sister. She thought that the sister's experience was **interested / interesting**.

5. Laila's sister's experience gave Maria some hope. She was **encouraged / encouraging** about the possibility of getting to know her neighbors.

B Complete the sentences with the *-ed* or *-ing* form of the verb in parentheses.

Crime was increasing in the neighborhood, and everyone felt ___frightened___.
 (frighten)
People were also _____ about the trash and litter problem. They said they
 (worry)
were _____ that the streets were so dirty. People were _____ of
 (frustrate)   (tire)
complaining, but the situation was _____. There was a special meeting at
                                    (depress)
City Hall. The meeting was _____. Everyone felt _____ that the
                           (encourage)   (satisfy)
city council was starting to make improvements.

Show what you know! Describe feelings about a neighborhood

STEP 1. Check (✓) three adjectives to describe how you feel about your neighborhood. Then write statements about your feelings.

☐ worried   ☐ frightened   ☐ excited   ☐ bored
☐ frustrated   ☐ encouraged   ☐ satisfied   ☐ other: _____

I'm excited about the different backgrounds of my neighbors.

STEP 2. GROUPS. Discuss.

1. Share your ideas from Step 1.
2. How many people in your group are happy in their neighborhood? How many are unhappy? What are the reasons?

Can you...describe feelings about a neighborhood? ☐

Give and follow directions

Life Skills

1 BEFORE YOU LISTEN

CLASS. Many community centers in the U.S. have after-school programs for children and teens. Discuss.

1. What kinds of activities do they offer?
2. Which activities are the most popular for young children? Which are popular among teenagers?

2 LISTEN

CD1 T30

A The director of the Hanson Park Community Center is returning a call to a parent. Listen to their conversation and take notes. What kinds of classes does the after-school program offer?

1. _____

2. _____

3. _____

4. _____

5. _____

CD1 T30

B Read the statements. Then listen to the conversation again. Write *T* (true) or *F* (false). Correct the false statements.

_____ 1. The Hanson Park Community Center offers tutoring in reading every day.

_____ 2. The Hanson Park Community Center is located in a building downtown.

_____ 3. The Hanson Park Community Center is open from 3 P.M. to 9 P.M.

_____ 4. Mrs. Suarez will enroll her daughter in the art classes.

_____ 5. Mrs. Suarez thinks her daughter will be interested in taking swimming lessons.

_____ 6. To enroll children in classes, parents should mail a letter to the director of after-school classes.

_____ 7. Classes at the Hanson Park Community Center are free.

A Look at the map. Look at the compass rose. What do the letters *N*, *E*, *W*, and *S* stand for?

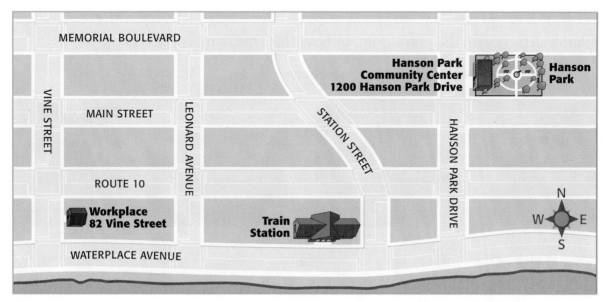

CD1 T31

B Jenna Smith, the director of Hanson Park Community Center, is giving a parent directions to the center. Listen and mark the route on the map.

C Look at the map. Circle the correct words. (If necessary, listen to Jenna Smith's directions again.)

1. The parent should go **north / south** on Vine Street to get to the Hanson Park Community Center.

2. The director tells the parent to drive **east / west** on Route 10.

3. The Hanson Park Community Center is **northwest / northeast** of her workplace.

4. The nearest cross-street to the Hanson Park Community Center is **Hanson Park Drive / Memorial Boulevard**.

D ROLE PLAY. PAIRS. Role-play these situations.

1. **Student A:** You need directions to the Hanson Park Community Center from your home. You live on Memorial Boulevard between Vine Street and Leonard Avenue.
   Student B: Look at the map and give directions.

2. **Student B:** You need directions to the Hanson Park Community Center from your home. You live on Waterplace Avenue by the train station.
   Student A: Look at the map and give directions.

Can you...give and follow directions? ☐

Listening and Speaking

1 BEFORE YOU LISTEN

A Match the pictures with the words from the box. Write the numbers next to the words.

_____ graffiti _____ a pothole _____ garbage _____ a vacant lot

1

2

3

4

B CLASS. Which of the things in Exercise A do you see on your way to school? Where do you see them? Do you think they are problems? Why or why not?

2 LISTEN

CD1 T32

A Jamil Hadad and Linlin Yang work at the same company. Listen. What's the topic of their conversation?

CD1 T32

B Read the statements. Then listen to the conversation again. Write *T* (true) or *F* (false). Correct the false statements.

_____ 1. Last week, the garbage truck came to Linlin's house on schedule.

_____ 2. Both Linlin and Jamil have a problem with their garbage pick-up.

_____ 3. The fast-food restaurants throw their garbage in the vacant lot.

_____ 4. Linlin and Jamil agree that it's OK for teenagers to hang out in the park.

_____ 5. Linlin is upset because there aren't enough after-school programs.

C PAIRS. Discuss. Linlin says that the trash in the vacant lot is a *health hazard*. What does she mean?

3 CONVERSATION

CD1 T33

Jamil and his wife Maryam are talking. Listen and read.

Jamil: I had lunch with Linlin at work today. She has a problem with the garbage pickup. They don't pick up the garbage at her house on schedule.

Maryam: Oh, yeah? The same problem we have.

Jamil: Yeah. And I told her about our problem with the vacant lot. We both wish there were more after-school programs in the community.

Maryam: Do you mean activities for young children?

Jamil: That would be good, but we also need sports for teens.

Maryam: Do you know what I wish?

Jamil: No. What?

Maryam: I wish they had a swimming pool.

4 PRACTICE

A PAIRS. **Practice the conversation.**

B PAIRS. **Use the conversation as a model to make similar conversations. Use the information in the wish lists.**

Wish List 1	Wish List 2	Wish List 3
educational programs	services for senior citizens	concerts
homework help	health and fitness classes	movies and art shows
computer classes	free hot lunches for anyone over 65	a chess club

C MAKE IT PERSONAL. **Think about community services.**

STEP 1. GROUPS. **Discuss.**

1. List six important community services.
2. Which community services are the most important? Number them from *1* (most important) to *6* (least important).

STEP 2. CLASS. **Share your results. Which are the three most important community services?**

Grammar

Wish in the present and future	
I **wish**	(that) we **had** a swimming pool in this community.
We **wish**	(that) the Sanitation Department **would come** to our neighborhood.
I **wish**	(that) there **were** more after-school programs at the community center.

Grammar Watch

- Use *wish* + simple past to talk about things that you want to be true now, but that are not true.
- Use *wish* + *could* or *would* (not *can* or *will*) to talk about things that you hope will be true in the future.
- Use *were*, instead of *was*, after *wish*.

1   PRACTICE

A Some people are not satisfied with the services at their public library. Circle the verb *wish*. Underline the verb in the *wish* clauses.

Carlos: We (wish) the library opened earlier in the morning.

John: I wish it didn't close at 4:00 P.M. on Fridays.

Millie: I wish the movie selection at the library were better. I wish the movies weren't so old. How about some new releases?

Yusef: I don't have a computer. I wish the library would get more computers.

B A local newspaper interviewed people about problems with traffic. Complete the sentences with the correct form of the verbs.

Tim: The traffic is getting worse. I wish I ___didn't need___ a car.
(not need)

Gladys: I just wish there _____ more free parking downtown.
(be)

Andre: The streets are in bad condition. I wish the city _____ the potholes.
(fix)

Julio: I wish that people _____ so fast.
(not drive)

Bo: We need more stop signs. I wish we _____ a stop sign on every corner.
(have)

Jack's family is talking at the dinner table. Read what they're saying. Then rewrite each person's opinion as a wish. More than one answer is possible.

Jack: I think we need a hospital in the neighborhood.

Fran: The streets are so noisy. What do you think, Jason?

Jason: I agree, but public transportation is the biggest problem for me. The buses should run more frequently—every ten minutes would be great.

Carol: Well, I'd just like to be able to go to the park more often!

Sarah: I want swings and slides in the playground.

Mark: I'd like a place to play baseball. How about you, Uncle David?

David: A baseball field is a good idea, Mark, but I don't know why this family complains so much.

1. Jack wishes _____*there were*_____ a hospital nearby.

2. Fran wishes the streets _____ so noisy.

3. Jason wishes the buses _____ every ten minutes.

4. Carol wishes she _____ to the park more often.

5. Sarah wishes the playground _____ more equipment.

6. Mark wishes _____ a baseball field in the neighborhood.

7. David wishes his family _____ so much.

Show what you know! Talk about making changes in a community

STEP 1. **Complete these two sentences about your neighborhood.**

I wish _____ now.

I wish _____ in the future.

STEP 2. GROUPS. **Tell each other your wishes.**

STEP 3. CLASS. **Share your wishes. What three neighborhood changes were the most common?**

Can you... talk about making changes in a community? ☐

Reading

1   BEFORE YOU READ

A CLASS. Discuss. Are there community gardens in the area where you live? Who plants these gardens?

B Read the title and the headings in the article. Predict. What is the main idea?

2   READ

CD1 T34

Listen and read the article. Was your prediction about the main idea correct? What is the author's opinion about community gardens?

Green Is the Way to Go
by Jo Atkinsen, Freelance Contributor

Today, communities around the U.S. are going green. For some, that means paying attention to the **environment** by recycling or controlling pollution. But others are turning their neighborhoods green by planting community gardens.

Green Brings Benefits

A growing number of government and community leaders point out that gardening is a great way to improve the appearance of a neighborhood and the **value** of homes and businesses. It also unites neighborhood residents. Research at Texas A & M University and the University of Illinois shows that city areas with more green have less crime.

One Neighborhood's Story

Norris Square in Philadelphia is a neighborhood that has benefited from a community garden. In the 1980s, Norris Square was known for its **run-down** buildings and vacant lots filled with trash. Then a group of Puerto Rican women planted vegetables and flowers in one vacant lot. Soon there was also an outdoor kitchen and colorful murals showing rural life in Puerto Rico.

The Las Parcelas Community Garden became a place of beauty and a source of fresh food for Norris Square **residents**. It also became a source of neighborhood **pride**. Soon people were working together to do home repairs, clean up other vacant lots, remove graffiti, and plant more trees and flowers throughout the neighborhood.

Today, instead of fights in the park, there are festivals. Instead of **abandoned** cars along the streets, there are trees. People can now enjoy a neighborhood that is cleaner, safer, and more beautiful.

Plant Your Own Seeds

If you want to start a community garden in your area, you can get information from the Community Gardening Association at www.communitygarden.org.

A Complete the sentences. Circle the correct answers.

1. Residents of Norris Square planted the Las Parcelas Community Garden in _____.
   a. a lot   b. a park   c. a building

2. Norris Square residents started the Las Parcelas Community Garden in _____.
   a. the 1970s   b. the 1980s   c. the 1990s

3. Members of the community _____ in the Las Parcelas Community Garden.
   a. planted fruit trees   b. built an outdoor kitchen   c. painted grafitti

B Read the Reading Skill. Then answer the question.

Did crime probably increase, decrease, or stay the same in Norris Square because of the Las Parcelas Community Garden? Explain.

> **Reading Skill:** Making Inferences
>
> If an author doesn't give information directly, use what you read to make a logical guess about what is probably true.

4 WORD WORK

Find these boldfaced words in the article. Circle the definition that matches the meaning in the article.

1. environment
   (a.) the natural world   b. the people and things around you

2. value
   a. the importance of something   b. the money something is worth

3. run-down
   a. in very bad condition   b. very tired and not healthy

4. residents
   a. doctors in training   b. people who live in a particulat place

5. pride
   a. a feeling that you are better than others   b. a feeling of satisfaction

6. abandoned
   a. not being used or taken care of   b. illegally parked

Show what you know! Talk about community involvement

GROUPS. Discuss. Would you like to start a community garden? List reasons for and against starting a garden.

Listening and Speaking

1 BEFORE YOU LISTEN

A **PAIRS.** You are going to listen to a discussion at a city council meeting. The council members use the following words. Match the words with the definitions.

___d___ 1. convince   a. make the size or amount of something larger

_____ 2. urge   b. say who someone is or what something is

_____ 3. identify   c. try hard to persuade someone to do something

_____ 4. increase   d. persuade; get someone to agree

_____ 5. investigate   e. make the size or amount of something smaller

_____ 6. reduce   f. try to find out the truth about something

B **CLASS.** Look at the picture. What is the purpose of the ad?

2 LISTEN

CD1 T35

A Clara Ramos is a city council representative. She is answering Hugo Lopez's questions. Listen to their conversation. What are Clara Ramos and Hugo Lopez talking about?

CD1 T35

B **PAIRS.** Read the questions. Listen to the conversation again. Then answer the questions.

1. What did Clara Ramos ask the mayor and the chief of police to do?

2. What answer did she receive?

3. How can neighborhood residents help the police?

4. Why is there usually less crime as a result of community policing?

C **PAIRS.** Read this quote: "Safety is the responsibility of everyone in the community, not just the police." Who would probably make the statement, Clara Ramos or Hugo Lopez? Explain.

3 CONVERSATION

CD1 T36

A Listen to the phrases and sentences. Notice the weak pronunciation of *to*. Then listen again and repeat.

to come with me   I'd like you to come with me.

to make a difference   This is our chance to make a difference.

want to ("wanna")   We want to ("wanna") have better services.

going to ("gonna")   Now you're going to ("gonna") tell me to go to the meeting.

CD1 T37

B Eva Lopez is talking with her husband Hugo one week after the city council meeting. Listen and read.

Eva: You know what this neighborhood needs? More streetlights, especially in the school parking lot.

Hugo: If you really feel that way, Eva, why don't you do something about it?

Eva: Now you're going to tell me to go to the community-policing meeting, aren't you?

Hugo: The meeting is tonight at 7:30. I'd like you to come with me.

Eva: Not tonight. I'm working on the community newsletter.

Hugo: You can work on the newsletter another night. This meeting is important. It's our chance to make a difference.

Pronunciation Watch

The word *to* usually has a short, weak pronunciation. In conversation, *want to* is often pronounced "wanna" and *going to* is often pronounced "gonna."

4 PRACTICE

A PAIRS. Practice the conversation.

B PAIRS. Do you think Eva will attend the community-policing meeting? Explain.

C PROBLEM-SOLVING. Think about neighborhood problems.

STEP 1. Read about Hugo. What is his problem?

Hugo Lopez saw several young men in his neighborhood breaking windows and writing graffiti on the wall at the community center. They live in the Southland neighborhood, so he knows them and their families well.

STEP 2. GROUPS. Discuss possible solutions to the problem. Make a list. Then decide on the best solution.

Grammar

Verb + object + infinitive		
We don't **want**	**the city**	**to take away** services.
He **urged**	**us**	**not to believe** everything we hear.

········· **Grammar Watch**

- An infinitive is *to* + base form of the verb. To make a negative infinitive, use *not* + *to* + base form of the verb.
- With verb + object + infinitive, use object pronouns (*me, you, him, her, it, us, them*).

1   PRACTICE

A   **Read the conversation from a community-policing meeting. Circle the verb, draw a line under the object, and draw two lines under the infinitive.**

Officer: My Name is Officer Brown. As part of our community-policing effort, I (urge) you to check on neighbors who might need help.

Mrs. Soliz: My neighbor, Mrs. Soto, is eighty years old. I always ask her to call if she needs anything, but she tells me not to worry. What should I do?

Officer: Continue what you're doing. And, please, if you notice any change in her daily routine, try to find out what's going on.

Mrs. Soliz: I've noticed that some senior citizens are too trusting. They open the door when strangers knock. I've told Mrs. Soto not to do that.

Officer: That can be a problem. We have a safety class for seniors at the community center. We teach them to ask for identification even when they've made a call for service. We remind them not to open their doors until they know it's safe.

B   **Cross out the noun object in each sentence. Then change the noun object to a pronoun object.**

1. The mayor doesn't want ~~the sanitation workers~~ *them* to go on strike.

2. The community-policing program encourages the residents in our neighborhood to work with the police.

3. Community council members urge residents not to miss meetings.

4. The police expect my neighbors and me to report anything unusual.

5. Tell Mrs. Soto not to leave her door unlocked.

6. Please ask Mr. Lee to check on Mrs. Soto once or twice a week.

A Captain Liu is telling an officer about a class he wants her to give on street safety. Complete each sentence with an object pronoun and the correct form of the verb.

STREET-SMART TIPS
- Be alert. Keep your eyes and ears open.
- Show that you're confident. If you're nervous, don't show it.
- Trust your instincts. If you think something is wrong, it probably is.
- Use your common sense. You know how to make the right decisions.

Prepare a list of "street smart" tips. Teach the people to follow the four basic rules. Also tell _____them to stay away_____ from areas like parking
(stay away)
lots and alleys that are empty or poorly lit. Remind _____ lots of cash. Advise
(not carry)
_____ careful with their wallets. Just last week I saw a man who was
(be)
a target for crime. I warned _____ his wallet in his back pocket.
(not keep)

B Complete the sentences about ways to improve safety. Include an object + infinitive.

1. All city parks close at 11:00 P.M., but there are people in Southland Park all night. The police should tell _____them to go home_____.

2. Women and senior citizens are often easy targets. Why don't we organize special self-defense classes, like karate? The classes will teach _____.

3. The vacant lot across from the park is full of litter. Let's talk to Mrs. Hyer, the owner of the lot. We can ask _____.

4. Mr. Torres likes walking his dog late at night. Someone should tell _____.

Show what you know! Identify community problems

STEP 1. GROUPS. Identify a problem in the neighborhood where you attend school. Discuss.

- Who can you talk to in order to find a solution to the problem?
- What will you say to get help?

STEP 2. CLASS. Share your ideas.

Can you...identify community problems? ☐

Writing

1 BEFORE YOU WRITE

A **GROUPS.** **Communities can create a sense of belonging. Discuss.**

1. What is an *outsider*? Why is it important NOT to feel like an outsider?
2. What can people do to feel like part of their community?

B **Read the writing model. What is a *block party*? What is the author's opinion of block parties?**

A Block Party That Made a Difference

In July 2008, I went to my first block party. My husband and I were living in a new neighborhood, and we felt like outsiders. Then came the big event. I had no idea a block party could be such a great experience. First of all, the party was fun. The city closed our street to traffic, and everyone came out. There were games for children, music for teens and adults, and food for everyone. Best of all, I really got a chance to talk to some of my neighbors. That brings me to the second reason I liked the block party: I learned a lot about my neighborhood. I found out about the best places to shop and eat. I heard about programs and services at the library and the community center. I also found out about neighborhood volunteer projects, like cleaning up the park and delivering hot meals to senior citizens. You may already know the last reason I am a big fan of block parties. My husband and I made some good friends that day, and we now feel like part of the community. A few weeks after the block party, I started volunteering in the neighborhood, and yes, I am on the planning team for this year's event.

C **PAIRS. Answer the questions.**

1. Why was the block party fun?
2. How did the block party change the author's life?
3. Would you like to attend a block party? Explain.

> **Writing Tip**
>
> Details are important in your writing. Examples are an excellent way to give details.

D **What is the second reason the author likes block parties? Draw one line under the author's reason. What are three examples that give details about her second reason? Write *1*, *2*, and *3* next to each example.**

E **GROUPS. Compare your answers.**

2 THINKING ON PAPER

A BRAINSTORM. Think about the neighborhood where you live. What do you like about the neighborhood? What do you dislike? Organize your reasons in a chart like this.

Things I Like in My Neighborhood	Things I Dislike in My Neighborhood
A.	A.
B.	B.

B Decide whether you want to write about what you like or what you dislike about your neighborhood. Plan and organize your paragraph. Give reasons for your like (or dislike). Give examples that support your reasons.

What I Like or (Dislike) Most About My Neighborhood: _____

A. Reason: _____

    1. _____

    2. _____

B. Reason: _____

    1. _____

    2. _____

3 WRITE

Write a paragraph about what you like or dislike most about your neighborhood. Use the information in your plan. Look at the writing model for an example.

4 CHECK YOUR WRITING

☐ Did you state the main idea, or subject, of your paragraph?

☐ Did you use words like *first*, *second*, and *third* to signal your reasons?

☐ Did you give examples to provide details?

☐ Did you use correct capitalization, punctuation, and spelling?

1 REVIEW

For your grammar review, go to page 247.

2 ACT IT OUT — What do you say?

STEP 1. CLASS. Review the conversation on page 59 (CD1, Track 37).

STEP 2. ROLE PLAY. PAIRS. Role-play this situation.

Student A: You are organizing a spring clean-up in the neighborhood park next Saturday. Explain the reasons that the spring clean-up is a good idea. Try to convince Student B to help.

Student B: You have Saturday off and you have a lot to do. You don't have time to go to the spring clean-up. Explain your reasons.

3 READ AND REACT — Problem-solving

STEP 1. GROUPS. Read about Lydia's problem.

Until recently, Lydia's neighborhood was an immigrant community, and residents shared the same language and culture. However, the area is changing. There are a lot of new residents who are not from Lydia's home culture. Lydia no longer feels at home in her community. She is afraid that these and other changes will make it difficult for her and her family to continue living in the neighborhood.

STEP 2. GROUPS. What is Lydia's problem? Discuss a solution. List three things that she and her family can do to solve the problem.

4 CONNECT

For your Community-Building Activity, go to page 258.
For your Team Project, go to page 265.

Which goals can you check off? Go back to page 45.

 Go to the CD-ROM for more practice.

On the Job

Preview

Read the title. Why are the people shaking hands? What do you think they are saying?

UNIT GOALS

- ☐ Communicate with supervisors and co-workers

- ☐ Interpret information about employee benefits

- ☐ Check your understanding of a situation at work

- ☐ Talk about common workplace injuries

- ☐ Ask and answer performance review questions

- ☐ Follow work-related instructions

- ☐ Write a memo to a supervisor

Listening and Speaking

1 BEFORE YOU LISTEN

A CLASS. Sandra Duval is a new teller at People's Bank. It's her first day at work. Discuss. How do you think Sandra feels?

B CD1 T38 Read and listen to the words. Which ones have you seen or heard before?

> automatically   endorse   firsthand   observe   procedure

C CD1 T38 Listen again and repeat.

2 LISTEN

A CD1 T39 Sandra is talking to Robert Stamov, her manager at the bank. Listen to the first part of their conversation. How does Sandra feel about having to observe Robert? Why?

B CD1 T40 Read the statements. Then listen to the whole conversation. Write *T* (true) or *F* (false). Correct the false statements.

___F___ 1. Sandra will receive on-the-job training from
         one week
        Robert for ~~two weeks~~.

_____ 2. Robert explains how to cash a check.

_____ 3. Robert explains the procedure for personal bank accounts.

_____ 4. The bank's customers deposit checks more often than cash.

_____ 5. The amount on the check and the deposit slip must be the same.

C Sandra says, "I'm a little nervous, but I'll get over it." What does she mean? What does the phrase *get over it* mean?

D PAIRS. Sandra asked Robert a lot of questions. Is it a good idea to ask so many questions on the first day of a job? Explain.

3 CONVERSATION

CD1 T41

A  **Listen to the sentences. Notice the stressed words. Then listen again and repeat.**

  • •   •   •   •   • •

Fill out the **form**.   **Fill** the **form** out.   **Fill** it **out**.

CD1 T42

B **Read the sentences. Put a dot (•) over the words in the underlined sections that would be stressed. Then listen and check your answers.**

1. Let me know if I can <u>help you out</u>.
2. I'm a little nervous, but I'll <u>get over it</u>.
3. <u>Turn the computer off</u> before you leave.
4. I already <u>turned it off</u>.
5. There's a lot to learn, but you're <u>picking it up</u> quickly.

> **Pronunciation Watch**
>
> In most phrasal verbs, both the verb and particle can be stressed. If there is a noun object, the noun may be stressed instead of the particle. If there is a pronoun object, the pronoun is not stressed.

CD1 T43

C **Sandra is talking to Jason, another teller. Listen and read their conversation.**

Sandra: There sure is a lot to learn for this job.

Jason: There *is* a lot to learn, but you're picking it up quickly. Let me know if there's any way I can help you out.

Sandra: Thanks, Jason. Right now, I need to find out about my health benefits.

Jason: You're in luck. There's a meeting tomorrow to discuss our health plan.

Sandra: Oh, yeah. I forgot. What time is the meeting?

Jason: Two o'clock. But you should check with Robert.

4 PRACTICE

A PAIRS. **Practice the conversation.**

B MAKE IT PERSONAL. **Think about your first day at a new job.**

STEP 1. GROUPS. **What do you expect to do? Make a list of four things.**

> 1. Get an orientation to the building.

STEP 2. CLASS. **Share your ideas.**

Grammar

Phrasal verbs

Separable phrasal verbs	Inseparable phrasal verbs
Fill out the deposit slip completely. **Fill** the deposit slip **out** completely. **Fill** it **out** completely.	I'll **get over** my nervousness. I'll **get over** it.

Grammar Watch

- A phrasal verb consists of a verb + a **particle**. Particles are words such as *up, down, on, off, after, by, in,* and *out*.

- For **inseparable phrasal verbs**, the verb and the particle must stay together.

- For **separable phrasal verbs**, the verb and the particle can stay together or be separated.

- Many phrasal verbs can take **objects** (nouns or pronouns). When the object of a separable phrasal verb is a noun, the object can come before or after the particle. When the object is a pronoun, the object must come before the particle.

- Inseparable phrasal verbs sometimes have two particles, for example, *get along with*.

- *See page 282-283 for a list of phrasal verbs and their meanings.*

1 PRACTICE

Read the conversation. Underline the phrasal verbs. Then write the correct phrasal verb next to each definition.

Robert: When the bank closes, there's still quite a bit of work for the tellers. Most evenings you'll work until 6:00. At the end of the day, don't <u>turn off</u> your computer or other equipment until we've put together our final report for the day. It's important that we have an exact record of all transactions.

Sandra: What if there's a problem and I can't figure it out?

Robert: For now, you'll talk it over with me or another teller. If we see any problems, we'll point them out. But I'm not worried. You're doing an excellent job.

Sandra: Thanks. You can count on me to do my best.

1. _____turn off_____ = stop

2. _____ = discuss

3. _____ = depend on

4. _____ = assemble

5. _____ = solve a problem

6. _____ = indicate, show

A Unscramble the sentences. Put the words in order. More than one answer is possible.

1. filled / The customer / out / the form

   The customer filled the form out. OR: *The customer filled out the form.*

2. the new employee / out / We / with her first assignment / to help / offered

   _____

3. he'll / over / He's / about the new schedule, / it / get / but / upset

   _____

4. me / on time / count / the job / can / You / on / to do

   _____

5. talk / should / with your manager / over / that problem / You

   _____

B Circle the object in each sentence. Then, on notepaper, rewrite each sentence using an object pronoun (*it, them, her,* or *him*).

1. Be sure to turn off (your computer) before you leave.

   Be sure to turn it off before you leave.

2. Can you point out the new employees?

3. Their accountants figured out the problem.

4. The managers put this plan together.

5. She can count on her co-workers.

Show what you know! Communicate with supervisors and co-workers

ROLE PLAY. PAIRS. **Role-play this situation. Use the phrasal verbs in the box.**

Student A: You are starting a new job. Discuss your responsibilities with your supervisor.

Student B: You are Student A's supervisor, and it is his or her first day on the job. Discuss Student A's job responsibilities.

count on	figure out	find out	get over	help out	pick up
point out	put together	take over	talk over	turn off	turn on

Can you...communicate with supervisors and co-workers? ☐

Life Skills

1 READ AN EMPLOYEE HANDBOOK

 CLASS. New employees often receive a handbook on the first day of work. Discuss. What kind of information is usually included in an employee handbook?

 Read part of a company's employee handbook. Which benefits are probably different for part-time employees?

ACE Computer Solutions

Employee Benefits Overview

Welcome to Ace! We are pleased to provide you with information about your employment here. (Note: This information applies only to full-time employees.)

PAYROLL: All employees are paid bi-weekly, that is, at the end of every 2 weeks.

HOURS: The normal workday is 8 hours with one hour for lunch. You are expected to work Mon.–Fri.

OVERTIME: Here at Ace, we work overtime only when necessary. Full-time employees are allowed to work a maximum of 10 hours of overtime per week. The company pays employees one and one-half times their hourly rate for overtime work. Supervisors must approve all overtime.

PAID TIME OFF (PTO): After 90 days of service, you are eligible for PTO:

- **Sick leave:** 10 paid sick days per year. Please note that if you are out sick longer than 2 days, you must supply a doctor's note describing the nature of the illness and saying that you can return to work.

- **Vacation:** Vacation days are based on length of service (less than 5 years = 10 days per year; 5–10 years = 15 days per year; 11–19 years = 20 days per year; 20 or more years = 24 days per year).

- **Personal days:** You are allowed 5 personal days per year. If possible, please get permission from your supervisor at least 10 business days in advance.

- **Holidays:** Ace is closed on these holidays: New Year's Day, Martin Luther King Jr. Day, Memorial Day, Independence Day, Labor Day, Thanksgiving, and Christmas.

A Read the questions. Circle the correct answers.

1. How many times a month do Ace employees usually receive a paycheck?
   a. one
   b. two
   c. four

2. How many hours do full-time Ace employees normally work a day?
   a. seven
   b. eight
   c. ten

3. Imagine you're an Ace employee. You were home sick for four days. What do you have to do before you go back to work?
   a. get permission from your supervisor
   b. see a doctor
   c. notify a co-worker

4. Justin, an Ace employee, has been with the company for thirteen years. How many vacation days can he take?
   a. ten
   b. fifteen
   c. twenty

5. Silvia, another Ace employee, wants to take a personal day on her birthday, June 30. What is the last day she can ask for permission from her supervisor?
   a. May 30
   b. June 1
   c. June 16

6. Which is NOT a paid holiday for Ace employees?
   a. Presidents' Day
   b. Memorial Day
   c. Labor Day

B GROUPS. Discuss.

1. Do you think that Ace has good employee benefits? Explain.

2. This page is only a small part of an employee handbook. What other information do most employee handbooks include?

3. Why do you think Ace doesn't want employees to work overtime for more than ten hours?

4. What are some reasons employees take personal days?

Can you...interpret information about employee benefits? ☐

Check your understanding of a situation at work

Listening and Speaking

1 BEFORE YOU LISTEN

CLASS. Look at the picture of the doctor, the resident (someone who has almost finished training as a doctor), and the nurse.

1. What job duties do you think each person has?

2. The resident is holding a patient's chart. What kind of information is in a patient's chart?

2 LISTEN

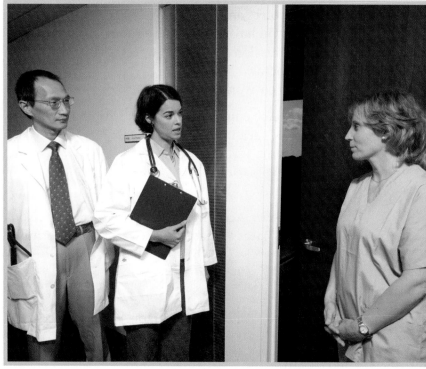

A CD1 T44

Listen to two conversations at a hospital. A doctor and a resident are a talking to a nurse. What kind of nurse is Carolina—responsible or not responsible? Explain.

B CD1 T44

Listen again to the first conversation. Complete the statements. Choose the correct words.

1. The resident doesn't see Mr. Cordova's **chart / vital signs**.

2. The nursing assistant probably **forgot to write / wrote** Mr. Cordova's vital signs in the chart.

3. Carolina **remembers to write / offers to take** Mr. Cordova's vital signs.

C CD1 T45

Read the statements. Listen again to the second conversation. Write *T* (true) or *F* (false). Correct the false statements.

_____ 1. Mrs. Worth had a gall bladder operation yesterday.

_____ 2. Mrs. Worth needs to wait for a while before she walks.

_____ 3. The nurses have helped Mrs. Worth to walk.

_____ 4. There are a lot of nurses on duty on Carolina's floor.

_____ 5. Carolina doesn't have time to help Mrs. Worth.

3 CONVERSATION

CD1 T46

A 🎧 **Listen to the sentences. Notice that the /t/ sound is often very quiet at the end of negative contractions. Then listen again and repeat.**

Pronunciation Watch

Auxiliary verbs (such as *have, can,* and *could*) usually have a strong pronunciation, with a clear vowel sound, in negative contractions and at the end of a sentence. They have a weak pronunciation, with a short, quiet vowel sound, when they come before another word in a sentence.

Can't she see Mr. Singer? — Yes, she **can**. She **can** see him today.

Couldn't he wait? — Yes, he **could**. He **could** wait until tomorrow.

Haven't they taken her out of bed? — Yes, they **have**. Where **have** they taken her?

CD1 T47

B 🎧 **Listen to the sentences. Circle the words you hear.**

1. **Has / Hasn't** Mrs. Worth been out of bed?
2. **Did / Didn't** the nurse take her vital signs?
3. **Could / Couldn't** we look at her chart?
4. **Have / Haven't** any of the nurses walked with her?
5. I **can / can't** help her right now.

CD1 T48

C 🎧 **Two nurses are talking at the nurse's station. Listen and read.**

Valerie: Carolina, Mr. Singer would like to talk with Dr. Paige. Have you seen her?

Carolina: I don't think she's on call today. Wasn't she on call last night?

Valerie: I don't know. I was pretty sure she was on the schedule for today.

Carolina: Let me check. See. She was here last night. Dr. Garcia is on duty today. Can't he see Mr. Singer?

Valerie: He could, but Dr. Paige is her doctor. Mr. Singer really wants to talk to her. He wants to know the results of his recent tests.

Carolina: Well, in that case, tell him that Dr. Paige will be in tomorrow. Couldn't Mr. Singer wait until then?

Valerie: I think so. I'll explain that to him.

4 PRACTICE

A PAIRS. **Practice the conversation.**

B ROLE PLAY. PAIRS. **You are co-workers at Greenville General Hospital. Read your part, but don't read your partner's part. Solve the problem.**

Student A: You're looking for some bandages in the supply closet. A co-worker told you that Student B had put them in there. Speak to Student B about the bandages.

Student B: You aren't in charge of the bandages. Another person stocks them in the supply closet.

Grammar

Negative *yes/no* questions

Questions	Responses
Didn't the nurse take Mr. Cordova's vital signs this morning?	No, she didn't. They're not on the chart.
Haven't they tried to take her down the hall?	Yes, they have. They walked with her last night.

⋮

Grammar Watch

- Negative *yes/no* questions begin with negative forms of *be* or negative forms of auxiliary verbs, like *do, did, have, can, will,* and *should*. Use contractions in negative questions.
- Use negative *yes/no* questions to check information that you think is true.
- Use short answers to respond to negative questions. Answer with *yes* if the information is true and *no* if it is not true.

1 PRACTICE

A Match the questions that fast-food workers ask one another with the answers.

___b___ 1. Didn't you train for the cashier job?

_____ 2. Didn't he give you the schedule you wanted?

_____ 3. Don't most of the workers get along?

_____ 4. Aren't the uniforms ready?

_____ 5. Hasn't payroll given you your paycheck?

a. Yes, they do. They're good friends.

b. No, I didn't. I trained to take orders.

c. No, they're not. They're at the cleaners.

d. No, they haven't, and I need it now!

e. No, he didn't. I'm working nights again.

B Unscramble the questions. Put the words in the correct order.

1. they / about the schedule change? / you / tell / didn't

   _Didn't they tell you about the schedule change?_____

2. yet? / arrived / hasn't / the cleaning crew

   _____

3. about that? / won't / complain / the customers

   _____

4. get / part-time employees / don't / health insurance?

   _____

A **Write negative questions. Use the prompts and the correct form of the verb.**

1. _____Didn't you clock in_____ yet?
   (you / did clock in)

2. _____ the morning shift instead?
   (I / can work)

3. _____ your uniform?
   (you / did bring)

4. _____ soon?
   (we / should close up)

5. _____ your break yet?
   (you / have taken)

6. _____ the counters?
   (they / should clean)

B **Read each response. Then write a negative *yes/no* question that one co-worker asked another. Use the words in parentheses.**

1. **A:** _____? (you / finish the report / yet)
   B: No, I haven't. I'm still working on it.

2. **A:** _____? (he / about the problem / tell his supervisor)
   B: No, he didn't. He didn't want her to know.

3. **A:** _____? (we / prepare / for the meeting)
   B: Of course we should. The director will be there.

4. **A:** _____? (they / for the holiday season / hire more workers)
   B: No, they can't. They're already over budget.

Show what you know! Check your understanding of a situation at work

ROLE PLAY. PAIRS. **Role-play a conversation between two employees at work.**

Student A: You are talking to a new employee. That employee is having difficulty meeting one of the requirements described below. Find out what his or her problem is. Use one of the phrases in the box.

Student B: You are the new employee. Answer Student A's question about the difficulty you are having.

get your building pass	establish your work hours
read the safety manual	try on your safety equipment
watch the training video	arrange to receive your paycheck

Can you...check your understanding of a situation at work? ☐

Reading

1 BEFORE YOU READ

A CLASS. A company's *fulfillment center* stores products in a warehouse and then packs them and sends them to customers. Discuss. What kinds of injuries can happen at a fulfillment center?

B CLASS. Adjustable computer screens and adjustable tables are two examples of *ergonomic* work equipment. What is the meaning of *ergonomic*?

2 READ

CD1 T49

Listen and read the article. What is the main idea?

Another Way to Stay Healthy

It is sometimes known as RSI (repetitive stress injury), RMI (repetitive motion injury), or MSD (musculoskeletal disorder). The name may change, but the problem remains the same. All of us here at We Pack, We Ship (WPWS) must be careful at work. We are all **at risk** of suffering from work-related injuries.

WPWS has always been concerned about the health and well-being of our **associates**. We realize how serious RSI can be. The severe pain caused by RSI often makes it necessary for employees to miss work and lose income. In order to reduce the amount of missed work time due to RSI, one year ago we formed the Safety Committee. The committee's **recommendations** have already led to several steps to control RSI. The first improvements were made in the office, where we created comfortable and well-lit workspaces for the office staff. Each workstation has ergonomic furniture, and all computers include an adjustable monitor and an ergonomic keyboard.

WPWS Safety Committee members discuss ways to avoid workplace injuries.

And good news for the warehouse staff, too! We're reorganizing the space so that workers can reach merchandise more easily and use machines to move heavy materials whenever possible. Other changes include conveyor belts that carry boxes from packing stations to the shipping area and adjustable tables that allow packers to avoid unnecessary bending, lifting, and twisting.

The Safety Committee has announced that it will be offering a series of workshops on ways to decrease our chances of developing carpal tunnel syndrome, tendonitis, and other **debilitating** RSIs. The workshops will provide training on the correct use of tools and equipment and the best ways to complete various tasks. The workshops will also teach exercises to keep us strong and healthy. The committee members haven't yet decided on the schedule of workshops, so look for more information in next month's newsletter.

A Complete the sentences. Circle the correct answers.

1. We Pack, We Ship (WPWS) created the Safety Committee to _____.
   a. write a safety handbook   c. save the company money
   b. make sure employees knew the rules   d. improve employees' attendance

2. Tendonitis is a type of _____.
   a. RSI   c. exercise
   b. ergonomic equipment   d. safety procedure

3. Employees can get a safety-workshop schedule _____.
   a. on page 6 of the newsletter   c. from the Safety Committee right now
   b. in next month's newsletter   d. at packing stations

B Read the Reading Skill. Then match each statement to one that has the same, or almost the same, meaning.

_____ 1. The first improvements were made in the office.

_____ 2. We created comfortable, well-lit spaces for the office staff.

_____ 3. Each workstation has ergonomic furniture.

a. Tables and chairs help employees work quickly and easily.
b. Changes to make work conditions better began in the office.
c. We made the work areas relaxing and bright.

> **Reading Skill:**
> Recognizing Restatements
>
> When you read, look for information that the author repeats or explains again with different words.

4 WORD WORK

Find the boldfaced words in the article. Guess their meanings from context. Choose the best definition.

1. **at risk**   a. in danger   b. protected from   c. afraid
2. **associates**   a. managers   b. customers   c. co-workers
3. **recommendations**   a. improvements   b. suggestions   c. problems
4. **debilitating**   a. causing anger   b. causing weakness   c. frightening

Show what you know! Talk about common workplace injuries

GROUPS. Make a list of three activities that will probably take place at the workshops that the Safety Committee is planning. How can those workshop activities help reduce RSIs?

Listening and Speaking

1 BEFORE YOU LISTEN

CLASS. Many companies give their employees regular performance reviews. Discuss.

1. Why are performance reviews important?
2. Why are performance reviews especially important for new employees?

Best Bakers

Employee Performance Review

Employee: _____ Supervisor: _____ Date: _____

4 = Exceeds Job Requirements   **2** = Needs Improvement
3 = Meets Job Requirements   **1** = Unacceptable

					Comments
Does quality work	1	2	3	4	
Meets quotas	1	2	3	4	
Follows instructions	1	2	3	4	
Has a positive attitude	1	2	3	4	
Works as a team member	1	2	3	4	
Follows safety procedures	1	2	3	4	
Is punctual	1	2	3	4	

2 LISTEN

CD1 T50

A Dennis Mack is a supervisor at Best Bakers. He is giving a performance review to Helena Gorecki, a new employee. Listen. Then look at the Employee Performance Review. In which category of job requirements does Helena need improvement?

CD1 T50

B Listen again. Circle the numbers in the performance review above, based on what Tim says. He hasn't yet covered all the categories.

C PAIRS. Compare your answers.

3 CONVERSATION

CD1 T51

Listen and read this part of Helena's review.

Dennis: First of all, I want you to know that we're happy in general with your work.

Helena: Oh, thank you!

Dennis: Yes, the quality of your work is very good. And you're meeting your quotas, which is really important. I gave you a "3" in both categories.

Helena: Thank you. I understand how important it is to get all the packages out on time.

Dennis: Exactly. And you're good at following instructions. I gave you a "3" there, too.

Helena: Sometimes I have to ask for clarification.

Dennis: That's great. You should always ask if you're not sure. It's better to ask than to do the wrong thing.

Helena: OK. Good.

4 PRACTICE

A PAIRS. **Practice the conversation.**

B ROLE PLAY. PAIRS. **Role-play this situation. Use the conversation as a model.**

Student A: You are a supervisor at Best Bakers. You are giving a performance review to one of your employees. Fill out the Employee Performance Review form before you begin. Make up the information.

Student B: You are an employee at Best Bakers. You are meeting with your supervisor to discuss your performance review. Respond to your supervisor's comments.

Grammar

Indirect instructions, commands, and requests

Direct speech	Indirect speech		
	Reporting Verb	**Object**	**Indirect Request**
"Ask a question if you're not sure."	He **said**		**to ask** a question if **we're** not sure.
"Leave your earrings and rings at home."	She **told**	**us**	**to leave our** earrings and rings at home.
"Please don't wear jewelry on the job."	She **asked**	**them**	**not to wear** jewelry on the job.
"Wear shoes that will protect your feet."	Company policy **requires**	**us**	**to wear** shoes that will protect **our** feet.

Grammar Watch

- When direct instructions, commands, and requests change to the indirect form, the verb changes to the infinitive form. Pronouns may also change to preserve the original meaning of the speaker.

- Use reporting verbs, such as *advise, ask, instruct, order, say, tell,* and *warn,* to introduce indirect instructions, commands, and requests.

- Most verbs that report indirect instructions, commands, and requests have an object. However, the verb *say* does not.

1   PRACTICE

Read the statements about performance reviews. Circle the reporting verbs. Underline the indirect requests and commands.

1. My supervisor (asked) me <u>to speed up my production</u>. I'm not meeting my quotas.

2. He also told me to think about safety and cleanliness. He specifically asked me to keep my work area cleaner.

3. My manager told me not to take such long breaks. She said to limit my breaks to twenty minutes.

4. She reminded me to wash my equipment at the end of my shift.

5. My boss warned me not to be late again or I might lose my job.

6. My supervisor asked me to check my work more carefully.

7. At the start of my review, my boss told me to relax.

Felix attended classes on office procedures. Read the notes he took about using office e-mail. Then change the direct commands into indirect instructions and requests.

E-mail Procedures

1. Click on the program icon to open the program.
2. Enter your password when prompted. Don't share your password with anyone.
3. Enter the e-mail address of the person you're writing to in the "To" section.
4. Don't forget to complete the "Subject" line.
5. Compose your message in the open section below "Subject."
6. Click on "Send" after completing the e-mail.
7. Remember, log out once you're done so that your privacy is protected.

1. The teacher told _us to click on the program icon_ to open the program.

2. He told _____ when prompted and warned

   _____ with anyone.

3. Next he said _____ in the "To" section.

4. He reminded _____ the "Subject" line.

5. He then instructed _____ in the open section below "Subject."

6. He told _____ after completing the email.

7. Finally, he advised _____ to protect our privacy.

Show what you know! Follow work-related instructions

PAIRS. Give instructions for a simple procedure, such as how to use a copy machine or how to check voice mail.

STEP 1. Student A: Write the steps to follow to complete the procedure.

STEP 2. PAIRS. Student A: Read the instructions to Student B. Student B: Write the instructions.

STEP 3. CLASS. Student B: Describe the procedure using indirect instructions.

Can you... follow work-related instructions? ☐

Writing

1 BEFORE YOU WRITE

A CLASS. Have you ever written a memo to your supervisor at work? Why did you write the memo? What happened after your supervisor read the memo?

B GROUPS. Why is it important to be concise and clear in a memo to a supervisor?

C Read the writing model. What problem does Lev Shepel describe? How many solutions does he offer?

> **Writing Tip**
>
> Most memos are short. They contain language that is direct and clear. The purpose of a memo is usually stated in the first paragraph. Information is often presented in a list instead of a paragraph.

Memo   **ILEA Furniture**
_____

To: Henry Avalos, Warehouse Manager
From: Lev Shepel, Delivery Associate
Date: 6/17/10
Re: Improving Furniture Delivery Times

The purpose of this memo is to offer several simple solutions to the problem of late furniture deliveries.

In my last performance review, you pointed out that over 50% of my deliveries were behind schedule. I believe that other drivers are having similar problems with their deliveries because of the following reasons:
- increased traffic along our delivery routes
- poorly planned delivery routes
- road construction in many areas.

We can't control traffic or road conditions, but we can take these steps to increase on-time deliveries:
- install GPS (navigational systems) to help drivers get around traffic jams and avoid construction delays
- plan delivery routes so that drivers spend less travel time going from one delivery location to the next.

Thank you for considering my suggestions. I hope that you will allow me to present my ideas at our staff meeting next week.

D PAIRS. Answer the questions.

1. Why do you think Lev Shepel is worried about the problem of late furniture deliveries?

2. How can GPS help to solve the problem that Lev describes?

3. What does Lev want his supervisor to do?

E Another driver at Ilea Furniture also wrote a memo. His subject line was "Deliveries." Why is Lev's subject line better?

A BRAINSTORM. Think about problems you have at work. Make a list in a chart like this.

Problems That My Supervisor Should Know About
1.
2.
3.
4.

B Choose one of your problems. Plan and organize your own memo. Write the reasons for the problem and ideas for solutions in a chart like this.

Most Important Work Problem: _____	
Reasons for the Problem	My Ideas for Solutions
•	•
•	•
•	•

3 **WRITE**

Write a memo about the most important problem where you work.
Use the information in your plan. Look at the writing model for an example.

4 **CHECK YOUR WRITING**

☐ Did you include a clear subject line?

☐ Did you state your purpose in your first paragraph?

☐ Did you present your reasons and solutions as a list in order to make your memo easy to read?

☐ Did you use correct capitalization, punctuation, and spelling?

1 REVIEW For your grammar review, go to page 248.

2 ACT IT OUT What do you say?

STEP 1. CLASS. **Review the conversation on page 66 (CD1, Track 40).**

STEP 2. ROLE PLAY. PAIRS. **Role-play this situation.**

Student A: You are a new employee at a credit-card customer service center. You would like more information about employee benefits. Your manager gave you the Employee Handbook, but you received so much information that you are confused. You have decided to talk to an experienced co-worker.

Student B: You have worked at the customer service center for three years. You want to help your new co-worker. Look back at the Employee Handbook on page 70 for ideas of what to explain.

3 READ AND REACT Problem-solving

STEP 1. GROUPS. **Read about Raquel's problem.**

Ariana Cordeiro works at a large hotel. Last week, Ariana's manager changed her work schedule. Ariana used to work from 4:00 P.M. to midnight, but now she has to work the day shift—from 8:00 A.M. to 4:00 P.M. With her new schedule, Ariana can't go to her English class. She also has a problem with child care.

STEP 2. GROUPS. **What is Ariana's problem? Discuss a solution. List three things that she can do.**

4 CONNECT For your Planning for Learning, go to page 258.
For your Team Project, go to page 266.

Which goals can you check off? Go back to page 65.

 Go to the CD-ROM for more practice.

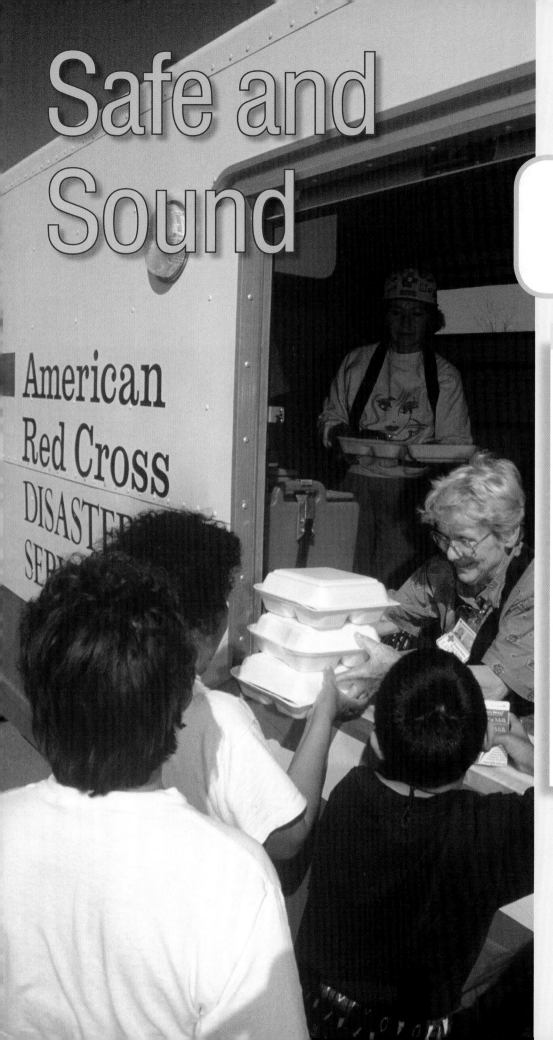

Safe and Sound

5

Preview

Read the title. Look at the picture. Why do these people need help?

UNIT GOALS

- ☐ Identify ways to prevent fires

- ☐ Talk about what to do in case of fire

- ☐ Talk about dangerous weather

- ☐ Discuss weather reports

- ☐ Talk about planning for a hurricane

- ☐ Interpret an evacuation map

- ☐ Communicate in a 911 emergency

- ☐ Write a plan for an emergency situation

Listening and Speaking

1 BEFORE YOU LISTEN

A CLASS. Discuss. What do you think the people in a fire-safety class want to learn?

B GROUPS. Find a *smoke alarm, a CO₂ detector,* and a *fire extinguisher* in the picture. How does each device help with safety in a home?

2 LISTEN

CD1 T52

A Lt. Tyrone Jefferson is teaching the first of four fire-safety classes. Listen. What is the focus of tonight's class?

CD1 T52

B Read the statements. Then listen again. Write *T* (true) or *F* (false) based on Lt. Jefferson's instructions. Correct the false statements.

_F_ 1. Lt. Jefferson will first talk about fire safety
  kitchen
  in the ~~bedroom~~ and then discuss fire safety
  in other parts of the home.

_____ 2. Cooking is the main cause of fires in homes
  in the U.S.

_____ 3. It's probably a good idea to wear a shirt with
  short sleeves when you're cooking.

_____ 4. If food catches fire, you should throw water on it.

_____ 5. If the phone rings in another room, Lt. Jefferson suggests that you ignore it.

_____ 6. Children should always be in the kitchen when you're cooking.

C PAIRS. What is one question that you would like to ask Lt. Jefferson?

3 CONVERSATION

CD1 T53

A Listen to the sentences. Notice the intonation. Then listen again and repeat.

If we want to keep our home safe, / what do you recommend?

When you're in the kitchen, pay attention to what you're doing.

CD1 T54

B Read the sentences. Add a comma where the voice should go up or down a little and pause. Then listen again and check your answers.

1. If a pan of food catches fire put a lid over it.
2. When you finish cooking remember to turn off the stove and oven.
3. If you have children you should be extra careful.
4. If you use a space heater don't put it too close to your bed.
5. When you leave the room don't forget to blow out the candle.

CD1 T55

C Lt. Jefferson is asking the class questions. Listen and read.

Lt. Jefferson: Let's continue talking about how to prevent home fires. Can anyone think of other possible dangers?

Mr. Sokolov: Cigarettes can be a cause of fires, right?

Lt. Jefferson: That's correct, especially if people smoke in bed.

Mr. Sokolov: A fire can also start if a smoker leaves a cigarette burning in an ashtray.

Lt. Jefferson: Right again.

Mr. Sokolov: So, if we live with someone who smokes and we want to keep our home safe, what do you recommend?

Lt. Jefferson: One thing you can do is to ask smokers to smoke outside.

4 PRACTICE

A PAIRS. Practice the conversation.

B PAIRS. Discuss. Talk about situations that can cause fires. Use the ideas in the pictures or your own ideas.

C MAKE IT PERSONAL. Think about fire safety.

STEP 1. GROUPS. Discuss. What are some ways to improve fire safety in your own home?

STEP 2. CLASS. Share your ideas.

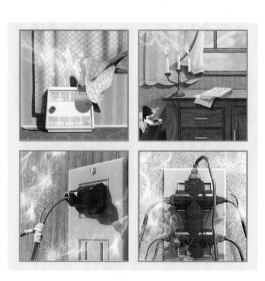

Grammar

Present real conditionals

If clause	Result clause
If a pan of food **catches** fire,	**put** a lid over it and **turn** the stove off.
If you **have** children,	you **should be** extra careful.
If you **don't have** a smoke detector,	your home **isn't** safe.
If we **want** to keep our home safe,	what **do** you **recommend**?

Grammar Watch

- Present real conditional sentences describe true situations that occur under real or possible conditions. They are also used to give instructions or advice under these conditions.
- Conditional sentences can begin with either the *if* clause or the result clause. Use a comma between the clauses only when the *if* clause comes first: *If you have children, you should be extra careful.* BUT: *You should be extra careful if you have children.*
- For present real conditional questions, use question word order only in the result clause.

1 PRACTICE

Read the poster that Lt. Jefferson used during his class on fire safety. Draw one line under the *if* clause and two lines under the result clause.

What to Do in CASE of FIRE

- If you see smoke coming under the door, don't open the door! Don't open the door if it is very hot or warm! Go to another exit.

- If the door is cool, open it slowly.

- If there is smoke along your escape route, drop to the floor and crawl on your hands and knees below the smoke.

- If you are trapped, close the doors between you and the fire. If you can get to a phone, dial 911 and ask for the fire department. If you can't reach a phone, go to a window and signal for help with a sheet or a flashlight.

A Combine the two clauses to make a conditional sentence about fire safety. Keep the clauses in the same order and add *if* to one clause. Include a comma if necessary.

1. (a fire occurs / leave your home immediately)

   If a fire occurs, leave your home immediately.

2. (you have small children / tell them not to hide under a bed in case of fire)

   _____

3. (family members can't escape by themselves / make plans to help them)

   _____

4. (don't open a door / it is hot to the touch)

   _____

5. (your clothes catch fire / drop to the floor and roll back and forth)

   _____

B PAIRS. These statements about fire safety at work are false. Make changes to each underlined result clause so that each statement will be true.

1. If you don't know where the fire exits in your building are, ~~don't worry~~. *find out*

2. If you hear the fire alarm, <u>don't leave your work area until firefighters arrive</u>.

3. <u>Get your coat and other personal belongings</u> if you don't have them with you.

4. If you work on the 10th floor, <u>take the elevator to exit the building</u>.

5. <u>Keep walking forward</u> if you see smoke.

Show what you know! Talk about what to do in case of fire

STEP 1. GROUPS. What should you do if there's a fire at home or at work? Make a list stating what you should and shouldn't do in case of fire.

STEP 2. CLASS. Share your ideas.

Can you...talk about what to do in case of fire? ☐

Reading

1 BEFORE YOU READ

A CLASS. What happens during an earthquake?

B Skim the title, the first paragraph, and the last paragraph of the article. Predict. What is the main idea of the article?

2 READ

CD1 T56

Listen and read the article. What three things should be part of a good earthquake emergency plan?

What You *Don't Know* May *Hurt* You

Many of us have the wrong idea when it comes to earthquakes. Unfortunately, our **misconceptions** may affect the way that we prepare—or even worse, do not prepare—for this very dangerous natural disaster.

Belief #1: In the U.S., earthquakes happen only on the West Coast, in states like California. Although scientists cannot predict earthquakes, research shows that earthquakes can happen anywhere, anytime. That's why it's important to have an earthquake emergency plan. The first step in your plan should be to make your home safe. For example, use the bottom shelves of cupboards and bookcases for items that are heavy or breakable. Make sure that heavy furniture and electronic equipment, like television sets, won't fall during an earthquake.

DUCK

COVER

HOLD

Belief #2: The safest place to be during an earthquake is in a doorway. In most buildings today, an inside wall is safer than a doorway. It's even better to get under a piece of furniture such as a table or a desk. As part of your emergency plan, practice "duck, cover, and hold."

Belief #3: After the shaking of an earthquake stops, the danger is over. Earthquakes can cause serious damage, so even after a quake, the situation will remain dangerous. Your emergency plan should include **evacuation routes** so that you and your family can have a safe way to leave your home after the shaking has ended. Also learn about work and school emergency plans, and agree on a place where the family can meet when it's safe to be outdoors.

Don't be **fooled** by these or other common misconceptions. Plan, prepare, and practice so that you'll be ready when an earthquake occurs.

A Read the Reading Skill. Then complete this statement. Circle the correct answer.

> In this reading, the author's purpose is to _____.
> a. persuade   b. entertain   c. inform

> **Reading Skill:** Identifying an Author's Purpose
>
> Think about an author's objective or purpose. Is it to *entertain* you by telling a story? Is it to *inform* you by giving facts? Is it to *persuade* you to agree with a specific opinion?

B Complete the sentences. Circle the correct answers.

1. To prepare for an earthquake, you should put heavy items and items that can break _____.
   a. under a table   b. on a low shelf   c. in a doorway

2. As part of your earthquake plan, you should _____.
   a. find out when the next earthquake will happen
   b. read several books about preparing for an earthquake
   c. include a way to leave your home during the earthquake

3. The author probably thinks that some people _____.
   a. are not afraid of earthquakes
   b. are not prepared for earthquakes
   c. don't know anything about earthquakes

C PAIRS. Why is it a good idea to "duck, cover, and hold" during an earthquake?

4 WORD WORK

Find the boldfaced words in the article. Use the context to figure out the meaning of each word. Write the meaning.

1. misconceptions _____

2. evacuation routes _____

3. fooled _____

Show what you know!   Talk about preparing for natural disasters

STEP 1. PAIRS. Discuss. What kinds of natural disasters like earthquakes, tornadoes, or floods occur in the area where you live?

STEP 2. What can you do to prepare for them?

Listening and Speaking

1 BEFORE YOU LISTEN

A CLASS. Discuss. What do you know about hurricanes? What do you know about tornadoes?

B GROUPS. Read the hurricane warning. What do the boldfaced words mean?

"**Meteorologists** at the **National Weather Service** have issued a severe weather **warning**. People who live in **coastal** areas should be prepared to **evacuate** their homes and go to a safe inland location. **Tides** will be high, and rain will be extremely heavy. Residents in areas near rivers and lakes should be prepared for **floods**."

2 LISTEN

A CD1 T57

Henry Ponce is the host of the radio show *Know Your World*. His guest today is meteorologist Dr. Kay Wilkins. Listen to the first part of their conversation. When does hurricane season in the Atlantic Ocean officially start and finish?

Starts: _____ Finishes: _____

B CD1 T58

Read the questions. Then listen to the whole conversation. Circle the correct answers.

1. What is <u>not</u> a danger of hurricanes?
   a. wind and rain   b. high waves   c. fires

2. Where do hurricanes generally cause the greatest damage?
   a. inland   b. on the coast   c. over water

3. Where do hurricanes get their power?
   a. inland   b. on the coast   c. over water

C CD1 T58

What is the difference between a hurricane watch and a hurricane warning?

STEP 1. Listen to the conversation again.

STEP 2. GROUPS. Discuss the difference.

D GROUPS. Discuss.

1. Which hurricanes have you either heard about or experienced personally?
2. How did the hurricane affect peoples' lives?
3. What can people do to prepare for a hurricane?

3 CONVERSATION

Two friends are talking about the weather. Listen and read.

Man: Can you believe this weather?

Woman: It's been really bad lately. Now there's a flood watch.

Man: I know. I heard it on the radio before I left home this morning.

Woman: The National Weather Service says there could be three more inches of rain. There's a severe weather watch that lasts until midnight.

Man: Wow…this could be very dangerous.

Woman: Yeah. It's probably a good idea to keep checking the weather report for updates.

Man: You're right. On days like today, it pays to be prepared.

4 PRACTICE

A PAIRS. Practice the conversation.

B MAKE IT PERSONAL. Think about your experiences in bad weather.

STEP 1. GROUPS. Describe an experience that you have had in bad weather.

STEP 2. CLASS. Share your experiences.

Grammar

Adverb clauses of time

Adverb clause (time)	Main clause
When there is the possibility of a hurricane in the next 36 hours,	the National Weather Service issues a hurricane watch.
As soon as you hear the warning,	make sure that your emergency preparations are complete.
Before I left home this morning,	I heard about the flood watch.
Until the weather service cancels the storm watch,	you should check the weather report regularly.
After they hit land,	hurricanes lose strength.

1 PRACTICE

A **Read the sentences about thunderstorms. Underline the adverb clauses.**

1. <u>After lightning flashes in the sky</u>, you hear the sound of thunder.
2. The sky usually turns dark before a thunderstorm begins.
3. When there's a thunderstorm, you should not stand under a tree.
4. Get inside a building or a car as soon as you see lightning.
5. You should stay inside until the thunderstorm ends.

Grammar Watch

- Adverb clauses of time tell when one action happened in relation to another action.
- Sentences can begin with the adverb clause or the main clause. Don't use a comma between the clauses when the adverb clause comes at the end. *Hurricanes lose strength after they hit land.*

B **Complete the paragraph about weather forecasting. Use *when, before, until,* or *after*.**

_____*When*_____ scientists predict storms quickly and correctly, they save lives. _____ they had technology to help them do their job, meteorologists worked slowly. Their work became easier and faster _____ they began using computers. Today, weather forecasters give up to thirty minutes' advance warning _____ a tornado actually arrives. As a result, people have time to find a safe place to stay _____ the storm is over. For example, _____ powerful tornadoes passed through Oklahoma in 1999, only 44 people died. However, 695 people lost their lives and 2,000 more were injured in 1925 because the tornadoes went through just a few minutes _____ they received the tornado warning.

A Read the following facts about tornadoes. Decide which of the events in brackets occurred first. Mark one event *1* (occurred earlier) and the other event *2* (occurred later).

               2   1

1. [Tornadoes occur] [when cold, dry air from Canada meets warm, moist air from the Gulf of Mexico.]

2. [After the winds of a tornado begin to turn in a circular direction,] [they move faster and faster.]

3. [Before a tornado arrives in an area,] [you will usually hear a loud warning siren.]

4. [Until scientists learned some basic facts about tornadoes,] [they had trouble predicting them.]

5. [When the violent winds of a tornado hit buildings,] [serious structural damage often occurs.]

6. [Weather Service personnel use weather radar to confirm a potential tornado] [before they issue a tornado warning.]

B Combine the two sentences with the adverb in parentheses. Include a comma if necessary.

1. The military used radar during World War II. / They wanted to know the location of planes and ships. (when) *The military used radar during World War II when they wanted to know the location of planes and ships.*

2. Radar worked well. / There was bad weather. (until)

3. It began to rain or snow. / Radar operators noticed that something strange happened with their equipment. (as soon as)

4. Scientists began to use radar to look at weather. / The war ended. (after)

5. Modern tools like radar were used to predict the weather / Forecasting was much less reliable than it is today. (before)

Show what you know! Discuss weather reports

Watch a weather report on television or on the Internet. Take notes about the information the meteorologist gives. Describe what happened during the weather report to a partner. Use adverb clauses of time.

Can you...discuss weather reports? ☐

Talk about planning for a hurricane

Life Skills

1 INTERPRET AN EVACUATION MAP

A What supplies would you need for a hurricane or other natural disaster? List items for each category at the right.

B PAIRS. Discuss. Are you prepared? Which items do you already have? Which ones do you need to get? What other supplies would be useful?

C CLASS. Look at the map. In what areas are hurricanes especially dangerous? Why is it important for people to know how to interpret an evacuation map?

- [ ] water
- [ ] food
- [ ] first aid supplies
- [ ] personal care items
- [ ] child care supplies
- [ ] cleaning supplies
- [ ] communication devices
- [ ] documents

2 PRACTICE

A Look at the map. Circle the correct answers.

1. What color are the evacuation routes?
   a. red   b. blue   c. tan   d. green

2. You live in Miami Beach. A major hurricane is coming, and you need to evacuate. In which direction do you need to go in order to evacuate?
   a. northeast   b. northwest   c. southeast   d. southwest

3. You live in Miami-Dade County on SW 136th Street, west of State Highway 997. In which direction do you need to go in order to evacuate?
   a. east, then north   b. east, then south   c. west, then north   d. west, then south

4. You live in the Florida Keys. Which two routes can you take to evacuate?
   a. Card Sound Road and U.S. Highway 41   c. U.S. Highway 1 and Card Sound Road
   b. U.S. Highway 1 and State Highway 994   d. U.S. Highway 1 and U.S. Highway 41

B In which direction do most evacuation routes travel from Miami-Dade County? Why?

C GROUPS. Think about what you learned earlier about hurricanes. How will you prepare for a coming hurricane? Make a list.

1. _____   3. _____

2. _____   4. _____

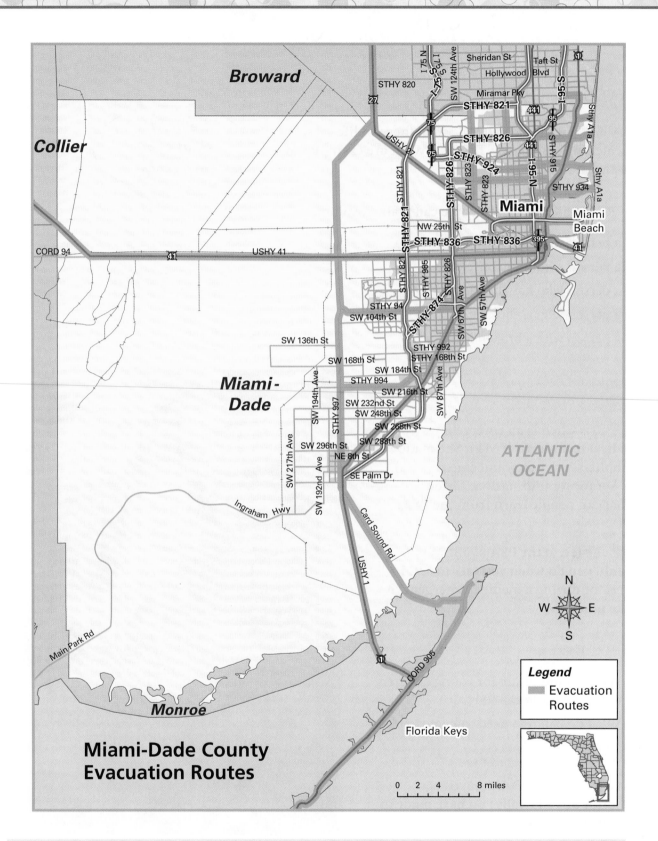

Miami-Dade County
Evacuation Routes

Broward

Collier

STHY 820

27

I 75 N

I-75-S

I-75-S-LI

SW 124th Ave

Sheridan St

Hollywood Blvd

Taft St

S-5-1

441

Miramar Pky

STHY 821

75

95

STHY 826

441

Sthy A1a

USHY 27

75

STHY 924

STHY 826

STHY 823

STHY 823

I-95-N

STHY 915

STHY 934

Miami

Miami Beach

Sthy A1a

STHY 821

STHY 821

NW 25th St

STHY 836

STHY 836

395

41

CORD 94

USHY 41

41

STHY 821

STHY 985

STHY 826

STHY 874

SW 67th Ave

SW 57th Ave

STHY 94

SW 104th St

SW 136th St

STHY 992

SW 168th St

STHY 168th St

SW 87th Ave

SW 184th St

SW 194th Ave

STHY 994

SW 216th St

Miami-Dade

STHY 997

SW 232nd St

SW 248th St

SW 268th St

SW 296th St

SW 288th St

SW 217th Ave

NE 8th St

SW 192nd Ave

SE Palm Dr

ATLANTIC OCEAN

Ingraham Hwy

Card Sound Rd

USHY 1

Main Park Rd

Monroe

1

CORD 905

Florida Keys

N
W   E
S

Legend

Evacuation Routes

0   2   4   8 miles

Can you...talk about planning for a hurricane? ☐

Listening and Speaking

1 BEFORE YOU LISTEN

A CLASS. You should call 911 when there's a life-threatening emergency. Discuss. What are examples of life-threatening emergencies?

> *Hello. 911. What's your emergency?*

B PAIRS. Which of these people can't talk? Explain.

- ☐ a person who is bleeding
- ☐ a person who is unconscious
- ☐ a person who has allergies
- ☐ a person who is choking
- ☐ a person with a broken leg

2 LISTEN

CD1 T60

A 💿 Iris Chen is an emergency medical technician (EMT). She made a public-service announcement (PSA) for her local radio station. Listen. What can people learn from the PSA?

CD1 T60

B 💿 Listen to the PSA again. What should you do when you talk to a 911 operator during a medical emergency? Take notes.

C PAIRS. Discuss.

1. Why is it important for young children to know how to call 911?

2. What do children need to know to place a 911 call?

D MAKE IT PERSONAL. PAIRS. Describe any 911 calls you have made or have heard about.

The vowel sound /i/ (as in *eat*) is usually spelled with the letter *e*. The vowel sound /ɪ/ (as in *it*) is usually spelled with the letter *i*.

CD1 T61

A Listen to the words. Notice the underlined vowel sound in each group of words. Then listen again and repeat.

/i/	/ɪ/
<u>ea</u>t	<u>i</u>t
br<u>ea</u>the	w<u>i</u>ll
bl<u>ee</u>ding	m<u>i</u>nutes

CD1 T62

B Listen and circle the word you hear.

1. eat / it   2. feel / fill   3. leave / live   4. seat / sit   5. steal / still

CD1 T63

C Pattama Somsiri is talking to a 911 operator. Listen and read.

Operator: Ma'am, I have your address and phone number. The ambulance will be there in a few minutes.

Pattama: OK…but what should we do until it arrives?

Operator: Is your sister still having trouble breathing?

Pattama: Yes, but my husband is helping her. He took a first-aid class last year, so he must know what to do.

Operator: Your sister may be having an allergic reaction.

Pattama: Well, she's allergic to nuts, but she was eating chocolate cake when the problem started. There weren't any nuts in the cake, so that couldn't be the problem.

Operator: If the cake is from a bakery, there might be nuts in it. I'll tell the EMTs about your sister's allergy.

4 **PRACTICE**

A PAIRS. Practice the conversation.

B ROLE PLAY. PAIRS. Role-play this conversation. It takes place during an emergency 911 call.

Student A: You are at home. You just walked into the living room and found your grandfather on the floor. He is unconscious, but he's breathing. You know that your grandfather has a heart problem. You call 911. Answer the 911 operator's questions.

Student B: You are a 911 operator. You just received an emergency medical call. Find out who the victim is and where he is. Ask if the person is breathing or bleeding. Also ask if the caller can put the victim in a comfortable position.

Communicate in a 911 emergency

Grammar

Expressing degrees of certainty

There weren't any nuts in the cake, so that	**can't** **couldn't**	be the problem.
A 911 call	**could** **may** **might**	save the life of someone you love.
In an emergency, some people	**may not** **might not**	be thinking clearly.

My husband took a first-aid class, so he **must** know what to do.
She didn't have an allergic reaction, so the cake **must not** contain any nuts.
Could it be an allergic reaction?

Grammar Watch

- Use *can't* or *couldn't* to show that something is almost impossible.
- Use *could, may (not)*, and *might (not)* to show that something is possible but NOT certain.
- Use *must* to show that something is almost certainly true. Use *must not* to show that something is almost certainly NOT true.
- Use *could* (not *may* or *might*) for questions.

1   PRACTICE

Mrs. Johnson fell down the stairs in her home. Decide which sentence shows more certainty. Circle your answer.

1. a. Mrs. Johnson's leg may be broken
   b. Mrs. Johnson's leg must be broken.

2. a. She might be in a lot of pain right now.
   b. She must be in a lot of pain right now.

3. a. She could need medical attention.
   b. She must need medical attention.

4. a. She may not be close enough to the phone to call 911.
   b. She couldn't be close enough to the phone to call 911.

5. a. There might not be anyone else at home with Mrs. Johnson.
   b. There couldn't be anyone else at home with Mrs. Johnson.

Complete the conversation between an EMT and a 911 operator. Use the phrases in the box.

couldn't be   could have   ~~may be~~   might be able to   might not know   must be coming

Operator: I have a caller on the line. He's reporting a bicycle accident.

It sounds like there _____*may be*_____ serious injuries.

EMT: Can you give me the location of the accident?

Operator: I have no phone number or street address on my computer screen.

That means the call _____ from a cell phone.

EMT: Did you ask the caller for the information?

Operator: Yes, but there's a problem. I think he's a tourist. He _____

exactly where he is. He says he's at the north end of Centennial Park, but that

_____ the correct location. The north section of the park is closed.

EMT: How about the police? We _____ get information from

the officer in the area.

Operator: The police have already been contacted.

EMT: Great. Please tell the caller not to move the victims. They _____

broken bones.

Show what you know!   Communicate in a 911 emergency

STEP 1. Read the suggestions about what to do after a 911 call. Then write your own suggestion.

- Have someone wait outside until the emergency team arrives.
- Turn on an outside light, even during the day.
- Stay with the injured person and reassure him or her that help is on the way.

- _____

STEP 2. GROUPS. Discuss the suggestions. Explain why it's important to follow each suggestion.

Can you... communicate in a 911 emergency? ☐

Writing

1 BEFORE YOU WRITE

A CLASS. Where can you find information about what to do during an earthquake or other emergency situation?

B Read the writing model. How did the writer learn what to do during an earthquake?

> An Earthquake Survival Guide
>
> I just moved to California, so I've never lived through an earthquake. However, I talked to members of my family who have been here for many years. I learned about their emergency plan and what to do during and after an earthquake. First, if you're outside, move away from buildings or other things that can fall on you. If you're inside, stay there. Get under a table, desk, or other large piece of furniture and hold on. After the shaking ends, carefully check for injuries and damage to your home. Give first aid and turn off the water, electricity, and gas if necessary. Then take your emergency supplies and leave the building. When you're outside, be careful. There may be dangers such as falling bricks or pieces of broken metal and glass. If the members of your family are not all with you, go to the meeting place that you agreed on. Call one family member who doesn't live in the earthquake area to let them know you're OK. Finally, work with your neighbors. Together, you can help those who need it and survive until life returns to normal. Earthquakes are frightening, but I feel better knowing what to expect.

C PAIRS. Answer the questions.

1. What should you do if you're outside during an earthquake?

2. If you're at home, what's the first thing you should do after the earthquake ends?

3. Why should you call a family member who lives in another city or state after an earthquake instead of calling a family member who lives nearby?

4. Why is the author glad that he learned what to do during and after an earthquake?

D Write *1–5* to show the order of steps in "An Earthquake Survival Guide."

_____ When it's safe, take your emergency supplies and leave your house.

_____ Go to the place where you agreed to meet your family.

_____ Finally, work with your neighbors so that you can help one another.

_1_ Give first aid if there are any injuries.

_____ Watch out for things like falling bricks when you're outside.

Writing Tip

When you write about how to do something, put the steps in a logical order.

A RESEARCH. Find out what to do during and after a tornado, blizzard, flood, wildfire, or other natural disaster. Ask someone who has had personal experience or ask your teacher how to get information at the library or on the Internet.

B Plan and organize your paragraph in a chart like this. Write your steps in time order.

What to Do During and After a _____	
Steps	**Details**
Step 1	
Step 2	
Step 3	

3 WRITE

A Write an introduction that explains how you learned about your topic. Look at the writing model for an example.

B Complete your paragraph about what to do during and after a natural disaster. Use the information in your plan. Look at the writing model for an example.

4 CHECK YOUR WRITING

☐ Did you include an introduction?

☐ Did you list specific steps in time order?

☐ Did you include a conclusion?

☐ Did you use correct capitalization, punctuation, and spelling?

1 REVIEW   For your grammar review, go to page 249.

2 ACT IT OUT   What do you say?

STEP 1. CLASS. Review the conversations on pages 86 and 87 (CD1, Tracks 52 and 55).

STEP 2. ROLE PLAY. PAIRS. Role-play this situation.

> **Student A:** You just took a fire-safety class at the local community center. You are visiting your cousin. Tell your cousin what you learned. Include information about how to prevent a fire in the home and what to do if there is a fire emergency.

> **Student B:** You want to learn about fire safety. You know that your cousin just took a fire-safety class at the community center. You want to know if you should take the course. Ask questions about it. You're especially worried about fires because several members of your family smoke.

STEP 3. PAIRS. Talk about fire safety at home and at work.
Use the ideas from your role play or your own ideas.

3 READ AND REACT   Problem-solving

STEP 1. Read about the problem.

You are beginning to prepare emergency supplies to be ready for a hurricane, an earthquake, or other disaster. However, the items that you need are expensive. Next month you'll be able to buy more supplies, but this month you can spend only $50 on your emergency items.

STEP 2. GROUPS. Decide which emergency supplies to buy this month. Use the price list. Explain your choices.

ITEM	PRICE
First-Aid Kit	$18.95
Radio	$24.98
Flashlight	$9.99
Batteries	$9.29 a pack
Water	$1.50 per gallon
Canned Fruit, Vegetables, Beans	average $1.25 each
Rain Ponchos	$10 each
Sleeping Bags	$24.99
Medicine	$50
Other:	

4 CONNECT   For your Organizing and Planning for Learning, go to page 259.
For your Team Project, go to page 267.

Which goals can you check off? Go back to page 85.

 Go to the CD-ROM for more practice.

Moving In

Preview

Read the title. What are these people doing? What do you think they are talking about?

UNIT GOALS

- ☐ Identify tenant responsibilities
- ☐ Interpret a lease
- ☐ Talk about landlord responsibilities
- ☐ Check that information is correct
- ☐ Talk about moving
- ☐ Discuss problems with neighbors
- ☐ Write about a housing problem

Listening and Speaking

1 BEFORE YOU LISTEN

CLASS. **When you rent a house or an apartment, you are responsible for certain things. Discuss.**

1. What are some tenant responsibilities? Make a list.
2. Tenants often have to give the landlord a *security deposit* when they move in. What is a security deposit for?

2 LISTEN

CD1 T64

A 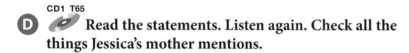 **Jessica is talking to her mother. Listen to the first part of their conversation. What is the conversation about?**

CD1 T64

B **Read the statements. Then listen again. Write *T* (true) or *F* (false). Correct the false statements.**

_____ 1. Each roommate will have her own bedroom.

_____ 2. The rent is $1,100.

_____ 3. They have to pay for water and electricity.

_____ 4. The security deposit is two months' rent.

CD1 T65

C **Listen to the whole conversation. How does Jessica's mother feel about Jessica's moving out?**

a. excited   b. annoyed   c. worried

CD1 T65

D **Read the statements. Listen again. Check all the things Jessica's mother mentions.**

☐ Jessica and her roommates may damage the apartment.

☐ They may not be safe.

☐ They may have problems with the building manager.

☐ They may have noisy neighbors.

E PAIRS. **Do you think parents and grown children should live together, very near each other, or farther away? Explain.**

CD1 T66

Jessica is talking to her new landlord, Harry. He is telling her about the building rules. Listen and read.

Jessica: I forgot to ask you: Does the apartment come with parking?

Harry: Yes, each tenant is allowed one parking space.

Jessica: Oh, then I guess we'll have to take turns. Where's the parking lot?

Harry: Behind the building. You can park in spot number 11. Make sure to hang this permit on your mirror. That way I know it's yours.

Jessica: Thanks. What if I have visitors?

Harry: Visitors aren't allowed to park in the tenant lot. If they do, their cars will be towed away. They have to park in the street. We have strict rules so no one will take the tenants' spots.

Jessica: OK.

4 **PRACTICE**

A PAIRS. Practice the conversation.

B ROLE PLAY. PAIRS. Look at the pictures. Role-play situations 1, 2, and 3. Use the conversation as a model.

Student A: You are a tenant.

Student B: You are the landlord. Tell the tenant each building rule.

Grammar

Expressing obligation, expectation, and permission

Tenants	are	required to	recycle glass, metal, and paper.
		supposed to	be considerate of their neighbors.
Tenants	are not	allowed to	smoke in the hallways.
		permitted to	have pets.
Are	visitors	**allowed**	to park in this lot?

Grammar Watch

- Use *be required to* when you talk about obligations, or things that people must do.
- Use *be supposed to* when you talk about expectations, or things that people should do.
- Use *be allowed / be permitted to* when you talk about permission, or things that people may do (things that are not against the rules).
- *Be permitted to* means the same thing as *be allowed to*, but it is more formal.

1 PRACTICE

Read the apartment building rules. Circle the tenant responsibilities that show obligations. Underline the expressions that merely show expectation. Use a double underline below the expressions that show permission.

480 Cumberland Drive

- Tenants (are required to) pay their rent on the first of the month.

- Tenants who pay their rent late are required to pay a late fee of $25.

- Tenants are not supposed to make noise in their apartments after 10:00 P.M.

- Tenants are not allowed to keep bicycles or strollers in the hall. They are supposed to keep them in their apartments.

- Tenants are permitted to use the laundry room only between the hours of 8 A.M. and 10 P.M.

A Complete the rules. Use the correct form of one of the phrases in the box. More than one answer may be possible.

> (not) be permitted to   (not) be required to   (not) be supposed to

1. Tenants _are not permitted to_ make changes to the apartment.

2. No one _____ smoke in the building.

3. If the rent is paid late, the tenant _____ pay a late fee of $20.00.

4. Tenants _____ entertain guests in the common areas of the apartment building. No one _____ have parties after 10 P.M.

5. New tenants _____ move in between the hours of 10 A.M. and 6 P.M.

6. Tenants _____ keep the front door of the building locked at all times.

7. Tenants _____ give three month's notice if they plan to move out.

8. All tenants _____ dispose of garbage in trash containers.

9. Tenants _____ put glass, cans, and paper in the green recycling containers.

10. Tenants _____ return all keys at the end of their lease term.

B GROUPS. Look at the rules in Exercise A. Discuss.

1. If you ever rented an apartment, which rules were true where you lived?

2. Do you think the rules are reasonable or unreasonable? Explain.

Show what you know!   Identify tenant responsibilities

CLASS. **Discuss tenant responsibilities from the point of view of a building manager. What are the five most important things that tenants should be required to do? Number them from 1 to 5, with 1 being the most important and 5 being the least important.**

Can you...identify tenant responsibilities? ☐

Life Skills

1 INTERPRET A LEASE

A GROUPS. When people rent an apartment or a house, they usually sign a *lease*. The lease describes the tenant's and landlord's rights and responsibilities. What things do you think leases include? Make a list.

B CLASS. Read the first part of the lease. Does the lease decribe any of the things you mentioned?

2 READ

Look at the lease again. Complete the sentences. Circle the correct answers.

1. _____ is going to live in the apartment.
   a. Vaslav Nowak
   b. Anita Cruz

2. The lease is for _____.
   a. one year
   b. five months

3. The rent is _____ per month.
   a. $1,500
   b. $1,000

4. The rent is due on _____.
   a. April 1
   b. the 5th day of each month

5. The landlord _____ the security deposit after the tenant moves out if the apartment is damaged or dirty.
   a. can keep
   b. must return

6. The _____ has to pay for damage caused by normal everyday use.
   a. landlord
   b. tenant

PARTIES: The parties to this agreement are:
___Vaslav Novak___, herein referred to as LANDLORD, and ___Anita Cruz___, herein referred to as TENANT.
TERM: This agreement is to begin on ___April 1___, ___2009___, and is:

___ month-to-month

✔ an agreement for the specific term of _12_ months, ending on ___April 1, 2010___.

1. RENT: Rent: ___$1,500___/month. Rent is payable in advance by the _5th_ day of each month, and will be delivered to ___Vaslav Novak, 1000 Center St., Apt 40B, Mountain View, CA 94040___.

2. SECURITY DEPOSIT: Tenant has paid to landlord, and landlord acknowledges receipt of ___$1,500___ as a cleaning and security deposit. The landlord may keep all or any part of this deposit upon termination of this rental agreement for any of the following reasons:
   i) to cover unpaid rent owed to the landlord
   ii) to pay the cost of repairing any damage to the premises resulting from abuse, misuse, or neglect, not including normal wear and tear.

A Read the second part of the lease. What does it descibe?

B Read the statements. Write *T* (true) or *F* (false). Correct the false statements.

_____ 1. The landlord pays for electricity and water.

_____ 2. The landlord is required to make sure appliances work and fix them if they break.

_____ 3. Both the landlord and the tenant are supposed to keep the apartment clean and safe.

_____ 4. The tenant is not supposed to make changes to the apartment without permission.

_____ 5. The tenant is not allowed to smoke in the hallways, but is allowed to smoke in his or her apartment.

_____ 6. The tenant is not allowed to use the laundry room after 8 P.M.

3. UTILITIES: The tenant agrees to pay for all utilities except ___water___, which shall be paid by the landlord.

4. PETS: Tenants shall not keep a pet on the premises.

5. THE LANDLORD SHALL:
   i) keep the public areas in a clean and safe condition.
   ii) keep the appliances in the rental unit in good working order.
   iii) paint the rental unit every three years.
   iv) supply a smoke alarm and CO detector in each rental unit.

6. THE TENANT SHALL:
   i) pay rent promptly when due.
   ii) keep the rental unit in a clean, safe, and habitable condition.
   iii) place garbage and refuse in the containers provided.
   iv) park only in the parking spot provided in the tenants' parking lot.

7. THE TENANT SHALL NOT:
   i) alter the premises (for example, paint) without permission of the landlord.
   ii) smoke on the premises.
   iii) use the laundry facilities between the hours of 10 P.M. and 8 A.M.

C GROUPS. Before you sign a lease, it's important to read it carefully. Don't sign it if you don't agree with the terms (rules). Discuss what problems might occur if you didn't know the answers to the following questions.

1. How long is the lease for?

2. Who will be living in the apartment (whose names will be on the lease)? Can other family members or other roommates be added later?

3. Can you get out of the lease if you need to move early, for instance, because of a job change or a family emergency?

Can you...interpret a lease? ☐

Listening and Speaking

1 BEFORE YOU LISTEN

GROUPS. **Where can you go if you have a problem with your landlord? What agencies in your community might provide free assistance?**

2 LISTEN

CD1 T67

A Manuel Rodríguez is a guest on *This Week,* **a radio talk show. Listen to the first call. What kind of questions does Manuel answer?**

CD1 T67

B **Read the statements. Then listen to the first call again. Write** *T* **(true) or** *F* **(false). Correct the false statements.**

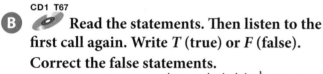

_F_ 1. Manuel is a ~~tenant with a problem~~. *tenant rights lawyer*

_____ 2. The caller wants his landlord to install new smoke detectors in his apartment.

_____ 3. The caller's smoke detectors aren't working.

_____ 4. The caller hasn't called his landlord yet to complain about his problem.

_____ 5. Manuel tells the caller to send a letter to his landlord.

CD1 T68

C **Listen to the second call. Circle the word or phrase that best completes each statement.**

1. The caller's landlord wants **to raise her rent / her to move**.
2. The caller's landlord **is not allowed to / is not going to** raise the rent right now.
3. The caller's lease is up **one year / six months** from now.
4. The caller **sometimes / never** pays her rent late.
5. The caller will probably **sign a new lease / look for a new apartment** when her lease is up.

D **GROUPS.** **Discuss. Why does Manuel ask the second caller if she has ever damaged the apartment or paid her rent late?**

3 CONVERSATION

CD1 T69

A Listen to the sentences. Notice the intonation of the tag questions. Then listen and repeat.

aren't you?   You're going to stay there with him, **aren't** you?

is he?   The repairman isn't there yet, **is** he?

doesn't he?   He has to replace the smoke detectors, **doesn't** he?

does she?   Your landlord doesn't pay for water, **does** she?

Pronunciation Watch

Add a short tag question like *aren't you?* or *doesn't he?* to check information. Use rising intonation to show that you are not sure the information is correct or that the other person will agree. Make your voice go up at the end of the tag question.

CD1 T70

B Lisa Ming is calling her building manager. Listen and read.

Max: Hello?

Lisa: Hi. This is Lisa Ming in Apartment 5F.

Max: Oh, hi, Lisa. What can I do for you?

Lisa: We don't have any hot water in the bathroom. Could you send someone over?

Max: Sure, I'll call the plumber right now. Will you be at home?

Lisa: No, I'm leaving for work in a few minutes.

Max: Then, is it OK with you if I let the plumber in?

Lisa: Yes, …but you're going to stay there with him, aren't you?

Max: Yes, I will.

Lisa: Because I don't want any strangers in our apartment while we're out.

Max: Don't worry. I'll be there while he does the work.

Lisa: Thanks, Mr. Cove.

4 PRACTICE

A PAIRS. Practice the conversation.

B ROLE PLAY. PAIRS. Role-play this situation. Use the conversation as a model.

Student A: You are a tenant. The lock on the door of your building is broken, and anyone can walk in. You ask the building manager to take care of the problem.

Student B: You are a building manager. You will send a locksmith to fix the door right away.

C MAKE IT PERSONAL. GROUPS. Discuss.

1. Did you or someone you know ever have a problem with a building manager? What was the problem?

2. What did you or that person do? What did the building manager do?

Grammar

Tag questions with *be*	
Affirmative statement	Negative tag
The repairman **is** on his way,	**isn't** he?
You**'re going to stay** there,	**aren't** you?
Negative statement	Affirmative tag
The repairman **isn't** there yet,	**is** he?
The landlord **wasn't** at home,	**was** he?

Tag questions with *do* as an auxiliary verb	
Affirmative statement	Negative tag
You **called** the landlord,	**didn't** you?
He **has to** replace the smoke detectors,	**doesn't** he?
Negative statement	Affirmative tag
Your landlord **doesn't pay** for water,	**does** she?
The repairman **didn't come** yet,	**did** he?

Grammar Watch

- Use tag questions to check that information is correct or when you are not sure the other person will agree.
- Use negative tags with affirmative statements. Use affirmative tags with negative statements.

1 PRACTICE

A Match the beginnings of the sentences with the endings.

  f   1. You called the landlord,   a. is there?

_____ 2. You didn't see mice in the apartment,   b. doesn't he?

_____ 3. The plumber fixed the sink,   c. is he?

_____ 4. The landlord has to paint the lobby,   d. did you?

_____ 5. There isn't any lead paint in the apartment,   e. didn't he?

_____ 6. The plumber isn't in the basement,   f. didn't you?

B Complete the sentences. Circle the correct words.

1. You checked the lease, **did / (didn't)** you?
2. The landlord wasn't in the office, **was / wasn't** he?
3. You're going to sign the lease, **are / aren't** you?
4. The building manager takes care of all the repairs, **does / doesn't** he?
5. You sent a letter to the landlord, **did / didn't** you?
6. There isn't any damage in your apartment, **is / isn't** there?
7. The landlord is responsible for keeping the building safe, **is / isn't** she?
8. The landlord and the plumber are finished with the work, **are / aren't** they?

CD1 T71

Complete the conversations with tag questions. Then listen and check your answers.

1. **A:** What's wrong, Li An?

    B: The landlord kept our security deposit because the carpet has stains on it.

    A: Oh … but we didn't stain the carpet, _____?

2. **A:** The landlord charged us for damage to the living room wall.

    B: But why? The living room wall isn't damaged, _____?

3. **A:** Let's get started. You cleaned the kitchen, _____?

    B: Yes, this morning. What else do we need to do?

4. **A:** You didn't like the apartment we saw this morning, _____?

    B: Yes I did. I liked it very much!

5. **A:** That apartment would be perfect for us! What did you think?

    B: I liked it, too. But it's kind of expensive, _____?

    A: The rent *is* a little high. But the landlord pays for gas and electricity, _____?

Show what you know!   Check that information is correct

ROLE PLAY. PAIRS. **Role-play this situation. Ask and answer questions, using information in the lease on pages 110–111.**

Student A: You are interested in an apartment. Make up a list of five tag questions for the landlord.

Student B: You are the landlord. Answer the tenant's questions.

> **Student A:** *The lease is for one year, isn't it?*
> **Student B:** *Yes, it is.*

Can you…check that information is correct?   ☐

Reading

1 BEFORE YOU READ

GROUPS. What are some reasons that people choose to move to a new city or town?

2 READ

CD1 T72

 Listen and read the article. Does it mention the reasons you guessed?

Americans on the Move

Ann Kramer is unusual. She was born and raised in Long Beach, California, and now lives there with her husband and children. Why is she unusual? Because these days, one in three Americans moves to a state different from where he or she was born. Why are so many Americans on the move?

One of the biggest reasons people **relocate** is to find jobs. When businesses close and jobs **disappear** in an area, people move. In recent years, people have moved away from places like Detroit, Buffalo, and Cleveland. Factories in these cities have closed, and hundreds of thousands of jobs have been lost. On the other hand, the population of Atlanta has grown because big companies like Home Depot and Coca Cola have created many new jobs there.

Another reason people move is the rising cost of cities. People have to live in places they can afford. As prices rise in some neighborhoods, people move to cheaper areas. In Harlem in New York and Logan Square in Chicago, some **lower-income** residents are moving away because rents are too high. As rents continue to rise in expensive cities like New York and San Francisco, more of the original populations may leave.

A third reason people move is **assimilation**. For example, 100 years ago, there were strong Italian communities in New York City, such as Little Italy in Manhattan. About 90 percent of the people who lived there were Italian and most spoke Italian or Sicilian. There were Italian newspapers, clubs, theaters, and Catholic churches. The children of these Italian immigrants stayed in the community. But gradually, the grandchildren of these immigrants became more fully part of American society. As this happened, the third generation started to move away. Now, many Italians have moved out of Manhattan to suburbs all over New Jersey and Long Island.

As Americans move out of one community and into another, they enrich the places they pass through. Stamford, Connecticut, was once home to Irish and Italian immigrants. Now families from Argentina, Uruguay, Poland, and Haiti live there. Fifty-four languages are spoken in the city public schools. The constant movement of Americans through cities and suburbs mixes classes, languages, and cultures, and continues to change the American landscape.

3 CHECK YOUR UNDERSTANDING

Reading Skill: Distinguishing an Author's Main Ideas from Details

Use the organization of a text to distinguish an author's main ideas from the details that explain or support those ideas.

PAIRS. **Read the article again. Answer the questions.**

1. What is the main idea of the article?

   _____

2. What are the author's answers to the question "Why are so many Americans on the move?"

   a. _____

   b. _____

   c. _____

3. Find one detail for each answer the author gives.

   a. _____

   b. _____

   c. _____

4 WORD WORK

Find the boldfaced words in the article. Figure out their meaning from context. Then write the definitions.

1. relocate _____

2. disappear _____

3. lower-income _____

4. assimilation _____

Show what you know!   Talk about moving

GROUPS. **Discuss.**

1. Have you ever moved? Why did you move? Were your reasons for moving described in the article?

2. What are some of the things that happen when people move to a new community?

Listening and Speaking

1 BEFORE YOU LISTEN

GROUPS. Discuss.

1. What kinds of problems can people have with their neighbors?

2. If you have a problem with a neighbor, what can you do?
   Who should you talk to?

2 LISTEN

CD1 T73

A   Oscar and Marta live in an apartment building. They are talking about their neighbors. Listen to their conversation. What is the problem?

CD1 T73

B   Read the statements. Then listen to the conversation again. Circle the correct answers.

1. Oscar and Marta **know / don't know** the neighbors well.

2. The neighbors were **rude / polite** when Marta asked them to be quiet.

3. **Oscar / Marta** is very angry about the situation.

4. Marta wants to call the **police / building manager**.

5. It **is permitted / is not permitted** to make noise in the building after 10 P.M.

6. Oscar and Marta decide to call the **police / building manager**.

C GROUPS. Discuss. What should Oscar and Marta do about their neighbors?

D MAKE IT PERSONAL. PAIRS. Have you ever had a problem with your neighbors? Describe your experience.

3 CONVERSATION

A  CD1 T74 **Listen to the sentences. Notice the intonation. Then listen and repeat.**

Oh, no!   That's horrible!   It's disgusting!

Pronunciation Watch

To show strong feeling, make your voice go up very high and then fall.

B CD1 T75 **Two neighbors are talking. Listen and read.**

Maria: I saw a mouse in the laundry room last night!

Rosa: Oh, no! That's horrible! Li Ping told me that she had mice in her building, too.

Maria: She did? It must be the construction next door. She said they were repairing the pipes.

Rosa: Come to think of it, there's some construction here, too, in the basement near the laundry room. I bet that's why there are mice.

Maria: Ugh! I can't stand mice! I'm going to call the landlord. I'll ask him to call the exterminator.

4 PRACTICE

A PAIRS. Practice the conversation.

B ROLE PLAY. PAIRS. Role play this situation. You are neighbors in the same apartment building.

Student A: A neighbor has parked in your parking spot three times this week, and you have had to park your car in the street. Tell Student B about your problem.

Student B: Tell Student A to find out who has been parking in the spot. Then tell Student A to talk to that neighbor and ask him or her to stop parking there.

C PROBLEM-SOLVING.

STEP 1. Read the problem. Think of a few possible solutions.

One of Pedro's neighbors, Leo, leaves for work very early in the morning. Leo's co-worker picks him up at 4:00 A.M. Many mornings, the co-worker honks his horn to let Leo know he's waiting. The horn wakes Pedro up, and he can never go back to sleep.

STEP 2. GROUPS. Discuss the problem. Share ideas about solving it. Vote on the best solution.

Discuss problems with neighbors

Grammar

Reported speech

Direct speech	Reported speech				
Lidia said, "You're too noisy."	Lidia	said			they were too noisy.
Lidia told her neighbor, "Your car is in my parking spot."		told	her neighbor	(that)	his car was in her parking spot.
The landlord said, "I'll fix it tomorrow."	The landlord	said			he would fix it tomorrow.

Grammar Watch

- Use reported speech to tell what a speaker says without using the exact words.
- In both direct and reported speech, the verb *tell* takes an object. The verb *say* does not.
- In formal English, when the reporting verb is in the past, the verb in the reported speech is often also in the past. In informal English, the verb in the reported speech does not change to the past, especially when speech is reported soon after it is spoken: *Lidia said they're too noisy.*
- Pronouns and possessives in reported speech usually change to keep the speaker's original meaning.
- *See page 283 for additional changes in verb tenses, pronouns, and possessives in reported speech.*

1 PRACTICE

A Read the advice column questions from two tenants. Underline the reported speech.

Q: One of my neighbors smokes all the time. I told him that <u>smoking wasn't allowed in the building</u>. I also told him that my children are getting sore throats. He said he would stop, but I can still smell smoke from his apartment. What should I do?

Q: The ceiling in our bathroom leaks every time our upstairs neighbors take a shower. The building manager said he would send a plumber, but it's been three days. I told my neighbors that they should call, too. They said they did, but nothing has happened. What should I do?

B Complete the statements. Use *said* or *told.*

My friend Inez called me last week. She was really upset. She ___told___ me that her neighbor had bought two big dogs. She _____ the dogs were always running in the halls. When they saw her, they jumped on her. She _____ she was terrified. I _____ her that she should complain to the landlord, but she _____ that she didn't like to complain. I _____ her I would call the landlord for her, but she _____ she would work it out.

A Read the tenants' problems. Rewrite them using *said* and informal English.

1. **Ivan:** "My neighbors' kids get up early and play and wake my wife and me up."

   <u>Ivan said that his neighbors' kids get up early and play and wake his wife and him up.</u>

2. **Victoria:** "The hallway in our building always smells of strong cooking odors from the restaurant next door."

   _____

3. **Adina:** "My neighbors have visitors at 2:00 and 3:00 in the morning, and they sometimes ring my doorbell by accident."

   _____

4. **Ming:** "We live right near a fire station, and the sirens wake our kids up all the time."

   _____

5. **Ibrahim:** "My neighbor parks her car in my space almost every weekend."

   _____

B Complete the paragraph about Sara's problem. Use the verbs in parentheses. Use formal English.

Last week, I spoke to the building manager about two problems. The first is with the front door. I told him that it <u>didn't close</u> properly and that this _____ a dangerous
                                        (not close)   (be)
situation. He said he _____ about the problem. I told him that he _____
                         (know)   (need)
to install an automatic lock. He said he _____ into it. The second problem is with
                                         (look)
the nightclub down the block. It closes late, and people make a lot of noise when they leave. The
manager said he _____ sorry but that he _____ to do anything about it.
                      (be)   (not be able)

Show what you know! Discuss problems with neighbors

PAIRS. Talk about a problem you have had with a neighbor. Use reported speech.

1. What did your neighbor do? What did you do or say?
2. How did you resolve the problem?

Can you...discuss problems with neighbors? ☐

Writing

1 BEFORE YOU WRITE

A CLASS. When a tenant has a problem in his or her apartment, he or she often writes a letter of complaint to the landlord to describe the problem. Why is writing a letter a good idea?

B GROUPS. Have you ever written a letter of complaint to a landlord? What did you complain about? What happened next?

C Read the writing model. Underline the complaint in the letter. Circle the solution to the problem.

> **Writing Tip**
>
> When you write a letter of complaint, clearly state the problem and ask for a solution to the problem.

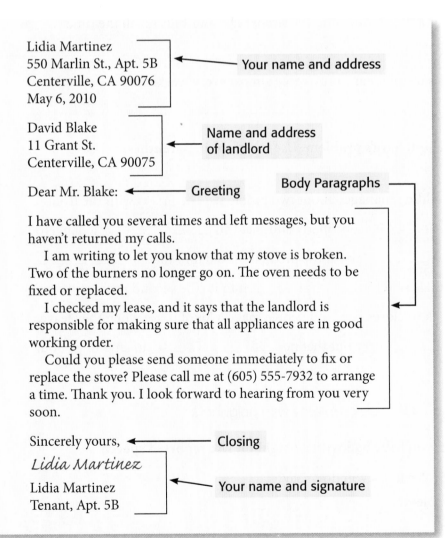

Lidia Martinez
550 Marlin St., Apt. 5B
Centerville, CA 90076
May 6, 2010
→ Your name and address

David Blake
11 Grant St.
Centerville, CA 90075
→ Name and address of landlord

Dear Mr. Blake: ← Greeting

Body Paragraphs

I have called you several times and left messages, but you haven't returned my calls.

I am writing to let you know that my stove is broken. Two of the burners no longer go on. The oven needs to be fixed or replaced.

I checked my lease, and it says that the landlord is responsible for making sure that all appliances are in good working order.

Could you please send someone immediately to fix or replace the stove? Please call me at (605) 555-7932 to arrange a time. Thank you. I look forward to hearing from you very soon.

Sincerely yours, ← Closing

Lidia Martinez
Lidia Martinez
Tenant, Apt. 5B
→ Your name and signature

2 THINKING ON PAPER

A BRAINSTORM. **Think about problems you might have in your house or apartment. Write a list of problems.**

Problem A: _____

Problem B: _____

B **Choose one problem. Think of possible solutions. Plan and organize your letter. Organize your ideas like this.**

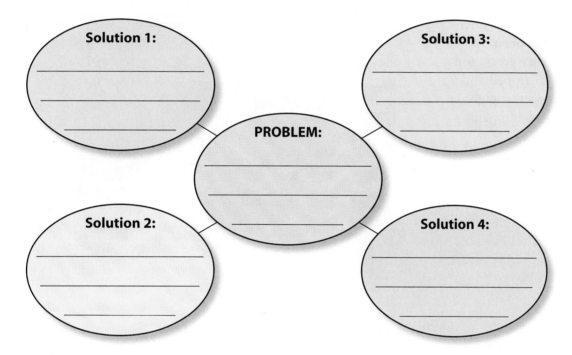

3 WRITE

Write your own letter of complaint. Focus on one problem and its solution.
Use the information in your plan. Look at the writing model for an example.

4 CHECK YOUR WRITING

☐ Did you clearly explain the problem?

☐ Did you ask for a specific solution?

☐ Did you include your name, address, and phone number?

☐ Did you use correct capitalization, punctuation, and spelling?

1 REVIEW   For your grammar review, go to page 250.

2 ACT IT OUT   What do you say?

STEP 1. CLASS. **Review the conversation on page 119 (CD1, Track 75).**

STEP 2. ROLE PLAY. PAIRS. **Role-play this situation.**

Student A: You are a tenant. The lobby in your apartment building has not been painted in twenty years, and the carpeting is ripped and stained. You meet a neighbor in the lobby and complain about the problem.

Student B: You are Student A's neighbor. Listen to Student A's complaints about the lobby and discuss what to do.

3 READ AND REACT   Problem-solving

STEP 1. **Read about Gustavo's problem.**

Gustavo moves into a new apartment that is closer to his place of work. He doesn't know anyone in the building. He would like to get to know his neighbors, but he finds them unfriendly.

STEP 2. GROUPS. **What is Gustavo's problem? Discuss a solution. List three things that he can do.**

4 CONNECT   For your Self-Evaluation Activity, go to page 259.
For your Team Project, go to page 268.

Which goals can you check off? Go back to page 105.

 Go to the CD-ROM for more practice.

Behind the Wheel

Preview

Read the title. How much does it cost to buy and own a car? What are some things that car owners have to spend money on?

UNIT GOALS

- ☐ Talk about things to consider when buying a car

- ☐ Describe preferences in cars

- ☐ Talk about buying car insurance

- ☐ Discuss car maintenance and repairs

- ☐ Discuss consumer-protection laws

- ☐ Describe a car accident

- ☐ Write about a good or bad purchase

Listening and Speaking

1 BEFORE YOU LISTEN

When you buy a car, you need to consider a lot of factors. Read the list of factors. Which ones are most important to you?

vehicle type = sedan, convertible, SUV, minivan, pickup, etc.

make and model = Ford Focus, Honda Civic, Toyota Corolla, etc.

safety features = seat belts, air bags, antilock brakes, etc.

optional features = CD player, power steering, air-conditioning sunroof, etc.

mileage = the total distance a car has traveled

gas mileage = miles per gallon (mpg) of gasoline

reliability = how well a car works; dependability

warranty = a written promise to fix or replace a product that doesn't work

2 LISTEN

CD2 T2

A   Listen to the first part of Mark and Eva Ortega's conversation. **What type of car do they want to buy? Why?**

CD2 T3

B   **Read the statements. Then listen to the whole conversation. Write *T* (true) or *F* (false). Correct the false statements.**

_____ 1. Mark and Eva think it's important for a car to have a warranty.

_____ 2. They want to buy a car with power steering.

_____ 3. They don't care about air-conditioning.

_____ 4. They agree that front airbags are enough to make a car safe.

_____ 5. Mark and Eva have agreed they want a red car.

CD2 T4

Read and listen to Mark and Eva's conversation with a salesperson at Tri-State Motors.

Salesperson: So, you're looking at the 2005 Ford Focus. It's a great little car, isn't it? I can let you have it for just under $9,000.

Mark: We've checked prices for this make and model. I think we can get the car for less.

Salesperson: I might be able to get you a lower price. I'll talk to my manager.

Eva: I see there are 58,000 miles on the car. How many previous owners have there been?

Salesperson: Just one. She drove the car mostly for shopping. Our mechanics have inspected the car. It's in excellent condition. Would you like to take a test drive? I can go get the keys for you.

Mark: Thanks, but not right now. We'd rather look at some other cars first.

4 **PRACTICE**

A GROUPS. Practice the conversation.

B MAKE IT PERSONAL. Think about the important factors in buying a car.

STEP 1. What are the three most important factors in buying a car? Write *1* (most important), *2*, and *3*.

_____ make and model   _____ gas mileage   _____ purchase price

_____ safety   _____ reliability   _____ other: _____

STEP 2. CLASS. Share your results. Explain your choices.

C GROUPS. Imagine that you want to buy a used car. Look at the pictures. Which car would you most like to have? Why?

Grammar

Would rather and would prefer to express preferences

Statements			
Mark and Eva **would rather**	**buy**	a compact	**than** a full-size car.
Mark and Eva **would prefer**	**buying**	a small car	(**to** a full-size car).
	to buy	a small car.	
They**'d rather not**	**have**	a large vehicle.	
They**'d prefer not**	**having**	a big car.	

Questions			
A: **Would** you **rather**	**drive**	a minivan	**than** an SUV?
B: Yes, I **would**.			
A: **Would** you **prefer**		a Ford	**to** a Toyota?
B: No, I **wouldn't**.			

> **Grammar Watch**
> - *Would rather* and *would prefer* both express preference.
> - Use the base form of the verb after *would rather*. Use an infinitive or a gerund after *would prefer*. The infinitive is more common than the gerund.
> - When comparing nouns with *would rather*, use *than* between the two nouns. When comparing nouns with *would prefer*, use *to* between the two nouns.

---

1 PRACTICE

I'd rather drive a sports car than a minivan any day!

Raul

I like this car, but I'd rather not drive a two-door model. And I'd really prefer a blue car to a yellow one.

Marina

2005 Hybrid
$10,999
Great Gas Mileage

I want a safe car, and I'd prefer not to spend money on car repairs.

Yuan

Look at the pictures. Check (✓) the statements that are true.

__✓__ 1. Raúl doesn't want to drive a minivan.

_____ 2. Marina is looking for a four-door car.

_____ 3. Marina really likes yellow cars.

_____ 4. Yuan wants a reliable car.

_____ 5. Yuan and Raúl like the same kinds of cars.

A Circle the correct words.

Auto FYI

by Art Jeffers, Columnist

When it's time for your next car, truck, or SUV, where (**would you rather** / **would you prefer** get your information? People don't always agree on the best way to become a smart auto shopper.

Some car buyers would prefer **read / reading** *Consumer Reports* and the *Kelley Blue Book*. Others would rather **use / to use** the consumerreports.org and kbb.com websites **to / than** spend hours looking at books and magazines.

Another group of car buyers would rather **learn / learning** from personal experience **than / to** read what the experts have to say. They **would rather / would prefer** do research by talking to friends and by paying attention to the cars they see on the road.

So, what about you? Would you prefer relying on your personal experience **to / than** using a website? Or would you rather **follow / following** the advice of experts? Whatever you do, get as much information as possible before you buy your next vehicle.

B Complete the conversation. Use *would rather (not)*, *would prefer (not)*, *would you rather*, or *would you prefer*.

Raúl: I love sports cars. I know they're expensive, and most people <u>would rather not</u> spend that much on a car. But I don't care. I _____ spend the money and drive a really cool car. How about you, Marina? What kind of car _____ having?

Marina: A hybrid. I like the combination of a gas engine and an electric motor with a battery. I _____ going to the gas station if I can avoid it.

Raúl: Hey, Yuan, how about you? What kind of car _____ drive?

Yuan: A safe car. I _____ have to worry about having an accident. I _____ having a car with a good safety record to anything else.

Show what you know! Describe preferences in cars

STEP 1. Write the make and model of the car you would prefer. Write three reasons.

STEP 2. GROUPS. Discuss your choices.

Can you...describe preferences in cars? ☐

Life Skills

1 READ A CAR INSURANCE RENEWAL NOTICE

CLASS. All drivers in the U.S. must have car insurance and must carry insurance identification cards in their vehicles. Discuss.

1. Why is car insurance so important?

2. What information is given in the identification card at the right?

3. The words *premium* and *deductible* appear on all insurance policies. What do these terms mean?

State.com	Phone Number: 1-800-188-5514
	NEW YORK STATE INSURANCE IDENTIFICATION CARD

Policy Number	Effective Date		Expiration Date	
0528-73-66-05	12/18/2008 (12:01 A.M.)		06/18/2009 (12:01 A.M.)	

Applicable with respect to the following Motor Vehicle.

GILBERT, LAURA S.	2004	JEEP	GRCHER LAR
1 SHADY LN.	Year	Make	Model
WHITE PLAINS, NY 10606			

Name & Address of issuer.	1J4GW48S64743281
STATE CAR INSURANCE COMPANY	Vehicle identification Number
ONE STATE PLAZA	Company Code: 639
Washington, DC 20076-0001	

2 PRACTICE

A Once or twice a year, car owners are required to renew their car insurance. Read this part of an insurance renewal notice.

B Read the questions. Circle the correct answers.

1. Who is Tom Russo?
   a. the insurance agent   b. the car owner

2. How long is the policy for?
   a. a month   b. a year

3. How much does the policy cost a year?
   a. $126.00   b. $1,512.00

4. How much does the owner pay before the insurance company begins to cover any expenses?
   a. $500.00   b. $126.00

State *Car Insurance*

Renewal Notice

Name of Insured
Tom Russo

Policy Number
12 4356 995 42

Policy Period
June 1, 2009–May 31, 2010

Vehicle Description: 2008 Ford Explorer
Deductible: $500
Monthly Premium: $126

Your agent is:
Josefina Blanco
Phone: (201) 555-2299
E-mail: jblanco@state.com

3 TALK ABOUT BUYING CAR INSURANCE

CLASS. Discuss.

1. How could you find out about car insurance?

2. What types of questions would you ask?

CD2 T5

A Tom's co-worker Amy is planning to buy her first car. Listen to their conversation. Tom and Amy mention three ways to find out about car insurance. What are they? Take notes.

1. _____

2. _____

3. _____

B PAIRS. What are some things that insurance companies ask when you want to get a quote, or price estimate, for car insurance? Check (✓) the information companies probably ask about.

☐ annual salary   ☑ type of car (year, make, and model, etc.)

☐ age   ☐ safety features

☐ marital status   ☐ when you bought the car

☐ checking account number   ☐ estimated number of miles you will drive each year

CD2 T6

C Now Amy and Tom are talking about getting a quote. Listen. Were your predictions in Exercise B correct? Change your answers if necessary.

CD2 T6

D Tom mentions several things that affect a person's car insurance. Listen again. List three things that can raise insurance premiums.

1. _____

2. _____

3. _____

E CLASS. Discuss.

1. Look back at the things you checked in Exercise B. Why do you think insurance companies want to know about these things?

2. Do you think it's fair for some drivers to pay higher premiums than others? Explain.

Can you...talk about buying car insurance? ☐

Listening and Speaking

1 BEFORE YOU LISTEN

A Read the tips from a website about car maintenance and repairs.

B CLASS. Discuss.

1. What do the boldfaced words in the tips mean?

2. What can car owners do to keep their cars in good condition?

2 LISTEN

CD2 T7

A Jake Alexander is the host of the radio show *All Things Auto*. Listen. In his opinion, what is his number one car-care tip?

CD2 T7

B Read the questions. Then listen to Jake Alexander again. Circle the correct answers.

1. How often should you change the oil in your car?
    a. once a week
    b. once a month
    c. once every three months

2. How often should you check your car's tires?
    a. once a week
    b. once a month
    c. once every three months

3. Where can you find out how much air to put in your tires?
    a. under the hood
    b. under the car
    c. in your owner's manual

4. What color is engine coolant?
    a. green or brown   b. green or yellow   c. red or black

5. What happens when you do regular car maintenance?
    a. You save money.   b. You spend more.   c. You drive more.

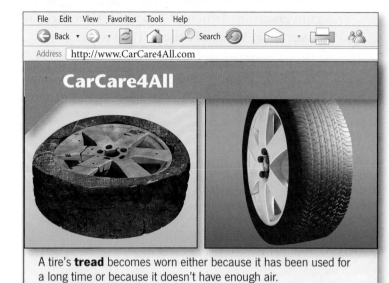

File   Edit   View   Favorites   Tools   Help

Back •   •   Search

Address http://www.CarCare4All.com

CarCare4All

A tire's **tread** becomes worn either because it has been used for a long time or because it doesn't have enough air.

Car Maintenance Tips

In addition to gas, don't forget the other things that you must put into your car. **Oil** keeps your car's engine running well. **Engine coolant** keeps the engine from getting too hot. Other **fluids** that you should check and add to your car when necessary are **transmission fluid** and **brake fluid**. And then there's the **washer fluid**. After all, you need to see out your windows. Finally, remember that the **air pressure**, or amount of air in your tires, is important. Also keep in mind that what goes in sometimes comes out, so be on the lookout for **leaks**.

Pronunciation Watch

Use stress and intonation to show which word in a clause or sentence is the most important. Make your voice go up on that word and make the vowel extra long. The most important word is often the last word in a clause or sentence.

CD2 T8

A 🔊 **Listen to the sentences. Notice how the stress and intonation highlight the most important word. Then listen again and repeat.**

Can you tell me what the **prob**lem is?

When I looked under the **car** this morning, I noticed a dark **stain.**

You might have an **oil** leak.

I'll see you to**mo**rrow, then.

CD2 T9

B 🔊 **Listen to these sounds: a squeal, a squeak, and a ping. Have you ever heard any of these sounds in a car?**

CD2 T10

C 🔊 **Lester is calling an auto repair shop. Listen and read.**

Mechanic:	Osman's Auto Repair. How can I help you?
Lester:	I want to know if I can bring my car in tomorrow.
Mechanic:	Sure. Can you tell me what the problem is?
Lester:	When I looked under the car this morning, I noticed a dark stain.
Mechanic:	You might have an oil leak. Bring the car in tomorrow morning, and we'll take a look at it. We open at 7:00 A.M.
Lester:	Thanks. I'll see you tomorrow, then.

---

4 PRACTICE

A PAIRS. **Practice the conversation.**

B MAKE IT PERSONAL. **What do you know about car maintenance?**

STEP 1. **Write four car-care tips.**

STEP 2. CLASS. **Share your car-care tips.**

Grammar

Embedded *wh-* Questions

Direct question	Embedded *wh-* question		
What is the problem?	Can you tell me	**what**	**the problem is**?
Why does the "Check Engine" light go on?	Could you explain	**why**	**the "Check Engine" light goes on**?
When did the noises start?	I don't know	**when**	**the noises started**.
What time will my car be ready?	I wonder	**what**	**time my car will be ready**.
How much will the repairs cost?	I want to know	**how**	**much the repairs will cost**.

1 PRACTICE

Grammar Watch

- Use embedded questions to ask for information politely or to express information about which you are uncertain.

- Put embedded questions inside questions such as *Do you know…?* inside statements such as *I don't know….* and

- Use statement word order (subject + verb) for most embedded questions.

A Read the conversation. Underline three embedded *wh-* questions.

A: Do you know if the car will be ready tomorrow?

B: Yes, it will. I'm a little worried. I don't know how much the repairs are going to cost.

A: I can't believe you didn't get a written estimate from the mechanic! He should tell you what it's going to cost before he begins work on your car.

B: Of course you're right. I don't know why I didn't think of that.

B Complete the conversation. Put the words in the correct order to form questions—both direct and embedded.

Katy: Do you know <u>where the receipt from the mechanic is</u> ?
(is/the/receipt/where/the/from/mechanic)

Doug: I don't remember _____ when I came home.
(it/with/what/did/I)

Katy: Mark, please tell me. _____?
(is/where/receipt/that)

Doug: It's probably in my wallet. Can you tell me _____?
(so/why/it/is/important)

Katy: I want to know _____ in the radiator.
(coolant/how much/the/put/mechanic)

Doug: _____?
(do/need/you/know/to/why/that)

Katy: There's steam coming from the hood. I want to find out

_____. Maybe he put in too much coolant,
(the/is/what/problem)
or not enough.

Embedded Yes/No Questions

Direct question	Embedded Yes/No question		
Does my car need an oil change?	Can you tell me		my car needs an oil change?
Can I bring my car in tomorrow?	I want to know	if whether	I can bring my car in tomorrow.
Did they fix the problem?	Do you know		they fixed the problem?

2 PRACTICE

A Circle one embedded *Yes/No* question in Exercise 1A.

B Pilar is shopping in an auto parts store. Change the direct questions in parentheses to embedded questions. Include a period or a question mark.

Pilar: Can you tell me _if you have windshield wipers for a 2006 Honda Accord?_
(Do you have windshield wipers for a 2006 Honda Accord?)

Salesperson: Yes, ma'am, we do. They're in Aisle 6.

Pilar: Do you know _____
(Are they on sale?)

Salesperson: I'm not sure _____ I'll find out.
(Did the sale end yesterday?)

Pilar: Could you also find out _____
(Will I need a special bulb for the turn signal?)

C Correct the mistakes in the embedded questions about car maintenance and repairs.

1. He wants to know ~~does~~ the car ~~need~~ new brakes.
    if   *needs*

2. They asked whether was it safe to drive with a damaged tire.

3. Can you tell me does the engine need more coolant?

4. We wonder that the leak is coming from the radiator.

5. The mechanic wasn't sure did they have the parts he needed to repair my car.

Show what you know! Discuss car maintenance and repairs

CLASS. What other things do you want to know about car maintenance and repairs? Write some embedded questions. Then take turns asking and answering them.

Can you...discuss car maintenance and repairs? ☐

Reading

1 BEFORE YOU READ

PAIRS. Look at the title and the headings for each section of the article. Predict. What is the article about?

2 READ

CD2 T11

Read and listen. Was your prediction correct? What do you think a "lemon" is? What happened to Shawn Chastain?

A Sour Purchase Turns Sweet

When Shawn Chastain came home with his new SUV, he thought he had bought the car of his dreams. Shawn had recently become a new father, and it was important for him to have a safe, **reliable** vehicle for his family. However, in just a few months, his dream turned into a nightmare when the "Check Engine" light came on and never went off. Shawn's SUV was a lemon.

No one knew what the problem was.

As soon as the trouble started, Shawn followed the procedures in his warranty. He took his SUV to the dealership where he had made his purchase, but the mechanics there couldn't figure out why the "Check Engine" light was on. They made several repairs, but nothing solved the problem, and Shawn wondered if his vehicle was safe. Shawn kept written records of what

happened on each of his trips to the dealership—all six of them! Then he decided it was time to contact the Texas Department of Transportation (TexDOT).

TexDOT provided a solution.

In Texas, if a vehicle is a lemon, the manufacturer must repair it, replace it, or buy it back. However, the owner has **responsibilities**, too.

According to TexDOT officials, Shawn Chastain gave them the proof they needed to **enforce** the Texas law. He

had kept a complete record of all his **interactions** with the manufacturer and dealer, including all repair orders, letters, and phone calls. Because of Shawn's careful record-keeping, TexDOT was able to reach an agreement with the manufacturer.

Shawn's problem caused him months of **aggravation**, but he finally got satisfaction. In the end, the manufacturer bought back his SUV. Thanks to that money, Shawn and his family finally own a car they can trust.

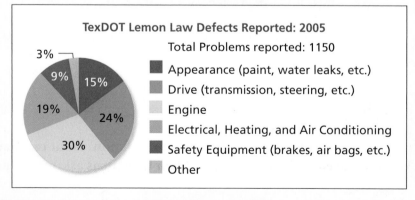

TexDOT Lemon Law Defects Reported: 2005

Total Problems reported: 1150

3%
9%
15%
19%
24%
30%

■ Appearance (paint, water leaks, etc.)
■ Drive (transmission, steering, etc.)
■ Engine
■ Electrical, Heating, and Air Conditioning
■ Safety Equipment (brakes, air bags, etc.)
■ Other

CHECK YOUR UNDERSTANDING

A **Complete the statements. Circle the correct answers.**

1. Shawn Chastain was worried about _____.
   a. the appearance of his SUV   b. the safety of his SUV   c. the speed of his SUV

2. Shawn Chastain used the Texas lemon laws _____.
   a. as soon as his problems started
   b. before he went to TexDOT
   c. after he had given the dealer many opportunities to fix his SUV

3. Shawn took the money that he received from the manufacturer and probably _____.
   a. got another SUV in the same make and model
   b. did research before he bought another vehicle
   c. repaired his SUV

B **Read the Reading Skill. Then look at the pie chart on page 136 and answer the questions.**

1. What was the total number of problems reported to TexDOT?

2. What was the most common problem reported? What percentage of defects were related to safety equipment?

> **Reading Skill:** Use Visuals
>
> Use charts, graphs, and other visuals to learn important facts.

4 **WORD WORK**

Find the boldfaced words in the article and guess their meanings from the context. Then complete the sentences using the correct forms of those words. Circle the correct words.

1. TexDOT decided it was the manufacturer's **responsiblity / responsible** to buy back Shawn's car.

2. **Reliablility / Reliable** is an important factor to consider when buying a new or used car.

3. Many cars have an **interaction / interactive** navigational system that gives drivers directions.

4. The Department of Transportation is responsible for the **enforcement / enforce** of certain laws.

Show what you know!   Discuss consumer-protection laws

Research lemon laws or other consumer-protection laws in the state where you live. Report to the class. Make sure your report describes
- what the law covers,
- what the manufacturer must do according to the law,
- whether the consumer has any responsibilities according to the law.

Listening and Speaking

1 BEFORE YOU LISTEN

PAIRS. Nora Peters and Frank Liu were involved in a fender bender (a car accident that isn't very serious). What do you think probably happened?

2 LISTEN

rearview mirror   lane

side mirror   lane

hood

turn signal   headlight

fender

bumper

CD2 T12

A Listen. Why did the accident happen? Check (✓) the cause.

☐ a. Nora was talking on her cell phone.

☐ b. Frank didn't put on his turn signal.

☐ c. Nora was speeding.

☐ d. Frank saw Nora's car too late.

CD2 T12

B Listen to Nora and Frank's conversation again. Then answer the questions.

1. Was anyone hurt in the accident?

2. Why did Nora want to find her cell phone?

3. Does Frank have insurance? How do you know?

4. What advice did Nora get from her insurance agent?

CD2 T12

C Listen to the conversation again. What four things did Nora and Frank go back to get from their cars?

1. _____

2. _____

3. _____

4. _____

D GROUPS. Discuss. What do you think Nora and Frank do next?

3 CONVERSATION

CD2 T13

A ⊘ **Listen to the sentences. Notice that the pronoun +'d is pronounced as only one syllable. Then listen again and repeat.**

'd = would   **I'd** rather drive a small car.

                  We'd prefer a safe car.

'd = had   **He'd** started changing lanes.

                  She'd already checked her car.

> **Pronunciation Watch**
>
> *Had* and *would* usually have a short, weak pronunciation when used with another verb. After a pronoun, use the contraction *'d* for either *had* or *would*.

CD2 T14

B ⊘ **Listen to the sentences. Circle the words you hear.**

1. **She / She'd** slowed down because of the rain.
2. **He / He'd** already started moving into the right lane.
3. **He / He'd** left his cell phone in the car.
4. **We / We'd** prefer to buy from a dealer.
5. **They / They'd** like the red car.

4 PRACTICE

CD2 T15

A ⊘ **Nora is talking to an officer. Listen and read. What does the officer ask to see?**

Officer: What can I do for you?

Nora: My name is Nora Peters. I was just involved in a car accident.

Officer: You'll have to fill out an accident report. Can I see your driver's license, vehicle registration, and insurance card?

Nora: Certainly. Here they are.

Officer: Thank you. Now, exactly where did the accident happen?

Nora: On Center Street, near Ashland Avenue.

Officer: Had anything unusual happened before the accident?

Nora: Not really. It was raining, and I had just slowed down. …

B PAIRS. **Practice the conversation.**

C ROLE PLAY. PAIRS. **Role-play this situation.**

Student A: You are talking to a police officer about a car accident. Tell the officer when, where, and how the accident happened. Describe the damage to your car.

Student B: You are a police officer at the Green Avenue Police Station. Get personal information and details about the accident that Student A was involved in.

Grammar

Past perfect statements

Nora **had** just **started** to slow down when she saw Frank's car.

Frank **hadn't noticed** the car coming from the opposite direction when he started to make his turn.

Past perfect questions and answers

A: Had Nora **looked** at the damage to her car before she talked to Frank?
B: Yes, she **had**.

A: When Frank and Nora called the police station, **had** they already **taken** pictures?
B: No, they **hadn't**.

A: Where **had** Frank **left** his cell phone?
B: He**'d left** it in his car.

Grammar Watch

Use the past perfect to show time order in the past. The past perfect shows that one action happened earlier than the other.

*Frank **had started** moving into the left lane before he saw Nora.*

| Frank started moving. | Then Frank saw Nora. | Now |

1 PRACTICE

There was an accident on Center Avenue yesterday evening. Read the sentences. Decide which action happened first and which one happened second. Mark the earlier action *1* and the later action *2*.

1   2

1. Sarah Miller had just gone into her favorite video store when she heard a loud crash.

2. She rushed out of the store. There had been a car accident at the corner.

3. Sarah had left her cell phone at home, so she went back to the store to call 911.

4. One of the drivers was yelling that another driver hadn't used his turn signal.

5. When Sarah came out of the store, all the drivers had gotten out of their cars.

A Match the clauses to describe what happened before a number of car accidents.

1. __d__ It had rained,

a. because she hadn't seen the red light.

2. _____ It was 10:00 P.M.,

b. but he hadn't used his turn signal.

3. _____ Lucy had dropped her cell phone,

c. right before she saw the cars in front of her.

4. _____ Bob Park moved into the left lane,

d. and the roads were wet.

5. _____ Victoria Gomez had stepped on the gas

e. but the streetlights hadn't come on yet.

6. _____ Kim Truong didn't stop at the intersection

f. so she reached down to get it.

B Complete the conversations. Use the past perfect.

1. **A:** What happened to your car?

   B: I had an accident last week. I ___had___ just ___pulled___ onto the highway
   (pull)
   when a truck ran into me.

   A: That's terrible! Did anyone get hurt?

   B: The truck driver had minor injuries because he _____ to put on his seatbelt.
   (not remember)

   A: _____ you ever _____ an accident before?
   (have)

   B: Yes. I was in a fender bender last year.

2. **A:** Felix and I were in an accident yesterday.

   B: Oh, no! Is everyone all right?

   A: Fortunately, no one got hurt. But you know, Felix is a terrible driver.

   B: I agree. _____ you ever _____ with him before?
   (drive)

   A: No, I _____. Yesterday was the first time—and the last!
   (not have)

Show what you know! Describe a car accident

GROUPS. Discuss. Talk about a car accident that you have been involved in or seen.

STEP 1. Describe what happened. Remember to use the past perfect to show time order in the past.

STEP 2. Ask and answer questions about the accidents.

Can you...describe a car accident? ☐

Write about a good or bad purchase

Writing

1 BEFORE YOU WRITE

A **GROUPS. Discuss.**
1. What is a *major purchase*?
2. What major purchases have you made? Make a list.

B **CLASS. Share your lists.**

C **Read the writing model. Why was the writer's purchase a good one?**

Down with Buyer's Remorse!

Some people suffer from buyer's remorse. They make major purchases quickly and then wonder if they did the right thing. I'm different. I shop carefully and feel good about my decision afterward. I recently used my shopping skills to buy an incredible used car. First, I did research on several different websites and looked at ads in the local newspaper. I knew that I would rather have a four-door than a two-door model, but I checked the prices for both. I also found out about important safety features. Next, I did more research to learn about repair costs and gas mileage. I decided to look for a small hybrid. Several weeks later, I found exactly what I wanted, but I didn't buy it immediately. I asked my brother's mechanic to inspect it, and I used the VIN (vehicle identification number) to see if the car had ever been in an accident. Finally, I was ready to buy. The car wasn't cheap, but I got a good deal. My new car is safe, reliable, and fun to drive. Besides, it's cute and saves me a lot of money on gas. I have absolutely no regrets.

> **Writing Tip**
>
> Use time words and phrases to signal the steps in a process.

D **PAIRS. Answer the questions.**

1. What is *buyer's remorse*?
2. What did the writer do before buying a car?
3. Why does the writer like her new car?

E **List four time words or phrases that the writer used to signal the steps in her process of buying a car.**

1. _____   3. _____

2. _____   4. _____

A BRAINSTORM. Think about your recent purchases—both large and small. Create a chart like this to record your ideas.

My Good Purchases	My Bad Purchases

B Choose one purchase to describe. Plan and organize your ideas in the space below. Use time words to show the order of the steps in your buying process.

My Best or Worst Purchase: _____

What I did right or what I did wrong

Step 1: First, _____

Step 2: Next, _____

Step 3: Then _____

Step 4: Finally, _____

3 WRITE

Write a paragraph about your good or bad purchase. Use your ideas and the steps you listed above. Use the writing model as an example.

4 CHECK YOUR WRITING

☐ Did you describe a good (or a bad) purchase?

☐ Did you clearly state your main idea?

☐ Did you use time words to show the order of the steps in your buying process?

☐ Did you use correct capitalization, punctuation, and spelling?

1 REVIEW For your grammar review, go to page 251.

2 ACT IT OUT What do you say?

STEP 1. **Review the conversation on page 139 (CD 2, Track 15).**

STEP 2. **ROLE PLAY. GROUPS.
Role-play this situation.**

Student A: You are the driver of a large SUV. You had just started backing out of a parking space when you heard a loud crashing noise. You hadn't seen the small car that was waiting for another parking space.

Student B: You are the driver of a compact car. You were waiting for a parking space when a large SUV backed into you. You are angry that the SUV damaged the passenger's side door of your car.

Student C: You are a police officer who was patrolling the neighborhood. Find out what the problem is. After the drivers give you the details of the accident, tell them that they must go to the police station to complete an accident report.

3 READ AND REACT Problem-solving

STEP 1. **GROUPS. Read about Maria's problem.**

María Campos is having a problem with the brakes on her car. She's not sure how much the repairs will cost, but she knows brake work is usually expensive and she doesn't have the money right now. She paid $500 to have her car repaired last month and $900 for car repairs four months ago. María lives far from her job, so she can't walk to work. She needs to decide what to do about her car.

STEP 2. **GROUPS. What is Maria's problem? Discuss a solution. Give reasons to explain your decision.**

4 CONNECT For your Planning for Learning go to page 260.
For your Team Project, go to page 269.

Which goals can you check off? Go back to page 125.

 Go to the CD-ROM for more practice.

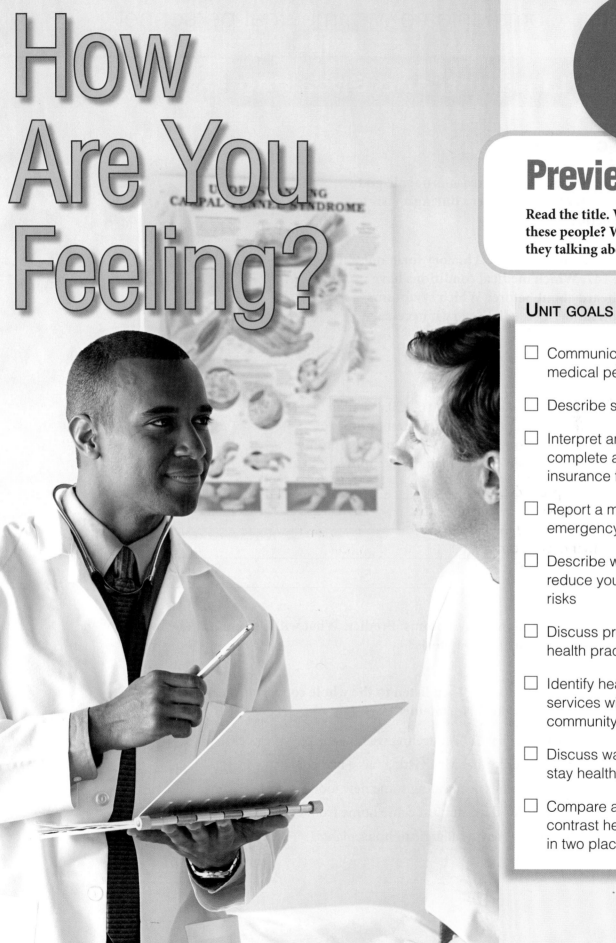

How Are You Feeling?

Preview

Read the title. Who are these people? What are they talking about?

UNIT GOALS

- ☐ Communicate with medical personnel
- ☐ Describe symptoms
- ☐ Interpret and complete a health insurance form
- ☐ Report a medical emergency
- ☐ Describe ways to reduce your health risks
- ☐ Discuss preventive health practices
- ☐ Identify health-care services within the community
- ☐ Discuss ways to stay healthy
- ☐ Compare and contrast health care in two places

Listening and Speaking

1 BEFORE YOU LISTEN

A CLASS. What are some reasons people go to see a doctor? What happens during a visit to the doctor?

B PAIRS. Read the medical history form on page 147. Which medical conditions have you heard about before? Which symptoms do you know? Use a dictionary if necessary.

2 LISTEN

CD2 T16

A  Irma Garcia is a patient at the City Center Clinic. She is talking to Dr. Kim. Listen to the first part of their conversation. What four symptoms has Mrs. Garcia been experiencing? Take notes.

1. _____

2. _____

3. _____

4. _____

B Think about Mrs. Garcia's symptoms. Predict. What will Dr. Kim say she has? What will be the doctor's diagnosis?

CD2 T17

C  Read the statements. Then listen to the whole conversation. Write *T* (true) or *F* (false). Correct the false statements.

_____ 1. Mrs. Garcia hasn't been feeling well for the past six weeks.

_____ 2. Dr. Kim thinks that Mrs. Garcia has a bad cold.

_____ 3. Mrs. Garcia has been eating some new foods lately.

_____ 4. Mrs. Garcia's daughter just came home from college.

_____ 5. Mrs. Garcia may be allergic to houseplants.

3 CONVERSATION

CD2 T18

A Listen to the words. Notice the groups of consonant sounds. Then listen and repeat.

sneezing	stomachache	clinic	drowsiness
sleepiness	stroke	question	prescription

CD2 T19

B Irma Garcia is talking with the pharmacist at a drugstore. Listen and read.

Irma Garcia: Excuse me. My name is Irma Garcia. Is my prescription ready yet?

Pharmacist: Let me check. Have you been waiting long?

Irma Garcia: About half an hour, I guess.

Pharmacist: I'm sorry. I have the prescription right here. Did Dr. Kim talk to you about this medication?

Irma Garcia: She told me to take one tablet daily.

Pharmacist: Did she explain the possible side effects, such as sleepiness?

Irma Garcia: Yes, and she told me that the medicine could also cause dry mouth.

Pharmacist: OK. Be sure to read the information on the label and follow the directions. Please give your doctor a call if you have any problems.

4 PRACTICE

A PAIRS. Practice the conversation.

B MAKE IT PERSONAL. Keep track of your medical history.

STEP 1. Fill out a medical history form like the one above. List other details of your medical history, such as immunizations, surgeries, medications, etc. Use this information the next time you go to the doctor.

STEP 2. GROUPS. Discuss why it's important to know your own medical history and the medical history of family members.

Pronunciation Watch

Many words and syllables begin with a group of consonant sounds. We say the consonants in a group closely together.

City Center Clinic	New Patient—Medical History

Name:_____

Address:_____

Phone #:_____

E-mail Address:_____

Medical Conditions (Check all that apply.)

	You	A Family Member
High blood pressure	☐	☐
High cholesterol	☐	☐
Heart disease	☐	☐
Diabetes	☐	☐
Stroke	☐	☐
Cancer	☐	☐
Allergies	☐	☐

Symptoms (Check all that you have been experiencing in the past six months.)

☐ tiredness	☐ vomiting
☐ sleeplessness	☐ nausea
☐ sneezing	☐ stomachache
☐ coughing	☐ headache
☐ congestion	☐ chest pain
☐ dizziness	☐ weakness in arms or legs
☐ aches and pains	☐ numbness in feet

Grammar

Present perfect continuous

Statements

I've **been sneezing** a lot lately.		
This **has been going on**	*for*	about two weeks.
I **haven't been feeling** well	*since*	my daughter came home.

Grammar Watch

- Use the present perfect continuous to show that an action started in the past and is still going on.
- To show how long an action has been going on, use the present perfect continuous with *for* + the length of time, or *since* + the time the action began.

Questions	Short answers
A: Has Mrs. Garcia **been feeling** tired recently?	**B:** Yes, she **has**.
A: Have you **been eating** any new kinds of food?	**B:** No, I **haven't**.
A: What **have** Mrs. Garcia and her husband **been doing** lately?	**B:** They**'ve** both **been working** in the family business.

1 PRACTICE

A Read these waiting room conversations. Underline the present perfect continuous.

1. **Receptionist:** It's nice to see you. Have you been feeling better since your last visit?
   Mr. Jackson: Yes, I have. My arm hasn't been hurting at all. I'm just here for a follow-up.

2. **Ms. Weber:** I've been seeing Dr. Kim for two years. Have you been coming here long?
   Mr. Owolabi: No. My wife made this appointment for me. I've been getting sleepy at work lately.

3. **Nurse:** Dr. Kim will see you now, Mrs. Garcia. I hope you haven't been waiting too long.
   Mrs. Garcia: I've been here about fifteen minutes, but that's OK. I've been reading an interesting article about allergies. Maybe I'll finish it after I see the doctor.

B Dr. Kim is talking to a new patient, Charles Owolabi. Circle the correct words.

Dr. Kim:	Good afternoon, Mr. Owolabi. What brings you here today? **Has / Have** you been having some health problems?
Mr. Owolabi:	I've been feeling very tired **for / since** the past few months.
Dr. Kim:	**You have / Have you** been experiencing any other symptoms?
Mr. Owolabi:	Yes, I **am / have**. I'm a carpenter, and I sometimes get cuts on my hands at work. The cuts **been / have been** taking longer to heal.
Dr. Kim:	You wrote here that there's a history of diabetes in your family.
Mr. Owolabi:	That's right. My grandmother was diabetic, and so is my mother. She **is taking / has been taking** insulin **for / since** 2005.

Mrs. Garcia and Dr. Kim are talking about Mrs. Garcia's allergy. Complete their conversation. Use the present perfect continuous.

Dr. Kim: Good morning, Mrs. Garcia. How ___*have*___ you ___*been doing*___
                                                                          (do)

                      since I saw you last month?

Mrs. Garcia: Great! I _____ much better. The congestion in
                               (sleep)

                      my nose is gone, and I _____ at night.
                                                     (not/cough)

Dr. Kim: _____ you _____ your medicine regularly?
                                            (take)

Mrs. Garcia: Yes. I _____ your instructions, Dr. Kim.
                                  (follow)

Dr. Kim: _____ the medication _____ any side effects?
                                                (cause)

Mrs. Garcia: No. Everything _____ perfectly.
                                  (go)

Dr. Kim: And your daughter?

Mrs. Garcia: Well, she _____ in the garden lately. She gave all
                                  (work)

                      her houseplants away when she learned about my allergy!

Show what you know!   Describe symptoms

STEP 1. Many students suffer from stress. Check (✓) any symptoms of stress that you have been experiencing.

- ☐ get headaches
- ☐ feel dizzy
- ☐ have stomachaches
- ☐ have difficulty sleeping
- ☐ get frequent colds
- ☐ other: _____

STEP 2. GROUPS. Talk about any symptoms of stress that you have been experiencing. Share ideas about things that can relieve stress.

Can you...describe symptoms? ☐

Life Skills

1 INTERPRET AN INSURANCE ENROLLMENT FORM

CLASS. Discuss. Many companies in the U. S. offer health insurance coverage to their employees.

1. What is health insurance?

2. Why is health insurance important?

2 READ

Read part of a health insurance enrollment form. Find and underline these words: *dependent, divorce, enroll in, spouse, waive.*

ABLE Phone Company   **Health Insurance Enrollment Form**

Open Enrollment Period: You must enroll in your health insurance plan within one month of your date of hire. You can make changes only during the first two weeks of January or the last two weeks of October.

Section 1: Employee Information

Name (first, last) *Patricia Noon*   Social Security Number *123-45-6789*

Address *112 East Street*   ☐ Male   ☒ Female   Birthdate *11/20/1980*

City, State, Zip *Middletown, CT 06457*   Marital Status ☐ Single ☒ Married

Phone Number *860-555-3263*   Employment Status ☒ Full-Time ☐ Part-Time

Starting Date *January 5, 2010*

Section 2: Type of Enrollment: Select (x) one.

☐ Waive (I do not wish to enroll in the company plan.)

☒ Enroll

☐ Change (I want a different type of plan.)

Section 3: Members Covered: Indicate who you wish to cover.

☒ Self   ☒ Spouse   ☒ Dependent(s)

Name (first, last) of all others to be covered   Birthdate

Spouse *John Noon*   *04/25/1979*

Dependent *Maria Noon*   *12/03/2007*

Dependent

Dependent

Section 4: Reason(s) for Changing Type of Plan (Mark all that apply.)

☐ New Employee ☐ Marriage ☐ Divorce ☐ Birth ☐ Change of Spouse's Employment

---

WORD WORK

Match the words you underlined in the form with their definitions.

_____ 1. dependent   a. the end of a marriage

_____ 2. divorce   b. a person for whom you provide food, clothing, housing

_____ 3. enroll in   c. officially join

_____ 4. spouse   d. choose not to have or do something

_____ 5. waive   e. a husband or wife

4 **CHECK YOUR UNDERSTANDING**

A **Look at the enrollment form again. Complete the sentences with information from the form.**

1. The employees at ABLE Phone Company can change their health insurance plan

   during the months of _____ and _____.

2. Patricia's Social Security number is _____.

3. Patricia was born on _____.

4. Patricia has been working at the company since _____.

5. Patricia's husband's name is _____. _____ is her daughter's name.

6. Patricia was 27 when her daughter was born. Her husband was _____ years old.

B PAIRS. **Discuss.**

1. Patricia is expecting her second child in December. When do you think she should change her health insurance plan?

2. One of Patricia's co-workers is going to waive his health benefits. What are some possible reasons for his decision?

C CLASS. **Discuss.**

1. Some companies offer health insurance to their employees, but many do not. What can people do when their company doesn't help pay for health insurance?

2. In some countries, the government pays for people's health care. Is that true in your country? Should the government pay for health care in the U.S.? Explain.

Can you...interpret and complete a health insurance form? ☐

Listening and Speaking

1 BEFORE YOU LISTEN

A Some medical conditions are serious or could become serious. These emergencies require a 911 call for an ambulance. Check (✓) the situations that you think are medical emergencies.

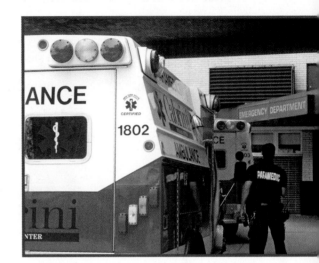

☐ sneezing and coughing   ☐ a stroke

☐ a stomachache   ☐ a heart attack

☐ a broken leg   ☐ congestion

B GROUPS. Compare answers. Discuss. What are some situations that would NOT require a 911 call?

2 LISTEN

CD2 T20

A Listen to the 911 call. What kind of medical emergency do you think the caller is describing?

a. broken arm   b. heatstroke   c. heart attack

CD2 T20

B Read the questions. Then listen to the conversation again. Circle the correct answers.

1. Which statement best describes the condition of the caller's husband?
   a. He is conscious and in no pain.
   b. He is conscious and sweating badly.
   c. He is unconscious.

2. What ongoing condition is the caller's husband taking medication for?
   a. diabetes   b. high blood pressure   c. pain

3. Why is the caller's husband having difficulty breathing?
   a. He is overweight.   b. He is diabetic.   c. He is having chest pain.

4. Which statement best describes the caller?
   a. She is calm.   b. She is frightened.   c. She is angry.

C GROUPS. Discuss. In your opinion, did the 911 operator handle the call well? Why or why not?

3 CONVERSATION

CD2 T21

A man has just called 911. Listen and read.

911 Operator: 911. What's your emergency?

Caller: It's my wife. Her legs are so weak that she can't walk.

911 Operator: Is your wife conscious, sir? Can she talk?

Caller: She's conscious, but she can't speak.

911 Operator: Can I have your exact address, please?

Caller: 1175 West Hampton Street, Apartment 12-B.

911 Operator: Thank you, sir. Now, can you tell me when the symptoms began?

Caller: Just a few minutes ago. At first, she had a bad headache. Then she couldn't stand up.

911 Operator: Everything will be OK, sir. I know it's hard in a situation like this, but stay calm. The paramedics are on their way. Please stay on the line.

4 PRACTICE

A PAIRS. **Practice the conversation.**

B GROUPS. **Discuss.**

1. Why did the 911 operator continue talking to the caller until the paramedics arrived?

2. Have you ever placed a 911 call? Describe the situation.

C ROLE PLAY. PAIRS. **Role-play this situation about a medical emergency. Use one of the ideas below or your own idea.**

- A family member may have food poisoning.

- A co-worker may have broken an arm or a leg.

- A friend or family member is bleeding heavily.

- A child has swallowed dish detergent or other cleaning fluid.

Student A: A family member, friend, or co-worker has just had a medical emergency, and you call 911. Tell the 911 operator what has happened and describe the person's condition and symptoms. Follow the instructions of the 911 operator.

Student B: You are a 911 operator and Student A calls you about a medical emergency. Listen as Student A describes the condition of the person who needs medical attention. Ask questions to find out information you need to know. Give Student A instructions about how best to handle the situation.

Grammar

Such . . . that and *so . . . that*	
It was **such** a terrible situation	**that** the caller couldn't remain calm.
The man had **such** serious symptoms	**that** his wife called 911.
His legs are **so** weak	**that** he can't walk.
You got to the ER **so** quickly	**that** we were able to give you excellent care.
He has **so many** vague symptoms	**that** it's difficult to say what the problem is.
I was in **so much** pain	**that** I couldn't move.

· · · Grammar Watch

- Use *such* with nouns.
- Use *so* with adjectives or adverbs.
- Use *so many* with plural nouns. Use *so much* with non-count nouns. *See page 284 for a list of non-count nouns.*

1 PRACTICE

A Read this information from a medical website. Circle the examples of *such . . . that* and *so . . . that*. Underline the clauses beginning with *that*.

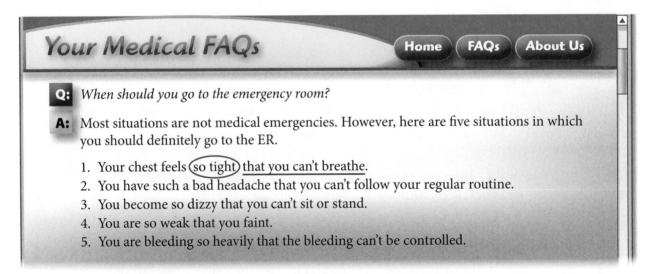

Your Medical FAQs | Home | FAQs | About Us

Q: *When should you go to the emergency room?*

A: Most situations are not medical emergencies. However, here are five situations in which you should definitely go to the ER.

1. Your chest feels so tight that you can't breathe.
2. You have such a bad headache that you can't follow your regular routine.
3. You become so dizzy that you can't sit or stand.
4. You are so weak that you faint.
5. You are bleeding so heavily that the bleeding can't be controlled.

B Six months ago Charles Owalabi's doctor told him he was at risk for diabetes. Read what Charles has done since then. Unscramble the sentences on notepaper.

1. worried / I / that / was / so / diabetes / I / might get / that I went on a strict diet.

   I was so worried that I might get diabetes that I went on a strict diet.

2. relief / It's / a / such / that my blood tests are normal now.

3. these days / eating / healthy foods / I'm / such / that I feel like a new person.

4. weight / so / I've / much / In fact, / lost / that people don't recognize me.

5. health problems / many / so / can / other / Diabetes / lead to / that it can be dangerous.

PRACTICE

A **A doctor wrote a letter to her local newspaper. Complete the letter with *so*, *such*, or *so many*.**

Dear Editor,

Your recent article on healthy living raised _____such_____ an important issue that I left copies in my waiting room for my patients. Many of them complain that they have _____ responsibilities at work that they have no time to eat healthy meals or get exercise. However, as your article points out, we can all make small changes _____ easily that there is no excuse not to.

Small changes can lead to big benefits. Let's take breakfast as an example. Medical experts say that breakfast is _____ an important meal that no one should skip it. But thousands of children start their school day on empty stomachs. This has become _____ a serious problem that many schools now serve breakfast. And what about adults? Why are _____ of us still skipping breakfast? We say we're _____ busy that we don't have time for breakfast. Well, it's time to find the time! This idea seems _____ simple that everyone should understand it.

B **Read these reasons for not getting enough exercise. Combine the sentences on notepaper using *such ... that*, *so ... that*, *so much ... that*, or *so many ... that*.**

1. I'm busy. I don't have time to exercise.
   I'm so busy that I don't have time to exercise.
2. Gyms are expensive. I can't afford to go to one.
3. Exercising is boring. It's hard for me to keep doing it.
4. I'm tired when I come home from work. I just want to eat and go straight to bed.
5. I have chores on the weekend. I can't find the time to work out.
6. I haven't exercised in a long time. I'll never be able to get back into shape.
7. I was in pain the last time I worked out. I never want to do it again.

Show what you know!   Describe ways to reduce your health risks

STEP 1. GROUPS. Discuss.

1. What are the two most important things a person can do to stay healthy?
2. What are five excuses people use for not exercising or eating a healthy diet? Make a list. Use *so . . . that* and *such . . . that* where possible.

STEP 2. CLASS. Share your ideas.

Can you...describe ways to reduce your health risks? ☐

Reading

Overweight Population in the U.S.

1976–1980
2003–2004

Percent

Adults 20–74　Teens 12–19　Children 6–11　Children 2–5

1 BEFORE YOU READ

A CLASS. Look at the graph. Discuss. What information does it show?

B Study the definitions.

life expectancy = the length of time that a person will probably live
decrease your chances = lessen the possibility
significant = large enough to be important
obesity = the condition of being too overweight, especially in a way that is dangerous
dramatically = noticeably

C Skim the first paragraph of the article. Predict the main idea.

2 READ

CD2 T22

Read and listen. Was your prediction correct?

The Long and Short of It

People in the U.S. have been living longer and longer. Consider this: In 1900, the average American lived to the age of 47. In 1950, the average lifespan was 68. In 2007, **life expectancy** was 77.9. So, what would it take to live to the age of 100? Some experts believe that we can find the answer if we look at the leading causes of death.

What the Numbers Say
The Centers for Disease Control and Prevention (CDC) is part of the U.S. Department of Health and Human Services. Recent CDC statistics show that heart disease, cancer, and stroke are the top three causes of death in the U.S. For every 100,000 people, 210.3 people died from heart disease, 184 died from cancer, and 47 died as a result of a stroke in 2005. That's the bad news. The good news is the number of deaths from heart disease, cancer, and stroke declined from 2004 to 2005 and the number could continue to drop.

What We Should Do
Researchers feel that doctors are getting better at diagnosing and curing diseases. They also say disease prevention is important, and that's where there's more bad news-good news. According to the CDC, 34 percent of people in the U.S. who are twenty or older are overweight. However, if we can control our weight, we have a better chance of keeping our blood pressure low and a better chance of avoiding heart disease and stroke. A healthy weight can also help prevent certain kinds of cancer.

In short, genetics certainly plays a role in how long we'll live, but the research is clear. The genes we receive from our parents are just part of the story. Modern medicine and what we do to prevent disease can make a big difference in whether or not we live to be 100.

A Weighty Issue
- If you are overweight, losing a small amount of weight (even 10 percent of your current weight) will help **decrease your chances** of having health problems such as high blood pressure or Type 2 diabetes.

- Statistics from 2003–2004 and 2005–2006 showed no **significant** increase in the number of U.S. adults who were overweight. However, **obesity** is still a problem in this country.

- It is not just adults who have weight problems. The number of children and teens in the U.S. who are overweight has gone up **dramatically** since the 1970s.

Reading Skill:
Scanning a List for Details

Read information in a bulleted list quickly to look for details such as facts and numbers.

A Read the Reading Skill. Then read the statements. Write *T* (true) or *F* (false). Scan the bulleted items on page 156 to find your answers.

_____ 1. You must decrease your weight by at least 20 percent to improve your health.

_____ 2. Being overweight can cause high blood pressure and Type 2 diabetes.

_____ 3. There were a lot more overweight adults in the U. S. in 2006 than in 2004.

_____ 4. The number of overweight children and teens has increased since the 1960s.

B Complete the sentences. Circle the correct answers.

1. In 1950, the average American lived to the age of _____.
   a. 47   b. 68   c. 77.9

2. In 2005, the number of people in the U.S. who died from heart disease, cancer, and stroke _____.
   a. increased   b. decreased   c. stayed the same

3. Since the 1970s, the number of overweight children and teens has _____.
   a. increased   b. decreased   c. stayed the same

4. People who are overweight probably have _____.
   a. low blood pressure   b. high blood pressure   c. a low risk for cancer

C Look again at the graph on page 156. Circle the statement that is NOT true.

a. From 2003 to 2004, more than 15 percent of children ages 6 to 11 were overweight.
b. From 1976 to 1980, 5 percent of children ages 2 to 5 and 5 percent of teens were overweight.
c. The percentage of overweight adults in the U.S. increased more than any other group between the two time periods shown.

4 **WORD WORK**

GROUPS. *Genetics* is the study of genes. What is a *gene*? List some characteristics that parents pass on to their children through genes.

Show what you know! Discuss preventive health practices

GROUPS. Discuss.

1. Do you have a healthy lifestyle? Does the information in the article make you want to change your lifestyle? Explain.

2. What other things can people do to live healthfully?

Listening and Speaking

1 BEFORE YOU LISTEN

A GROUPS. **What kinds of immunizations have you had? Why did you get these vaccinations?**

B PAIRS. **Look at the picture of a health fair. Discuss.**

1. What types of services might a health fair provide?
2. Why would people go to a health fair instead of to a doctor?

2 LISTEN

CD2 T23

A A radio news anchor is reading a public service announcement (PSA). Listen. What is the purpose of the announcement?

CD2 T23

B Read the questions. Listen to the PSA again. Then answer the questions.

1. According to state law, who must get specific vaccinations?
2. When is the immunization deadline for school children?
3. In addition to immunizations, what can children ages 5 to 12 get at the health fair?
4. What time does the health fair start on Saturday? What are the hours on Sunday?

C GROUPS. **Answer the questions.**

1. Which immunizations are required in schools where you live? (Look on the school district's website.)
2. Why do you think immunizations are required for all first-time students?
3. Where in your community can children can get their immunizations? (Ask the parents in your group, or check on the school district's website.)

Pronunciation Watch

In words that end in *-ical*, *-ity*, and *-tion*, stress the syllable just before the ending. In words that end in *-ize* and *-ate*, the stress is usually two syllables before the ending.

CD2 T24

A Listen to each word. Notice the stress. Then listen again and repeat.

medical   o**be**sity   immuni**za**tion   **im**munize   com**mu**nicate

CD2 T25

B Put a dot (•) over the stressed syllable in each word. Then listen and check your answers.

1. examination   2. physical   3. community   4. specialize   5. participate

CD2 T26

C A mother has called the nurse at her daughter's school. Listen and read.

Nurse: Good morning. This is Nurse Doyle speaking. How can I help you?

Mother: Good morning. I received a letter about my daughter. It says that she should get a medical check-up.

Nurse: What grade will your daughter be in when school starts?

Mother: Fifth grade.

Nurse: I see. Then your daughter must see a doctor. State law requires all fifth-grade students to have a physical examination. And your daughter's immunizations must be up to date, too.

Mother: OK. Then I guess I'd better make a doctor's appointment.

Nurse: Yes, and you'd better do it soon. We must receive the results of the medical exam and the list of immunizations no later than September 15th. That's the deadline.

4 PRACTICE

A PAIRS. Practice the conversation.

B ROLE PLAY. PAIRS. Role-play this situation.

Student A: You are a parent. You don't have medical or dental insurance. You received a letter from your child's school. It says that your second grader cannot go to class until he or she has gone to a dentist. You think the requirement to have a dental exam is unfair because you can't pay for the exam.

Student B: You are a school nurse. You must talk to any parent who received a letter saying that his or her child needs to go to the dentist before that child can come back to school. The dental exam is a state requirement for all students in the second grade. Suggest some places that might provide dental treatment free of charge.

Grammar

Should, ought to, had better, and must

For more information, you **should** visit the Radio WDKM website.
School officials say that parents **should not** wait until the last minute.
Parents **ought to** have their children immunized now.
I**'d better** make a doctor's appointment soon, or I'll miss the deadline.
You**'d better not** forget. It's very important.
Your daughter's immunizations **must** be up to date. It's a requirement.
A: Should I make an appointment today?   **B:** Yes, you **should**.

> **Grammar Watch**
>
> - Use *should* or *ought to* for advice, suggestions, and opinions.
> - Use *had better* (*'d better*) for strong advice or suggestions.
> - Use *must* when something is required or necessary.
> - For negative meanings, use *should not* (*shouldn't*) and *had better not* (*'d better not*).
> - Use *should* in questions.

1   PRACTICE

A   Two co-workers are talking about the importance of getting a flu shot. Read their conversation. Underline the examples of *should, ought to, had better,* and *must*.

A: I think that everyone <u>should</u> get a flu shot.

B: I agree, but the company ought to give us the shots for free.

A: You'd better not say that too loudly. You should be grateful that we can get the vaccine for just $10.

B: You're right. It's a good deal, especially for someone like me.

A: Why especially for someone like you?

B: I'm over fifty, and I have heart disease. They say that anyone over the age of fifty or with medical conditions like heart disease or diabetes should get a flu shot every year. It's already September 24. I'd better go to Smithson's soon.

A: Don't forget to take your ID card. The announcement says that you must have an employee ID to get the $10 price.

> **Attention Employees!**
>
> Flu shots will be available for all MRC Tire Company employees at Smithson's drugstores during the month of September. Show your employee ID card to get the special price of $10.

B   Look at the examples you underlined. For each example, write: *1* (advice, suggestion, opinion), *2* (strong advice, strong suggestion), or *3* (requirement).

A Unscramble the sentences on notepapper. Put the words in order.

1. annual / should / medical / Children / and / have / checkups / adults

   Children and adults should have annual medical checkups.

2. sleep / get / Everyone / seven to eight / ought to / of / hours

3. had better / their / find time / to / stress / in / lives / Adults / reduce

4. people / should / active / give up / an / Older / lifestyle / not

5. must / We / to / health / take steps / protect / our

B Read the health article from the Radio WDKM website. Find and correct six mistakes with *should, ought to, had better,* and *must.* The first mistake has been corrected for you.

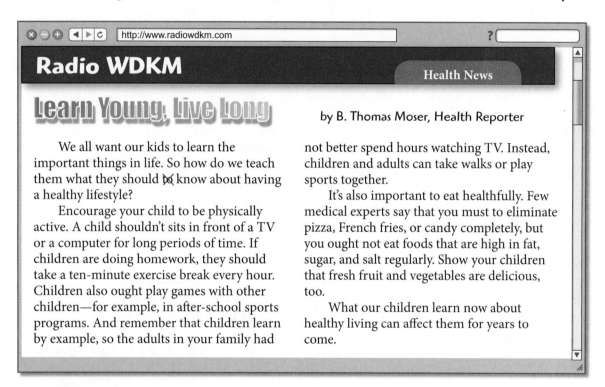

Radio WDKM

Health News

Learn Young, Live Long   by B. Thomas Moser, Health Reporter

We all want our kids to learn the important things in life. So how do we teach them what they should ~~to~~ know about having a healthy lifestyle?

Encourage your child to be physically active. A child shouldn't sits in front of a TV or a computer for long periods of time. If children are doing homework, they should take a ten-minute exercise break every hour. Children also ought play games with other children—for example, in after-school sports programs. And remember that children learn by example, so the adults in your family had not better spend hours watching TV. Instead, children and adults can take walks or play sports together.

It's also important to eat healthfully. Few medical experts say that you must to eliminate pizza, French fries, or candy completely, but you ought not eat foods that are high in fat, sugar, and salt regularly. Show your children that fresh fruit and vegetables are delicious, too.

What our children learn now about healthy living can affect them for years to come.

Show what you know!   Discuss ways to stay healthy

STEP 1. GROUPS. Discuss advice, suggestions, recommendations, or requirements for good health. Record your ideas on the board. Use full sentences.

STEP 2. CLASS. Which three ideas are most helpful? Take a vote.

Can you... discuss ways to stay healthy? ☐

Lesson 9   Describe a personal experience with health care

Writing

1 BEFORE YOU WRITE

A GROUPS. People sometimes have illnesses, injuries, or other health issues that require visiting a doctor or going to a hospital. What experiences have you had with medical personnel? Make a list.

B PAIRS. Describe one of your experiences. Use words that make the experience vivid, that is, words that express what it was like.

C Read the writing model. Underline the words that express what the experience was like for the writer.

A Visit to the Doctor

Last summer I fell on the sidewalk and sprained my ankle. After a week, it felt better. But last month, it started to hurt a lot again, and I was having trouble walking. I went to the clinic, but the doctor there said that I needed to see an orthopedist and recommended Dr. Nemec. I couldn't get an appointment until the next week. I was very worried and sat nervously in the waiting room. My ankle ached with pain, and I could barely put any weight on it. I limped into Dr. Nemec's examining room. It was cold, and I shivered while waiting to see her. Everything in the room was bright white or metal, and there was a lot of medical equipment that I did not recognize. What would this doctor do to me with all those machines?

When Dr. Nemec walked into the office, she smiled warmly. Her soft voice and firm but gentle manner immediately put me at ease. She examined me very thoroughly but without hurting me. She pressed gently where my ankle hurt and explained what she was going to do. Dr. Nemec was reassuring and competent, and this made all my fear—and even some of the pain—go away. I knew that everything would be all right.

> **Writing Tip:** Using Sensory Details
>
> When you write a personal narrative, use sensory details to help the reader see, hear, feel, smell, or taste what you are describing. Sensory details appeal to the reader's five senses.

D PAIRS. Answer the questions.

1. How does the writer feel before he sees the doctor? Circle the details that let you know.

2. How does the writer feel while and after the doctor examines him? Underline the details that let you know.

3. Find sensory details in the writing model. Which senses do they appeal to?

BRAINSTORM. **Think about your experiences with health care. Choose one of your experiences to write about. Use the sensory-details chart below to list details that make your experience vivid.**

Sensory details	
Sight	
Hearing	
Touch	
Smell	
Taste	

3 **WRITE**

In a personal narrative, a writer tells a story about a personal experience. Write a personal narrative about an experience you had with health care. Use the writing model as an example. Include the details from your chart to make your description come alive.

4 **CHECK YOUR WRITING**

☐ Did your narrative describe a personal experience you had with health care?

☐ Did you include sensory details to help the reader see, hear, feel, smell, or taste what you described?

☐ Did you use correct capitalization, punctuation, and spelling in your narrative?

1 REVIEW

For your grammar review, go to page 252.

2 ACT IT OUT What do you say?

STEP 1. Review the conversation on page 159 (CD2, Track 26).

STEP 2. ROLE PLAY. PAIRS. Role-play this situation.

Student A: You recently moved to a new city with your daughter, who has just started fourth-grade. You're at the City Center Clinic with your daughter because she has been having stomachaches. You talk to the person next to you, who tells you that all fifth-grade students in your state must have a medical exam.

Student B: You're at the City Center Clinic with your son because he needs to get the medical exam required for all fifth-grade students. You tell this to the person next to you. When you hear that this person's daughter is suffering from stomachaches, you tell him or her that your son had stomachaches when he started his new school.

3 READ AND REACT Problem-solving

STEP 1. GROUPS. Read about the problem.

We all know that diet plays an important role in preventing heart attacks, strokes, and some kinds of cancer. However, it is often difficult to make healthy changes in the way we eat. Why do people find it so hard to eat a healthy diet?

STEP 2. Keep a record of all the food that you eat for 24 hours. Bring your "food diary" to class.

STEP 3. Discuss. What are one or two changes that each member of your group can make to have a better diet? Give advice and explain your reasons.

4 CONNECT

For your Community-Building Activity, go to page 260.
For your Team Project, go to page 270.

Which goals can you check off? Go back to page 145.

 Go to the CD-ROM for more practice.

Partners in Education

Preview

Read the title. Why is it important for parents to be involved in their children's education?

UNIT GOALS

- ☐ Discuss a student's progress

- ☐ Talk about parents' involvement in school

- ☐ Interpret and respond to a report card

- ☐ Talk with school personnel

- ☐ Talk about improving schools

- ☐ Talk about after-school programs

- ☐ Discuss school safety

- ☐ Write a letter to the editor

Listening and Speaking

1 BEFORE YOU LISTEN

A GROUPS. In many places in the U.S., the school system has three levels: elementary school, middle school, and high school. Discuss. How are the schools organized in the area where you live?

B GROUPS. The word *grade* has two meanings. What is its meaning in each of these sentences?

1. My daughter is in the second **grade**.   2. Her **grade** on the spelling test was an A.

2 LISTEN

CD2 T27

A Mrs. Adamski is talking to Mr. Bowman, the guidance counselor at her children's school. Listen to the first part of their conversation. Then circle the correct answer.

Mr. Bowman made the appointment with Mrs. Adamski because _____.
a. her son is having some problems with his grades
b. her son will start high school this fall
c. he wants her daughter to be a better student
d. he wants to help her daughter go to college

B PAIRS. Now listen to the whole conversation. Predict. Why does Mr. Bowman say it's time for Monica to start thinking about college?

CD2 T28

C Read the statements. Then listen to the whole conversation. Write *T* (true) or *F* (false). Correct the false statements.

__F__ 1. Monika is ~~already~~ *not* making plans to go to college.

_____ 2. Monika might be able to get a scholarship to go to college.

_____ 3. Mrs. Adamski doesn't want her daughter to go to college.

_____ 4. There are special classes to help students prepare for college.

_____ 5. Mrs. Adamski will bring her husband on her next visit to the guidance office.

D PAIRS. Was your prediction correct? What did Mr. Bowman mean by "Yes and no"?

3 CONVERSATION

CD2 T29

A Listen to the sentences. Notice the stress on the information that is different in the second sentence in each conversation. Then listen and repeat.

A: Her daughter has problems with her grades.
B: No, her son has problems with his grades.

A: Her daughter is sixteen years old.
B: No, her daughter is thirteen years old.

Pronunciation Watch

Use stress to highlight information that is new or different, which is often the last important word in a clause or sentence. To correct or disagree with something, highlight the information that is different.

CD2 T30

B Mrs. Adamski is at a middle school parent-teacher conference. Listen and read the conversation.

Mr. Manning:	I'm so glad you could come to talk about your son. I'm Mr. Manning, Robert's math teacher.
Mrs. Adamski:	It's nice to meet you. Robert says he's having some problems with math.
Mr. Manning:	Well, Robert is a great kid, and he seems to enjoy the class. But, yes, I think he needs a little help.
Mrs. Adamski:	I saw his last test. He got a 70. I think it was because he didn't study enough.
Mr. Manning:	That's possible. Since he's having some trouble, it would be good for Robert to have a tutor.
Mrs. Adamski:	That sounds like a good idea. Will it be expensive?
Mr. Manning:	No! We have a free after-school program. Students help each other. It's peer tutoring.

C CLASS. Discuss. What is a parent-teacher conference? What is Parent-Teacher Night? How are these events different?

4 PRACTICE

A PAIRS. Practice the conversation.

B MAKE IT PERSONAL. GROUPS. Discuss. Have you had any experiences talking to teachers or other school personnel — either for your child or for yourself? Share your experiences.

Grammar

Adverb clauses of reason	
Main clause (result)	Adverb clause (reason)
I'd like Monika to start planning now	**because** she is one of our best students.
I want Robert to get some tutoring	**since** he is having some trouble in math.

Grammar Watch

Use a comma between the clauses when the adverb clause comes first: *Since he is having some trouble, I want Robert to get some tutoring.*

1 PRACTICE

A Read the statements from parents about Parent-Teacher Night. Draw one line under the reason. Draw two lines under the result.

1. "I always go to Parent-Teacher Night because I like the personal contact with my child's teachers."

2. "It's important to find out what the teachers are really like since my child spends so much time with these people every day."

3. "Since there's a chance to talk one-on-one with the teachers, I can ask about ways for my daughter to improve."

4. "Because our children's education is very important to us, my husband and I want to participate in school activities."

5. "I enjoy Parent-Teacher Night because it gives me a chance to meet other parents."

B Read the statements from teachers about Parent-Teacher Night. Combine the sentences using either *because* or *since*. Don't change the order of the clauses.

1. I'm happy to see parents at Parent-Teacher Night. It means they care.

   I'm happy to see parents at Parent-Teacher Night because it means they care.

   OR *I'm happy to see parents at Parent-Teacher Night since it means they care.*

2. I want parents to help their children at home. I always explain my requirements.

   _____

3. The teachers feel happy and proud. Most parents show a lot of respect for them.

   _____

4. Parents don't always know what's going on at school. Children don't tell them.

   _____

5. Home-school communication is important. Parents and teachers should talk often.

   _____

Infinitives and adverb clauses of purpose	
Main clause (result)	Adverb clause or infinitive (purpose)
You took off time from work	**to** meet with me.
I'll bring my husband	**so that** we can both talk to you.

Grammar Watch

- In the infinitive, *to* is followed by the base form of the verb.
- *So that* is followed by a subject and a verb.

2 PRACTICE

A Read part of the introduction to the West Apollo Elementary School Parents' Guide. Underline the infinitives and clauses that talk about purpose.

West Apollo Elementary School publishes this handbook <u>to provide</u> useful information for parents. It is especially important for you to look at the School Rules on page 8 so that you will understand West Apollo's policies and procedures. In addition, you should pay close attention to the calendar on page 11 so that you can make plans for days when school is closed. See the list of school personnel on page 10 to become familiar with our staff.

B Use *to* or *so that* to complete each school rule.

1. You must provide the name and phone number of a family member _so that_ the school can contact someone in case of emergency.

2. West Apollo Elementary School doors will be locked at 7:45 A.M._____ protect the safety of our students.

3. If your child misses school, you must provide a written note _____ explain the absence.

4. Cell phones are not permitted in school _____ classes are not disrupted.

5. Fire drills are conducted _____ everyone is prepared if there is ever a real fire in school.

Show what you know! Talk about parents' involvement in school

GROUPS. Discuss. Do you think it is important for parents to be involved in their children's schooling? Why? In what ways can parents get involved?

Can you... talk about parents' involvement in school? ☐

Interpret and respond to a report card

Life Skills

1 READ A CHILD'S REPORT CARD

A **CLASS. Discuss.**

1. How often do children receive report cards?

2. What kind of information normally appears on a report card?

3. What type of grading systems can be used?

B **PAIRS.** Read part of Manuel Medina's fifth-grade report card. Study the headings. Help each other with new vocabulary.

2 PRACTICE

A Read the statements. Write *T* (true) or *F* (false). Correct the false statements.

___T___ 1. Manuel was absent more often than he was late.

_____ 2. The lowest grade on Manuel's report card is in social science.

_____ 3. Manuel has a C in two classes.

_____ 4. Manuel has done well on all computer assignments.

_____ 5. Manuel's grade in science is a 70.

B **PAIRS. Answer the questions.**

1. What are Manuel's two best classes?

2. Which academic skill does Manuel need to improve the most?

3. Which "Habits & Attitudes" does Manuel need to improve?

Reporting Period 1

Student Name: Manuel Medina

Teacher Name: A. Brown

Days Absent: 3

Days Late: 1

Academics	Total Grade	Comments
English Language Arts	78	Needs to improve writing. Needs to read more
Mathematics	98	Excels in all aspects of math
Science	72	Has trouble with science vocabulary
Social Science	70	Difficulty with reading affects ability to perform well on tests
Computer	95	Has done an excellent job on all computer assignments
Habits & Attitudes		
Work Habits		
Follows directions		
Completes all class and homework assignments	X	Needs to turn in homework regularly and on time
Social Habits		
Works well in groups	X	Needs to participate in group activities
Shows respect for others		
Is responsible and reliable		
Assessment Key		

90–100 = A (Excellent)	69–60 = D (Poor)
80–89 = B (Good)	Below 60 = F (Failing)
79–70 = C (Average)	X = needs improvement

GROUPS. Discuss. What should a parent do if a child receives a low or failing grade on a report card?

4 READ

A Read the note that Manuel's mother sent to his teacher, Ms. Brown, after reading his report card. Why did she write the note?

B Now read Ms. Brown's note to Ms. Medina. How does she respond to Ms. Medina's request for a conference?

> Dear Ms. Brown,
>
> My husband and I looked at Manuel's report card yesterday. We are concerned about his grades in social science, science, and English. We have been trying to get him to read more, but it is difficult.
>
> Could we have a conference to talk about how to help him? I would prefer to meet in the early evening after work, but I can be available almost anytime.
>
> Thank you for your help.
>
> Sincerely,
>
> Bertha Medina

> Dear Ms. Medina,
>
> Thank you for contacting me about Manuel's grades.
>
> I would be happy to meet to discuss ways to help Manuel read more. I can be at the school in the evening so you don't have to miss work. Please call me at 310-555-9904 to set up a day and time for our conference.
>
> Sincerely,
>
> Arlene Brown

C Read both notes again. Then answer the questions.

1. What does Ms. Medina need to do now to arrange a meeting with Ms. Brown?
2. Are Ms. Medina and Ms. Brown going to meet in the morning, afternoon, or evening? Why?
3. What are Ms. Medina and Ms. Brown going to discuss?

5 WRITE

Write a note to your child's teacher about something you would like to discuss. If you don't have children, write a note to your English teacher about your own learning. Use Ms. Medina's note as a model.

Can you...interpret and respond to a report card? ☐

Listening and Speaking

1 BEFORE YOU LISTEN

A Discuss. If you were enrolling a child in a new school, what would you want to find out about the school?

B GROUPS. In some school districts, parents have to prove that their family lives in that district. Why? What things can they use to show their home address?

2 LISTEN

CD2 T31

A Mr. Lopez is talking to the secretary at West Apollo Elementary School. Listen to the first part of their conversation. Why is Mr. Lopez at school with his daughter?

CD2 T31

B Listen to the first part of the conversation again. Answer the questions.

1. Why is Marta changing schools?
2. How many days of school has Marta missed?
3. What grade is Marta in?

CD2 T32

C Read the questions. Listen to the whole conversation. Then circle the correct answers.

1. What does Mr. Lopez use to prove his address?
   a. his lease   b. a phone bill   c. an electric bill

2. What other information did Mr. Lopez bring with him?
   a. an emergency contact form   b. Marta's school-bus schedule   c. Marta's health records

3. What information does the secretary give Mr. Lopez?
   a. a list of school rules   b. a medical form   c. a list of school supplies

4. When will Marta begin school?
   a. today   b. next week   c. no information

CD2 T33

Mr. Lopez continues to speak with the school secretary. Listen and read.

Mr. Lopez: I have a question.

Secretary: Certainly.

Mr. Lopez: I heard that there's a free lunch program. Is that true?

Secretary: Yes. We have a free lunch program for students who need financial assistance.

Mr. Lopez: That's great. What do I need to do?

Secretary: Here's an application. You'll need to fill it out, and you'll need to provide documents that show income.

Mr. Lopez: No problem. One more thing.

Secretary: Sure.

Mr. Lopez: I'd like to talk with my daughter's teacher. Would that be possible?

Secretary: Yes, but you'll need to make an appointment.

Mr. Lopez: OK. Wednesday is best for me.

Secretary: First, let me get your daughter's name again and the teacher's name.

4 PRACTICE

A PAIRS. Practice the conversation.

B ROLE PLAY. PAIRS. Role-play this situation.

Student A: You are a parent. Call the school. Choose one of the reasons below for your call. Use the information below.

Student B: You are the school secretary. Answer the parent's questions. Also help the parent make an appointment.

Reasons for the call

a. You want information about the breakfast program, and you want to speak to the principal.

b. You want information about after-school programs, and you want to speak to your child's teacher.

c. You want information about the school calendar, and you want to speak to the guidance counselor.

C MAKE IT PERSONAL. GROUPS. Schools have many different programs for students. Discuss.

1. What kinds of school programs do you know about?

2. When and where do these programs take place?

3. What other programs do you think schools ought to have?

Grammar

Adjective clauses: Relative pronoun as subject of the clause

Main clause	Adjective clause	
	Relative pronoun—Subject	Verb (+ Object)
We have a free lunch program for students	**who/that**	need financial assistance.
I brought an electric bill,	**which/that**	has my name and address on it.

Grammar Watch

- Use *who* for people.
- Use *which* for things.
- Use *that* for both people and things.

1 PRACTICE

A Read the paragraph. Underline the adjective clauses. Circle the person or thing that the adjective clauses give information about.

The Parent-Teacher Association is an (organization) which works on both the national and local levels. At the local level, parents and other family members meet to share ideas that can improve student learning. The PTA members also work on special projects. For example, they sometimes sell candy, cookbooks, or tickets to a dance to earn money which can help the school buy new computers. In some cases, the money is used to pay guest speakers, who come to the school to teach students for a day. The local PTA does a lot of good, and it gives the people who participate in its activities a feeling of belonging to the community.

B Complete the sentences with *who* or *which*.

1. Schools in the U.S. have programs, __which__ help parents get involved in their children's education.

2. Parents _____ know what their children are doing in school can help them do better.

3. Parent-teacher conferences are important meetings _____ give parents one-on-one time with school personnel.

4. Parents can ask for a translator _____ speaks their language.

5. Guidance counselors _____ work at the school can request meetings with parents.

Adjective clauses: Relative pronoun as object of the clause		
Main clause	**Adjective clause**	
	Relative pronoun — Object	Subject + Verb
I need a phone number	**(which/that)**	we can call.
You're the person	**(who/that)**	I spoke with.

2 PRACTICE

A Read the letter to parents in West Apollo School District. Underline the relative pronouns. Circle the person or thing the relative pronoun refers to. Double underline the subject and the verb that follow the relative pronoun.

Dear Parent:

Please become involved in our schools! Here are examples of (things) that you can do.

1. Volunteer to go on one of the many field trips which our students make.

2. Find time to coach a sports team. Think about the future athletes that you can help.

3. Help organize a multi cultural night that students, parents, and teachers can attend.

Remember: Everything that you do helps all our children.

B Read the sentences. Cross out the relative pronoun if it can be omitted.

1. Silvia is the kind of mother who likes to be involved in her children's education.

2. Are there things which I can do to help my son with his schoolwork?

3. The project that Mrs. Bentley assigned shouldn't take more than an hour.

4. Parents should talk to their children about the work that they're doing in class.

5. Charlie told his mother the name of the teacher who helped him.

Show what you know! Talk about improving schools

GROUPS. Discuss.

What are at least five things parents can do to help their children's school? Take notes.

Can you... talk about improving schools? ☐

Reading

1 BEFORE YOU READ

A **CLASS.** What did you do after school when you were a child? If you are a parent, what do your children do after school?

B **GROUPS.** After-school programs need to pay for the teachers and supplies. The words below can be used to talk about money. Discuss their meanings.

cuts   budget   reduce   eliminate

2 READ

A Look at the highlighted quote. What do you predict the author will say about after-school programs?

CD2 T34

B Read and listen. Was your prediction correct? What does Meg Reitz think of after-school programs?

Commentary   MEG REITZ

What's the Real Cost of Cutting After-School Programs?

Because they have to make cuts in the annual budget, local school board officials are discussing whether or not to continue **funding** for after-school programs. As far as I can see, there should be no discussion about whether or not to continue paying for them. After-school programs are essential.

Today's parents, both mothers and fathers, have jobs, and they work long hours. So who's taking care of the kids until Mom or Dad gets home? A major benefit of after-school programs is safety. They keep young people **occupied**, and busy children usually stay out of trouble. However, after-school programs are more than a babysitting service. They provide educational, cultural, and personal advantages.

> ". . . after-school programs cost money, but they're worth every dollar."

Research has shown that students who participate in after-school programs have a better attitude, and as a result, they attend class regularly, get better grades, and have an increased chance of graduating from high school. Also, after-school programs allow time for art, music, and hands-on learning in math and technology. They can offer field trips to concerts, museums, and places that show the history of our city.

In after-school programs, young people can learn about themselves, too. They may find out what they're really interested in and decide on a future career. While they're having fun doing a science project or preparing for a dance performance, students can develop their creativity and communication skills. And many programs give students the chance to work together on a team.

Sure, after-school programs cost money, but they're worth every dollar. Besides, help is available. Our school board can ask for **support** from local business groups and apply for funds from the government. There's no good reason to reduce or eliminate programs that benefit our children.

CHECK YOUR UNDERSTANDING

A Read the statements. Write *F* (fact) or *O* (opinion).

_F_   1. School board officials are discussing whether or not to fund after-school programs.

_____ 2. It's important to keep after-school programs.

_____ 3. Students in after-school programs get better grades.

_____ 4. After-school programs cost money.

_____ 5. After-school programs are worth the cost.

B Complete the sentences.

1. Student safety after school is often a problem because _____

_____ .

2. Students who participate in after-school programs are more likely to _____

_____ .

3. After-school programs often provide opportunities for students to work directly with

_____ .

4. Money for after-school programs often comes from _____

_____ .

C GROUPS. Discuss. The title of the reading asks a question. Based on what the author says, what is the answer to that question?

4   WORD WORK

Find the boldfaced words in the article and guess their meaning from the context. Write a synonym for each word.

1. funding _____   2. occupied _____   3. support _____

Show what you know!   Talk about after-school programs

GROUPS. Discuss an after-school program that you know about. What are the advantages of the program?

Listening and Speaking

1 BEFORE YOU LISTEN

CLASS. What makes a school safe? What can school officials do to improve student safety?

2 LISTEN

CD2 T35

A The West Apollo Elementary School principal is talking to a group of parents, teachers, and community leaders. Listen. What does she want them to do?

Student Safety Matters

CD2 T35

B Read the questions. Listen to the principal again. Then circle the correct answers.

1. Before this evening, how many times had the committee met?
   a. none   b. one   c. two

2. How many improvements does the mayor want each school to make?
   a. three   b. four   c. five

3. Which places are **NOT** mentioned?
   a. classrooms   b. playgrounds   c. parking lot

CD2 T36

A 🔘 **Listen to the sentences. Notice the pronunciation of the past modals. Then listen and repeat.**

The teachers **should have** ("should of") stopped the fight.

They **shouldn't have** ("shouldn't of") allowed it to start.

You **must have** ("must of") heard about the plan.

> **Pronunciation Watch**
>
> When you say past modals such as *may have, must have, might have, should have, shouldn't have, could have,* and *couldn't have,* link the two words together and pronounce them as one word. *Have* usually sounds like *of* (or *a* in fast speech).

CD2 T37

B 🔘 **Listen to the sentences. Circle the words you hear.**

1. I **should have / shouldn't have** told her about the problem.
2. The teachers **could have / couldn't have** stopped the fight.
3. They **should have / shouldn't have** talked to the parents.
4. My son **could have / couldn't have** been involved in the fight.
5. You **should have / shouldn't have** gone to the meeting.

CD2 T38

C 🔘 **Two parents on the safety advisory committee are talking. Listen and read.**

Parent A: I was disappointed in our meeting tonight. I think we should have talked much more about playground safety.

Parent B: I agree. Too many kids get hurt on the school playground.

Parent A: Right. We need good-quality equipment. I'm not sure the swings and slides we have now are of good quality.

Parent B: And the children need better supervision. Who is watching them on the playground?

Parent A: I don't know. My son told me there was a fight last week. Nobody did anything about it. The teachers should have stopped it.

Parent B: Stopped it? The teachers shouldn't have allowed it to start!

4 **PRACTICE**

A **PAIRS. Practice the conversation.**

B **MAKE IT PERSONAL. Discuss ideas about school safety.**

GROUPS. Imagine you are members of a school safety committee. Which three things are the most important for safety? Use the list below. Add your own ideas.

☐ knowing what to do in case of fire   ☐ knowing what to do in case of bad weather

☐ supervising students on the playground   ☐ protecting students on the Internet

☐ making sure students do not use cell phones   ☐ other: _____

Grammar

Past modals: Expressing degrees of certainty about the past

Subject	Modal	Have	Past participle	
They	may (not) might (not) must (not) could (not)	have	noticed	the problems.

······· **Grammar Watch**

- Use *may (not) have, might (not) have,* or *could have* to show that you are not certain that something happened.

- Use *must have* to show that you are almost certain that something has happened.

- Use *must not have* to show that you are almost certain that something has NOT happened.

- Use *cannot have, could not have (can't have, couldn't have)* to show that you are certain that something has NOT happened.

1 PRACTICE

A Read the conversation between a student and teacher. Underline the past modal phrases.

Admir: Ms. Lee, I can't find my bike helmet. I <u>might have left</u> it here. Did you see it?

Ms. Lee: No, I'm sorry. I didn't. Could you have left it at home?

Admir: No, I was wearing it this morning.

Ms. Lee: Well, that's good. You should wear it whenever you ride. Maybe you left it in the cafeteria.

Admir: Oh, you're right! I got breakfast this morning. I must have left it there.

B Complete the sentences. Use *may have, may not have, must have,* or *couldn't have.*

1. **A:** Where is Mr. Chen?

   B: He was out yesterday, so he _____ heard about the safety meeting.

2. **A:** The superintendent of schools was here. She looked very pleased.

   B: She _____ noticed the safety signs.

3. **A:** I'm not sure the safety committee checked the equipment on the playground.

   B: They _____ been there yet. There are still no seats on the swings!

4. **A:** Did you see Victor at the meeting?

   B: He _____ been there, but I didn't see him.

Expressing advice or opinions about the past

Subject	Should (not)	Have	Past participle	
A teacher	**should**	**have**	stopped	the fight.
The teachers	**shouldn't**	**have**	allowed	it to start!

Grammar Watch

- Use *should have* to talk about actions that were advisable in the past but that did not occur.
- Use *should not have* to talk about actions that were NOT advisable in the past but that did occur.

2 PRACTICE

Some children behaved in unsafe ways on the bus. Write sentences saying what they should have or shouldn't have done.

1. The children played loud music. _They shouldn't have played loud music._

2. They didn't wear their seat belts. _____

3. They ran up and down the aisle. _____

4. They put their heads out the windows. _____

5. They didn't show respect for the driver. _____

6. They got out of their seats. _____

7. They didn't listen to the bus driver. _____

8. They threw candy wrappers in the aisle. _____

Show what you know!   Talk about school safety

Nine-year-old Tuan Le was having terrible back pains. The doctor said that the problem was Tuan's backpack.

STEP 1. Read about Tuan's problem.

STEP 2. PAIRS. Discuss Tuan's problem. Use past modals to answer the following questions.

1. What was the cause of Tuan's back pain? List as many possible causes as you can.
2. What should Tuan's parents have done? List anything that might have helped.

STEP 3. GROUPS. Share your ideas.

Can you...talk about school safety? ☐

Writing

1   BEFORE YOU WRITE

A   GROUPS. Parents sometimes disagree with decisions that their local school districts make. What can they do when this happens?

B Many newspapers encourage their readers to write *letters to the editor*. In a letter to the editor the writer expresses his or her feelings about an important topic. Underline three words that show how the person who wrote the letter below feels about the additional in-service days in the West Apollo School District.

Letter to the Editor:

As working parents of two young children, my wife and I were surprised and upset when we found out that the number of teacher in-service days (when teachers get training) in the West Apollo School District had increased from three to five days per year. As you know, when teachers have in-service days, the children are off from school.

I believe that students benefit from the work their teachers do during in-service. However, I am concerned about children whose parents cannot take time off from their jobs or pay for extra child care on the additional in-service days. One possible solution is for the school district to organize special activities for students on these days.

Non-teaching staff, such as classroom aides, could supervise these activities in the school cafeteria or gymnasium. A second possible solution would involve direct cooperation among parents. With careful planning, they could almost certainly find a stay-at-home mother, a grandparent, or another responsible family member to take care of small groups of children. The children could go to a different home on each in-service day so that everyone contributes to the child care.

I plan to talk to the principal of our children's school and to the president of my local PTA about this important issue as soon as possible. All parents should do the same.

C   PAIRS.   Answer the questions about the letter.

1. What is an advantage of teacher in-service days?
2. What is a disadvantage of teacher in-service days?
3. Do you agree or disagree with the writer? Explain.

Writing Tip

When a letter or an essay includes more than one paragraph, it's important to put similar information together. What kind of information did the writer put in the first paragraph? In the second paragraph? In the last paragraph?

A BRAINSTORM. Think about a decision in your child's school or in the school you are attending that you are unhappy about. Organize your ideas in a chart like this.

Decision I disagree with: _____	
Positive results	Negative results

B Choose the negative result that is the biggest problem. Think of solutions to that problem. Organize your ideas like this.

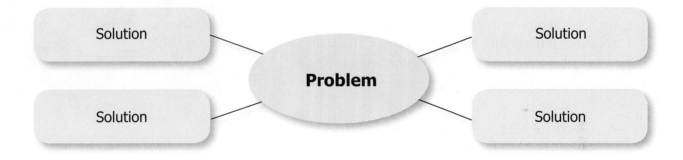

Write your own letter to the editor about a recent school decision that you did not agree with. Focus on the problem you chose in Exercise 2B and two solutions to that problem. Use the writing model as an example.

☐ Did you explain the decision and explain the reasons that it is a problem?
☐ Did you give possible solutions?
☐ Did you describe the actions you would take?
☐ Did you group similar ideas together?
☐ Did you use correct capitalization, punctuation, and spelling?

1 REVIEW

For your grammar review, go to page 253.

2 ACT IT OUT — What do you say?

STEP 1. Review the conversation on page 167 (CD2, Track 30).

STEP 2. ROLE PLAY. PAIRS. Role-play this situation.

> **Student A:** You are a parent who thinks that school is important. You know that your son's grades have fallen since he got a job. You want your son to succeed in school, but you also want him to work to make money. You are talking to your son's math teacher.

> **Student B:** You are a high school math teacher. You are talking to the parent of one of your favorite students. You think that his/her son should go to college, but it will be impossible for him to get a scholarship if his grades continue to drop. You want to find out what the problem is and find a way to solve it.

3 READ AND REACT — Problem-solving

STEP 1. GROUPS. Consider the problem.

You are a group of parents who live in the same neighborhood. Your children attend the same middle school. One of the parents just told you how many times she has gone to the school recently for events such as a PTA meeting, a parent-teacher night, and a student safety meeting. She also mentioned that there is going to be a family barbecue at the school next Friday evening. Some other parents in the group never received information about any of these events.

STEP 2. GROUPS. Discuss. What are the possible reasons that some of the parents didn't receive information from their children's school? What should the parents do?

4 CONNECT

For your Self-Efficacy Activity, go to page 261.
For your Team Project, go to page 271.

> **Which goals can you check off? Go back to page 165.**

> Go to the CD-ROM for more practice.

Safety First

10

Preview

Read the title. What types of accidents can occur at work?

UNIT GOALS

- ☐ Give a progress report
- ☐ Talk about work requirements
- ☐ Discuss workplace safety
- ☐ Talk about preventing accidents at work
- ☐ Interpret and complete an accident report
- ☐ Recognize requirements for promotions
- ☐ Make requests, suggestions, and offers at work
- ☐ Write about ways to improve workplace safety

Listening and Speaking

1 BEFORE YOU LISTEN

A **GROUPS.** Which things are most important to employers? Speed (how fast employees work)? Quality (how good employees' work is)? Make a list of things an employer wants or expects from an employee.

B When people or companies need to build something, they often hire a *contractor* to manage the project. The contractor often hires *subcontractors*. Look at the picture of a contractor and a subcontractor. What tasks do you think each person does?

2 LISTEN

CD2 T39

A Sam is a contractor. He is talking to his subcontractor, Oleg. Oleg is making kitchen cabinets for Sam. Listen to their conversation. What is the problem?

CD2 T39

B Read the statements. Then listen to the conversation again. Write *T* (true) or *F* (false). Correct the false statements.

_F_ 1. The wood arrived from the supplier a̶ ̶w̶e̶e̶k̶ ̶a̶g̶o̶. *yesterday*

_____ 2. Sam's work on this kitchen is one week late.

_____ 3. Oleg didn't call Sam to tell him about the problem.

_____ 4. Oleg needs to finish so work can be done on the counters.

_____ 5. Sam wants Oleg to hurry.

_____ 6. Sam and Oleg don't care about quality.

C **GROUPS.** Sam is upset because Oleg has not finished his work. Discuss.

1. What could Oleg have done differently?
2. What could Sam have done differently?

3 CONVERSATION

CD2 T40

A Sam is doing work at an apartment building. He called the building manager to give her a progress report. Listen and read.

Sam: Jan? This is Sam Baker. I wanted to give you a progress report on the work we're doing on the kitchens at 215 River Road.

Jan: Oh, good. I was just going to call you.

Sam: Well, here's the thing. I just spoke to Kurt, my subcontractor, and he's running a little behind schedule—but we're doing everything we can.

Jan: How much behind schedule? What's the problem?

Sam: Five sinks are on backorder. We got the supplier to rush the order, but we won't get them until next Monday.

Jan: Can you find a different supplier?

Sam: I had Kurt check around, and it doesn't look like anyone else has what we need. I'll have him check some other places, and I'll get back to you.

Jan: Call me tomorrow.

B PAIRS. **Practice the conversation.**

C ROLE PLAY. PAIRS. **Role-play this situation.**

A building manager has hired you to remodel twelve bathrooms in an apartment building.

Student A: You are a contractor. Your subcontractor is having problems. He is supposed to remodel one bathroom every two days, but he is behind schedule.

Student B: You are the building manager. Tenants are upset because the schedule for remodeling their bathrooms keeps changing. You want a progress report.

D MAKE IT PERSONAL. GROUPS. **Talk about your own job experiences or those of people you know. Discuss.**

1. Is there a lot of pressure on the job to work fast?

2. Is there a lot of pressure to do quality work?

3. Is it easy or difficult to make employers happy?

Grammar

Make/have/let/get + Verb

I	**made**	Kurt	**check** around.
	had	Boris	**call** you from the van.
You need to	**let**	the counter guy	**measure** the space.
We	**got**	the supplier	**to rush** the order.
We	**didn't get**	the supplier	**to rush** the order.

········· **Grammar Watch**

- Use *make* when someone requires another person to do something.
- Use *have* when someone asks another person to do something.
- Use *let* when someone allows another person to do something.
- Use *get* when someone persuades another person to do something, *get* is followed by the infinitive instead of the base form.

1 PRACTICE

A Read the first sentence. Then underline the correct noun or pronoun to make the second sentence true.

1. The manager had me drive the forklift.

   The manager / I drove the forklift.

2. Our boss let us go home early on July 3.

   Our boss / We went home early on July 3.

3. The supervisor made them work faster.

   The supervisor / They had to work faster.

4. Pam got Mei-Ling to work the night shift.

   Pam / Mei-Ling changed her shift.

B Complete the instructions for supermarket cashiers. Use the verbs in the box. Use one verb twice.

> get   have   let   make

1. If the customer has a store card, _____ her give you the card before you start scanning items.

2. If you need to check the price of an item, _____ your bagger to find the information, so you can continue helping the customer.

3. Always _____ the customer take her time getting her money out. Never _____ the customer hurry.

4. If the customer is paying by credit card, don't forget to _____ him or her sign the receipt.

A Read what each person said. Then state what the person wanted or allowed, using the verb in parentheses.

Supervisor: All employees must turn off their machines at night.

(*have*) The supervisor _had the employees turn off their machines at night._

Foreperson: Harry, remember to clean off your shoes.

(*make*) The foreperson _____

Boss: You can use the company van this weekend.

(*let*) My boss _____

Rafael: Sandra and Ben, please work until the job is finished.

(*get*) Rafael _____

Manager: New workers, please don't ask questions until the training is over.

(*not let*) The manager _____

Jocelyn: Dan, I want you to meet all the people working on the site.

(*have*) Jocelyn _____

B Rewrite the new sentences on notepaper, changing any object nouns to pronouns.

Show what you know! Talk about work requirements

STEP 1. GROUPS. What things has an employer asked or allowed to you to do at work? Discuss the ideas below or your own ideas.

- have you work late
- have you work on weekends
- make you wait for your paycheck
- make you work overtime

- make you work in unsafe conditions
- let you take several breaks
- let you leave work early
- let you try a new procedure

STEP 2. PAIRS. Do any of these issues pose problems for you? Choose one issue to discuss. What can you do to solve this problem?

Can you...talk about work requirements? ☐

Reading

1 BEFORE YOU READ

CLASS. Look at the pictures. Where have you seen these things? Why are they important?

exit door

fire extinguisher

sprinkler system

2 READ

CD2 T41

Read and listen. What did the Triangle Shirtwaist Factory fire make the American public realize?

---

http://www.onthejobsafety.com

Triangle Shirtwaist Factory Fire

On March 25, 1911, fire broke out in the Triangle Shirtwaist Factory in New York City. Inside the factory, the workers were all women, some only 15 years old. Some of them got out. But on the 9th floor, there were only two exit doors. One exit was filled with smoke. The other exit door was locked. The workers on that floor were trapped. One hundred and forty-eight workers were killed.

The Triangle Shirtwaist Factory fire made the newspaper headlines. People were **outraged** to learn of the working conditions there, in which women and children of 12 or 13 years old worked fourteen-hour shifts during a 60- to 72-hour workweek in dangerous and **unsanitary** conditions. The Triangle Shirtwaist Factory was typical of many unsafe workplaces in the early twentieth century. In factories, mills, and mines, workers, including children, worked long hours on dangerous machines with no clean air to breathe. In these workplaces, people were injured and sometimes even killed.

After the fire, the **public** became more aware of these conditions and asked the government to make workplaces safer. Workers organized into powerful **unions** that fought for safer conditions. Conditions improved gradually. But it wasn't until 1970 that the government created the Occupational Safety and Health Administration (OSHA). The purpose of OSHA is to prevent injuries and deaths in the workplace by enforcing rules for safety and health. For example, each workplace has to have a sprinkler system, fire extinguishers, and at least two exit doors. OSHA **inspectors** visit workplaces regularly to make sure companies follow the rules.

Today, if a company does not follow safety rules, it has to pay a fine. Workers can complain to OSHA about unsafe conditions. Thanks in part to OSHA, conditions for workers in the U.S. are now much safer than they used to be.

3

CONVERSATION

The words in a sentence are usually pronounced together without stopping. Link a consonant sound at the end of one word to a vowel sound at the beginning of the next word without stopping.

CD2 T43

A Listen to the sentences. Then listen and repeat.

He was out of work for a month.

That's awful.

I'll go back and read it again.

Good idea.

Do you have any questions?

CD2 T44

B Read the sentences. Draw a line (‿) to show where a consonant sound is linked to a following vowel sound. Then listen and check your answers.

1. These machines are dangerous.

2. Don't wear a bracelet when you're operating the press.

3. I'll take it off right now.

4. Make sure the guards are all on the machine.

CD2 T45

C Asad and Claudia are continuing their conversation. Listen and read.

Asad: You know, Luis cut himself badly last year and couldn't work for a month.
Claudia: Oh! That's awful!
Asad: I know. So that's why I want to be sure everyone is taking safety precautions.
Claudia: You're right. I think I'll go back and read the safety manual again. Maybe I'll make notes to myself to help me remember.
Asad: Good idea. There are some useful pointers in the manual. I don't want you to injure yourself.

4 **PRACTICE**

A PAIRS. Practice the conversation.

B MAKE IT PERSONAL. GROUPS. Discuss.

1. Have you ever worked in a dangerous workplace? What were the safety hazards?

2. What did you do to keep yourself safe?

Grammar

Reflexive pronouns

Subject pronoun		Reflexive pronoun	
I		**myself**	
You (singular) You (plural)		**yourself** **yourselves**	
He	hurt	**himself**	at work.
She		**herself**	
We		**ourselves**	
They		**themselves**	

· · · · · · · · Grammar Watch

- Use a reflexive pronoun when the subject and object of a sentence refer to the same people.
- Remember: If the subject and object are different, use an object pronoun: *The supervisor helped her at work.*
- You can also use a reflexive pronoun to emphasize that someone or some group did something alone. *By is* sometimes added: *I installed the safety equipment (by) myself.*
- *See page 284 for a list of verbs that can be used with reflexive pronouns.*

1 PRACTICE

Read what a nurse's aide wrote about her first day at work. Circle the reflexive pronouns and underline the nouns they refer back to.

My first day at work was OK, but I made a couple of mistakes. I was helping patients with their breakfast because some <u>patients</u> can't feed (themselves.) First, I helped a patient who couldn't hold her glass of juice by herself and I spilled it all over myself! It was embarrassing! Then I had to help another patient with his bandage. I know that when you work with sick people you have to protect yourself, but I forgot to put on my latex gloves to keep myself safe. Later I helped bathe a patient who couldn't wash himself. This time, I remembered to wear my gloves!

A Complete the conversations. Circle the correct words.

1. **A:** Wang burned **him / himself** on the bread oven today. I feel bad. I should have warned **him / himself** that the oven was really hot.

   B: Don't blame **you / yourself**. It was an accident.

2. **A:** Can you move those wires out of the way? People might trip on **them / themselves** and hurt **them / themselves**.

   B: OK, I will.

3. **A:** Never operate this forklift by **you / yourself**. Someone else should always be nearby in case you have an accident.

   B: I know. The supervisor already told **me / myself** that.

B Complete the sentences with the correct reflexive pronouns.

1. Salma is a deli worker. When she slices meat, she is careful not to cut ___herself___ .

2. Ironworkers often work high up on bridges and tall buildings. They take special care to keep _____ safe on the construction site.

3. The scaffold rope broke, and Hakeem lost his balance, but he kept _____ from falling.

4. The company doesn't want us to injure _____ on the machines.

5. You shouldn't use a tall ladder by _____. You should have someone hold it.

6. I have to attend the course so I don't hurt _____ on the new equipment.

Show what you know! Talk about preventing accidents at work

STEP 1. **Answer the questions.**

1. Have you ever hurt yourself on the job? What happened?
2. Do you know other people who have hurt themselves on the job? What happened?
3. If you hurt yourself at work, do you tell your boss? Why?
4. Do you do everything you can to keep yourself safe at work? Explain.

STEP 2. GROUPS. **Ask one another the questions and explain your answers.**

Can you...talk about preventing accidents at work? ☐

Life Skills

1 READ AN ACCIDENT REPORT

When people have an accident at work, they often fill out an accident report. What kind of accident did Charles have?

Employee's Report of Work-related Injury   To be completed immediately after the accident and submitted to your supervisor

Employee Name: _Charles Beaumont_   ID Number: _5673472_

Male [X] Female [ ] Date of Birth: _4/16/80_   Marital Status: _M_

Home Address: _18 Center Street Apt. 6B, Mountain View, CA 94040_
         Street   City   ZIP Code

Home Phone No. _650-555-4827_   Cell Phone No. _650-555-1029_

Job Title: _Roofer_

Employment Start Date: _5/1/2008_

Date of Accident: _2/25/10_

Location of Accident: _200 Blossom Ln., Mountain View, CA_

Describe in detail how the accident occurred:

I was repairing the roof of a barn. The ladder gave way because the ground was soft. I fell backwards approximately 35 feet to the ground.

(Describe the work you were engaged in, describe how the injury occurred, and explain the cause.)

Part of body injured: _lower back_

(be specific—example: right middle finger, left ankle, upper back)

Type of injury: _sprain_

(example: sprain, burn {degree of burn}, contusion, sutured)

Was medical treatment sought? If so: _Dr. Lao, 524 Filmore Street, Mountain View, CA 94040_   _650-555-1122_
      Name and Address of Medical Provider   Phone Number

No. of days missed from work: _3_

Return to work date (as stated by physician): _3/3/10_

Type of leave used: _sick days_

No. of days worked with restrictions: _0_

Name of witness (es): _Mike Cabrera_   Phone No. _650-555-8304_

Was safety equipment provided? Yes [X] No [ ]

Was safety equipment used? Yes [X] No [ ]

Signature of employee: _Charles Beaumont_   Date: _3/3/10_

Questions? Call 650-555-9827

A Read the report again. Then answer the questions.

1. Where does Charles Beaumont live and work?

   _____

2. What does he do?

   _____

3. How old is he?

   _____

4. How did the accident happen?

   _____

5. What was his injury?

   _____

6. What doctor did he see?

   _____

7. How long did he stay out of work?

   _____

8. Who saw the accident?

   _____

B PAIRS. Compare your answers.

C GROUPS. Discuss.

1. Why is it important to fill out an accident report form?
2. Is it good for the employer? Is it good for the employee? Explain your answers.
3. If you work, what procedures do you follow at your workplace when you have an accident or injure yourself?

D MAKE IT PERSONAL. Imagine that you had an accident at a job. Complete the accident report form on page 275. Make up the details.

Can you...interpret and complete an accident report? ☐

Listening and Speaking

1 BEFORE YOU LISTEN

GROUPS. What are reasons that a manager gives an employee a raise (more money) or a promotion (higher-level job)? Make a list.

2 LISTEN

CD2 T46

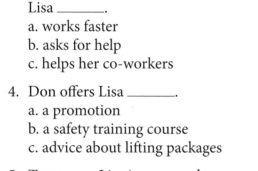

A Lisa works at Parcel Movers, a package-delivery service. She is talking to her manager, Don. Listen to their conversation. What good news does Don give her? What is one reason he gives?

CD2 T46

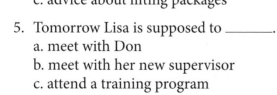

B Read the sentences. Then listen to the conversation again. Circle the correct answers.

1. Lisa started working as a sorter
   _____ ago.
   a. three months
   b. six months
   c. six years

2. Don says that Lisa is an _____ worker.
   a. efficient
   b. innovative
   c. inaccurate

3. When there is a lot of work to do,
   Lisa _____.
   a. works faster
   b. asks for help
   c. helps her co-workers

4. Don offers Lisa _____.
   a. a promotion
   b. a safety training course
   c. advice about lifting packages

5. Tomorrow Lisa is supposed to _____.
   a. meet with Don
   b. meet with her new supervisor
   c. attend a training program

C **GROUPS.** Think about the reasons Lisa has been promoted. Does your job or a job you know about have the same requirements for promotion? What do people need to do to get promoted?

3 CONVERSATION

CD2 T47

A 🔘 Listen to the words. Notice the pronunciation of the underlined letters. Then listen again and repeat.

n<u>o</u>	j<u>o</u>b	<u>o</u>ther
ag<u>o</u>	n<u>o</u>t	d<u>o</u>ne
prom<u>o</u>ted	<u>o</u>perate	c<u>o</u>mpany

CD2 T48

B 🔘 Listen to the words. Notice the pronunciation of the underlined letters. Write each word in the correct column in the chart in Exercise A.

1. <u>o</u>nly   2. st<u>o</u>p   3. d<u>o</u>n't   4. d<u>o</u>esn't   5. c<u>o</u>me   6. pr<u>o</u>blem

CD2 T49

C 🔘 Kay and Luis are talking about their jobs at Parcel Movers. Listen to their conversation.

Kay: You know, I've been working here for five years now, and they still haven't promoted me.

Luis: Wow, that's too bad. Do you have any idea why not?

Kay: Not really. I think I'm a good employee.

Luis: You don't come to work late, do you?

Kay: No, I come in on time every day. And I work hard. I don't think my manager likes me.

Luis: Why don't you ask for a transfer? You could come and work in our operations department. My manager is demanding but very supportive. And I think there's an opening.

Kay: I don't know. Maybe. Tell me more about the department. What's it like?

4 PRACTICE

A PAIRS. Practice the conversation.

B PROBLEM-SOLVING. GROUPS. Kay doesn't think her manager likes her. Discuss.

1. What might be some other reasons that Kay didn't get a promotion?

2. What do you think Kay should do?

Make requests, suggestions, and offers at work

Grammar

Could you/I . . . ? / Why don't you/I . . . . ? / Would you mind . . . ?

Questions				Affirmative answers	Negative answers
Could	I	talk	to you?	Yes, of course. Sure. No problem.	Sorry, I'm busy. Sorry, I can't.
Could	you	work	overtime tonight?		
Why don't	you	ask	the supervisor?	Good idea.	I don't think that's a good idea.
Why don't	I	help	you with that?	Thanks.	That's OK, I don't need any help.
Would you mind	working		on Saturday?	Not at all.	I'm sorry, but I can't. I'd rather not.

Grammar Watch

- Use *Could I/you* and *Would you mind* to make polite requests for permission or help.
- Use *Why don't you* . . . to make suggestions.
- Use *Why don't I* . . . to make offers.
- When someone makes a request with *Would you mind*, use a negative answer, *Not at all,* to say you agree to the request.

1 PRACTICE

A Match the requests or suggestions with the correct response.

__b__ 1. Could I take a break now? ☐R☐

_____ 2. Could you show me how to use this ladder? ☐

_____ 3. Why don't we clean up now? ☐

_____ 4. Would you mind saying that again? ☐

_____ 5. Why don't I help you with that box? ☐

_____ 6. Why don't you finish it tomorrow? ☐

_____ 7. Why don't I start that for you? ☐

a. Not at all. I said, put on your protective glasses.

b. No problem. You've been working a long time.

c. It's due today.

d. Thanks a lot.

e. Good idea.

f. Great. I'll finish later.

g. Sure. You hold it this way.

B Look at Exercise A again. Is each question a *request* (R), a *suggestion* (S), or an *offer* (O)?

Complete the questions with the correct expressions in the box. You will use some expressions more than once.

| Could I | Could you | Why don't I | Why don't you | Would you mind |

1. **A:** _____Why don't I_____ get that down for you?

   B: Thanks. I'd appreciate that.

2. **A:** _____ working on Sunday?

   B: I'm sorry, but I can't. I'm going to a wedding.

3. **A:** _____ answer the phones for me for a couple of minutes?

   B: Sure. No problem.

4. **A:** _____ borrow your copy of the safety manual?

   B: I'm sorry. I don't have it. I lent it to Sam.

5. **A:** _____ tell your supervisor your idea?

   B: I'm already planning to. I'll talk to her tomorrow.

6. **A:** _____ moving those boxes away from the exit?

   B: Not at all. They're a safety hazard where they are.

7. **A:** _____ carry a bottle of water with you so you don't get thirsty?

   B: Good idea. It's really hot out here.

Show what you know! Make requests, suggestions, and offers at work

ROLE PLAY. PAIRS. Role-play these situations. Take turns making requests or suggestions.

- You work in a clothing factory. You see a coworker using a sewing machine while wearing a long-sleeved sweater. Suggest that your coworker take off her sweater.
- You are a construction worker. You forgot to bring your protective glasses to work. Ask your supervisor if you can borrow his extra pair of glasses.
- You are a delivery driver. You don't feel well. Ask another driver to cover your shift for you.
- You work in a warehouse. Your back hurts, and you are unable to finish unpacking a shipment on time. A co-worker offers to help you.

Can you... make requests, suggestions, and offers at work? ☐

Writing

1 BEFORE YOU WRITE

A GROUPS. Sometimes workers have good ideas for making improvements at their workplaces. Discuss. What are some ways that workers can make their suggestions known to their bosses?

B Read the writing model. What is Lorenzo Herrera writing about? Who is he probably writing to?

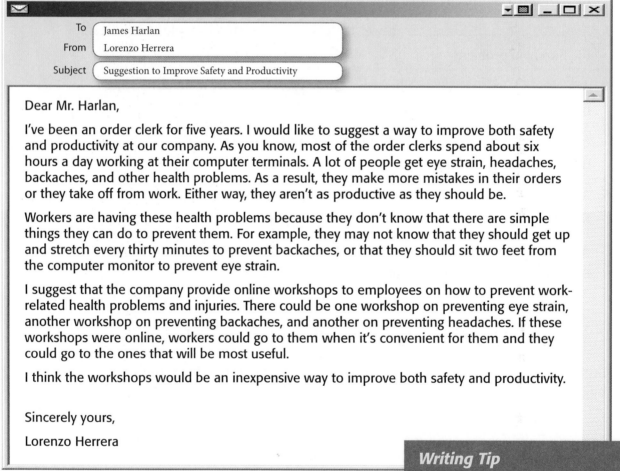

To   James Harlan
From   Lorenzo Herrera
Subject   Suggestion to Improve Safety and Productivity

Dear Mr. Harlan,

I've been an order clerk for five years. I would like to suggest a way to improve both safety and productivity at our company. As you know, most of the order clerks spend about six hours a day working at their computer terminals. A lot of people get eye strain, headaches, backaches, and other health problems. As a result, they make more mistakes in their orders or they take off from work. Either way, they aren't as productive as they should be.

Workers are having these health problems because they don't know that there are simple things they can do to prevent them. For example, they may not know that they should get up and stretch every thirty minutes to prevent backaches, or that they should sit two feet from the computer monitor to prevent eye strain.

I suggest that the company provide online workshops to employees on how to prevent work-related health problems and injuries. There could be one workshop on preventing eye strain, another workshop on preventing backaches, and another on preventing headaches. If these workshops were online, workers could go to them when it's convenient for them and they could go to the ones that will be most useful.

I think the workshops would be an inexpensive way to improve both safety and productivity.

Sincerely yours,

Lorenzo Herrera

C PAIRS. Answer the questions.

1. What is happening at the writer's workplace?
2. Why does the writer think workers are getting injured?
3. What suggestions does the writer make to his supervisor?

Writing Tip

When you write about a problem, follow these steps:

1. identify the problem
2. explain the cause
3. suggest a solution

D Read the writing model again. Underline the sentences in which Lorenzo identifies the problems, circle the sentences that explain the causes, and star (★) the sentence that suggests a solution.

2 THINKING ON PAPER

A BRAINSTORM. Think about potential safety-related problems at your school or workplace. Use the words in the box to get ideas.

burns   clutter   cuts   exits   falls   hazards   poisons   strain

B Choose one of the safety issues you thought of. Think of solutions to that problem. Organize your ideas in a diagram like this.

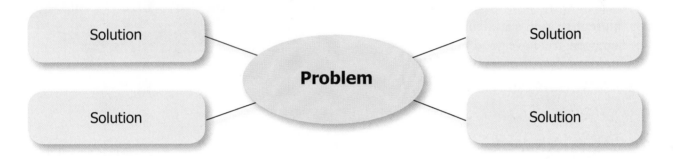

Solution

Solution

Problem

Solution

Solution

3 WRITE

Write an e-mail to a supervisor about an idea to improve safety at your school or your workplace. Use the writing model as an example.

4 CHECK YOUR WRITING

☐ Did you identify the problem and explain the causes?

☐ Did you suggest a solution?

☐ Did you use correct capitalization, punctuation, and spelling?

1 REVIEW For your grammar review, go to page 254.

2 ACT IT OUT What do you say?

STEP 1. **Review the conversation on page 198 (CD2, Track 46).**

STEP 2. **ROLE PLAY. PAIRS. Role-play this situation.**

> **Student A:** You've worked at your job for five years. You're hoping to get a promotion to supervisor.

> **Student B:** You're Student A's manager. You have good news! Student A is getting a promotion.

3 READ AND REACT Problem-solving

STEP 1. **Read the problem.**

Sometimes workers have accidents in the kitchen at Mangia Pizza. Last week a pizza cook slipped on some tomato sauce that had spilled on the floor. She was wearing sandals and a tank top. She fell against the pizza oven and burned her arm. And yesterday, a prep cook slipped on a piece of cheese and crashed into another kitchen worker, who was slicing onions. That worker cut himself with his knife.

STEP 2. GROUPS. **What is the problem? Discuss a solution. How can the workers at Mangia Pizza prevent accidents in the future?**

4 CONNECT For your Selt-Evaluation Activity, go to page 261.
For your Team Project, go to page 272.

Which goals can you check off? Go back to page 185.

 Go to the CD-ROM for more practice.

Know the Law!

Preview

Read the title. Look at the picture. Where are these people? What are they doing?

UNIT GOALS

- ☐ Identify misdemeanors
- ☐ Talk about legal problems
- ☐ Identify people in a courtroom
- ☐ Describe what happens in a courtroom
- ☐ Talk about DNA evidence
- ☐ Discuss traffic laws
- ☐ Write about different legal systems

Listening and Speaking

1   BEFORE YOU LISTEN

A   **PAIRS.** Look at the signs. They warn against misdemeanors, or crimes that are not very serious. What does each sign mean?

B   **GROUPS.** Discuss. Are the actions in the signs illegal in other countries?

2   LISTEN

CD2 T50

A   David is telling his cousin Solange about an experience he and his daughter had. Listen to the conversation. What happened to David and his daughter?

CD2 T50

B   Read the statements. Listen to the conversation again. Then write *T* (true) or *F* (false).

_F_   1. David's daughter got a fine for littering in the park.

____   2. The police called David shortly after 10 P.M.

____   3. The city has a 10 P.M. curfew for all teenagers.

____   4. Caroline and her friends were on their way to the movies at 10:15 P.M.

____   5. One of Caroline's friends was robbed.

____   6. David and Solange didn't know about the curfew.

C   **GROUPS.** Discuss. Do you think that a 10 P.M. curfew for teenagers is a good idea? Why or why not?

CD2 T51

David and Solange are talking about a problem Solange had with customs. Listen and read.

David: How was your trip? Did you have fun?

Solange: We had a great time, but we did have a bit of a problem on the way back.

David: Really? What happened?

Solange: We were going through customs when an officer stopped us and searched our bags. She found the mangoes I wanted to bring home.

David: They're worried about contaminating the food supply. I don't think you can bring in meat or bread, either.

Solange: Well, the officer threw all the mangoes out.

David: That's too bad. But she was just doing her job.

4 PRACTICE

A PAIRS. **Practice the conversation.**

B ROLE PLAY. PAIRS. **Role-play this situation.**

Student A: You are sitting on the front door step of an apartment building, waiting for some friends to pick you up in their car. Someone comes out of the building and asks you to leave. You refuse because you aren't doing anything wrong, and there is nowhere else to sit.

Student B: You own the building where Student A is sitting. You explain to Student A that it is illegal to trespass or loiter on private property. You tell him or her to leave.

C STEP 1. PAIRS. **Discuss. Which of the following misdemeanors do you think is most serious? Why do you think there are misdemeanor laws?**

- Driving without a valid license or insurance
- Improper disposal of trash
- Disturbing the peace
- Deliberately damaging someone's property

STEP 2. GROUPS. **Each of the actions above is not as serious as a felony, such as burglary or murder, but it is punishable by law. Discuss.**

1. Why do you think that these actions are illegal in the U.S.?
2. Are they illegal in your home country? If not, should they be? Why?

Grammar

Past continuous for interrupted action

Main clause	Time clause
I **got** a call on my cell	**while** I **was watching** the news.
We **were going** through customs	**when** an officer **stopped** us.

Grammar Watch

- Use the past continuous with the simple past to talk about an action that was interrupted by another action.
- Use *while* to introduce a time clause with the past continuous.
- Use the past continuous for the action that was interrupted.
- Use *when* to introduce a time clause with the simple past.
- Use the simple past for the interrupting action.
- A time clause can start or end a sentence. Use a comma after a time clause when it starts a sentence: *While I was watching the news, I got a call on my cell.*

1 PRACTICE

Read the sentences. Then read the questions and circle the correct answers.

1. Felipe was loitering in the hallway of the apartment building when the landlord came out of his apartment and asked him to leave.
   Who was in the hallway first?
   a. Felipe   b. the landlord

2. While Isaac was listening to loud music, his neighbor became angry and reported him to the police.
   What happened first?
   a. Isaac was listening to loud music.   b. The neighbor reported him to the police.

3. The Chang family was walking through a private garden when an elderly man told them that it was private property and asked them to leave.
   When did the Chang family start walking out of the garden?
   a. before the man talked to them   b. after the man talked to them

4. A security guard told Huang to put out his cigarette while he was standing in the lobby of the building.
   What happened first?
   a. The security guard talked to Huang.   b. Huang started smoking.

A Complete the conversations. Use the simple past and the past continuous.

1. **A:** So why did Kyle and Lenny get arrested?

   B: They _were having_ an argument at a restaurant when Kyle got mad at Lenny
             (have)

   and _____ over a table. The table _____ against a mirror on the
          (knock)   (fall)

   wall and _____ it. While a waiter _____ to clean up the mess,
          (smash)   (try)

   the owner _____ the police.
          (call)

2. **A:** Did you know that you can get a ticket if you don't clean up after your dog in this

   city? While my friend _____ his dog this morning, he _____ to
          (walk)   (stop)

   chat with a friend. While they _____, the dog _____ what dogs
          (talk)   (do)

   do. When my friend started to walk again without cleaning up after the dog, a

   policeman gave him a ticket.

   B: I guess he'll remember to clean up after his dog next time.

B Complete the conversation. Circle the correct words.

Marco is the owner of a restaurant. One day he double-parked his minivan outside the
restaurant and told his busboy, Emilio, to keep an eye out for a parking spot. While Emilio
looked / (was looking) for a spot, a car **pulled out / was pulling out** of a space nearby,
and Emilio **called / was calling** Marco. Marco told Emilio to move the car for him. But
while Emilio **moved / was moving** the car, a policeman **stopped / was stopping** him and
asked him for his driver's license. Emilio **didn't have / wasn't having** his driver's license
with him while he **drove / was driving**, which is illegal. The policeman **got / was getting**
suspicious while Emilio **tried / was trying** to explain the situation. He thought Emilio was
trying to steal the car. The policeman was about to take Emilio down to the station, when
Marco **arrived / was arriving** and explained what was going on. The policeman decided
not to give Emilio a ticket.

Show what you know!   Talk about legal problems

**GROUPS. Discuss. Talk about a legal problem you heard or read about. Describe
what happened. Use the simple past and the past continuous.**

Can you...talk about legal problems? ☐

Life Skills

1 IDENTIFY PEOPLE IN A COURTROOM

GROUPS. Look at this picture. Read the definitions. Write the name of the person next to the correct definition.

_____ = the person who watches prisoners and keeps order in the courtroom

_____ = the person who records what people say at a trial

_____ = the person who is accused of a crime

_____ = the lawyer who tries to prove that the defendant is not guilty

_____ = the official who is in charge of a court and who decides how crimimals should be punished

_____ = a group of citizens who decide if the defendant is innocent or guilty

_____ = the lawyer who tries to prove that the defendant is guilty

_____ = someone who describes what they know about a crime

_____ = the leader of the jury

2 PRACTICE

PAIRS. Take turns. Read a definition. Have your partner name the person it describes.

A Dan Jones is on trial for robbing a convenience store on March 8. Read each quote from his trial and write the name of the person who probably said it.

> bailiff   defendant   foreman   prosecutor
> court reporter   defense attorney   judge   witness

1. "Do you solemnly swear to tell the truth, the whole truth, and nothing but the truth?" *the bailiff* _____

2. "Mr. Jones, the jury has found you guilty. I hereby sentence you to one year in prison." _____

3. "I will show beyond a shadow of a doubt that Mr. Jones is guilty."
_____

4. "We, the jury, find the defendant guilty." _____

5. "I saw Mr. Jones running out of the convenience store. He was wearing dark clothes and a baseball cap, but I saw his face under the streetlight."
_____

6. "The prosecutor said, 'Where were you at 7:45 P.M. on the night of March 8?' The defendant replied, 'I was in the convenience store on March 8. I did not rob the store. I ran out of the store because I was in a hurry to catch my bus.'"
_____

7. "I will show that Dan Jones, for reasons that will be made clear, could not have committed this robbery." _____

B CLASS. Discuss.

1. Do you ever watch reality TV programs about trials or films about courtroom dramas? Decribe one show or film you have seen.

2. What have you learned about the American legal system from watching these stories?

Can you...identify people in a courtroom? ☐

Listening and Speaking

1 BEFORE YOU LISTEN

GROUPS. Have you ever seen a TV courtroom show? Do you think these shows present courtrooms as they are in real life? Explain.

2 LISTEN

CD2 T52

A Lisa and Alex are watching TV. Listen to their conversation. How does Lisa feel about TV courtroom shows?

CD2 T52

B Read the sentences. Then listen to the conversation again. Circle the phrase to complete each sentence.

1. Alex thinks courtroom TV shows are about **real law and justice / bad relationships**.

2. Lisa thinks courtroom TV shows are about **real cases / made-up cases**.

3. In the TV court case, the man borrowed money from his roommate to pay his **rent / car payment**.

4. The man refused to pay his roommate back because **they had a fight / he didn't have enough money**.

5. **Alex owes Lisa / Lisa owes Alex** fifty dollars.

C GROUPS. Discuss. If you had to go to court, would you want the case to be shown on TV? Why or why not?

3 CONVERSATION

CD2 T53

A Listen to the sentences. Notice the weak pronunciation of *is, are, was,* and *were.* Then listen and repeat.

The program is watched by millions of people.

The cases are heard by judges.

The roof was damaged.

I heard you were involved in a court case.

CD2 T54

B Listen to the sentences. Circle the word you hear.

1. a. is   b. are   c. was   d. were
2. a. is   b. are   c. was   d. were
3. a. is   b. are   c. was   d. were
4. a. is   b. are   c. was   d. were
5. a. is   b. are   c. was   d. were

CD2 T55

C Gina and Nick are talking about a court case. Listen and read.

Gina: I heard you were involved in a court case recently. What happened?

Nick: Well, I painted a woman's house last summer. While I was there, some landscapers were working in the neighbor's yard. They cut down a tree, and it fell on the woman's roof.

Gina: Uh-oh. . .

Nick: Uh-oh is right! The roof was damaged pretty badly. I saw the whole thing. The woman took the landscapers to small claims court. She wanted them to pay for the repairs to the roof.

Gina: So you were called as a witness during the trial?

Nick: Yes. I told the judge what happened, and the woman won the case.

Gina: It's a good thing you were there!

4 PRACTICE

A PAIRS. Practice the conversation.

B MAKE IT PERSONAL. GROUPS. Have you ever witnessed a crime or been involved in a legal dispute? If so, were you called to court as a witness? What happened?

Grammar

Passives: Present passive and simple past passive

Simple present passive		
This show	**is watched**	all over the country.
These court cases	**are heard**	by judges on TV.
Simple past passive		
The case	**was decided**	by a judge.
	was heard	by a jury.
The roof	**was damaged**	pretty badly.

Grammar Watch

- We usually use the active voice in English: *The police* **asked** *Mr. Carlson to describe the crime scene.*

- Use the passive voice when you don't know who the *agent* (the person or thing that did the action) is or when you don't want to emphasize the agent: *Mr. Carlson* **was asked** *to appear as a witness.*

- Use *by* with the passive if you mention the agent: *Curtis was questioned* **by the lawyer for the defense**.

- Do not mention the agent if the agent is obvious: *A tree fell on the woman's roof. The roof was damaged pretty badly.*

1 PRACTICE

**Read the sentences. Is the sentence active or passive?
Write *A* (active) or *P* (passive).**

_P_ 1. The defendant was arrested by the police chief.

_____ 2. The police told the defendant he had the right
to remain silent.

_____ 3. The defendant was allowed to post bail.

_____ 4. The defendant was released by the judge.

_____ 5. The defendant entered a plea of "not guilty."

_____ 6. The case was dismissed because of lack of evidence.

> When defendants *post bail*, they leave money with a court of law to guarantee that they will come back when their trial starts.
>
> Defendants have the *right to remain silent* when they are questioned. They can refuse to answer some or all questions before or during a trial.

A Complete the sentences about criminal trials with the simple present passive.

Criminal trials ___are heard___ by a jury of twelve people. The defendant _____
            (heard)   (question)

by the prosecutor and the defense attorney. Then the witnesses _____. Evidence,
                                                                (question)

such as photos and documents, _____ to the jury. The case _____ by the
                                      (show)   (discuss)

jurors outside the courtroom. During the trial, jurors _____ to read, watch, or listen
                                                      (not/allow)

to stories about the trial. The outcome _____ by the jury.
                                          (decide)

B Read part of Vincent's e-mail to a friend about his experience with jury duty. Complete the e-mail with the simple past passive.

> *Jury duty is a period of time when U.S. citizens must be ready to sit on, or be part of, a jury.*

Sorry I didn't call you yesterday. I ___was called___ for jury duty. The case
                                       (call)

was unbelievable. A woman was suing the city because she broke her ankle when

she tripped over a bump in the sidewalk. She wanted the city to pay for her medical

expenses. But when she _____ in court, her story didn't make sense. When
                          (question)

she _____ where she was when she tripped, she couldn't remember. Then
       (ask)

her doctor _____ to the stand. He said that she told him that she had fallen
            (call)

down the stairs in her house! The case _____ soon after, and all the jurors
                                 (dismiss)

_____ home.
(send)

Show what you know!   Describe what happens in a courtroom

GROUPS. **Discuss a court case you read or heard about. Use the active and passive voice. Answer the questions.**

- Who was accused, and what was the person accused of?
- Was the case decided by a jury or a judge?
- What was the verdict? Was the defendant found guilty or not guilty?

Can you... describe what happens in a courtroom? ☐

Reading

1 BEFORE YOU READ

A **GROUPS.** Discuss. What kinds of evidence do police and lawyers use to prove that criminals are guilty of crimes?

B **GROUPS.** Read the definition for DNA. Discuss. What is DNA? How can it be used to find out whether someone committed a crime?

> DNA = deoxyribonucleic acid. DNA carries genetic information in a cell. Every person has different DNA.

2 READ

CD2 T56

Read and listen. Then review your answers to Exercise 1B. Was your background knowledge about DNA correct? Explain.

DNA and the Law

On May 7, 2008, three men robbed a bank in Waldorf, Maryland. They drove away in a van with a bag of money. They thought they had escaped. But the bank had put a pack of chemicals in the money bag, and the pack **exploded**. The robbers dropped the bag, got out of the van, and ran away. Soon afterward, the police arrested one of the robbers. How did the police find him so quickly? DNA from the robbers' blood was found on the bag of money.

DNA consists of genetic material that is found everywhere in our body, such as in our blood, skin, and saliva. DNA is our genetic fingerprint. All people have **similar** DNA, but no two people have the exact same DNA.

How is DNA used to identify a criminal when a crime has been **committed**? The testing works like this: After a crime occurs, police collect **evidence** from a crime scene. Some of this evidence may be DNA **samples**, such as hairs or blood. The police then compare this DNA to DNA samples from an FBI **database**. The FBI database is computerized, and it has over 4 million DNA samples in it. These DNA fingerprints are taken from people all over the country who have been arrested or convicted of crimes. If the DNA in the evidence matches someone's DNA fingerprint, that person is probably guilty of the crime. But if the evidence does not match, the person is probably innocent.

DNA testing is not perfect. If DNA evidence is not collected or stored properly, for example, the tests may give wrong results. But it is still more **reliable** than other types of evidence. Witnesses may identify the wrong person. Lawyers, jurors, judges, and the police can make mistakes. DNA testing is usually accurate. It is the best way we have to prove that someone is guilty or innocent of a crime.

Before DNA testing, some innocent people went to prison for crimes they did not commit. The police are now using DNA testing to overturn wrongful convictions. As of 2008, DNA tests have been used to free more than 200 innocent people in the U.S.

CHECK YOUR UNDERSTANDING

Ⓐ **Read the Reading Skill. Then draw lines to divide each sentence into "chunks."**

1. Soon after the robbers dropped the bag and ran away, the police arrested one of them.

2. If the DNA in the evidence matches someone's DNA profile, that person is probably guilty of the crime.

Break long sentences into smaller "chunks" to make them easier to understand. One way to do this is to look for punctuation such as commas or connecting words such as *when, before, after, although,* and *if.*

Ⓑ **Read the sentences. Circle the correct word or phrase to complete each sentence.**

1. The **bank / police** put a pack of chemicals in the money bag.

2. The bank robbers ran away from the van **with / without** the bag of money.

3. The police used DNA evidence to catch **one / all** of the bank robbers.

4. Two people **never / almost never** have the same DNA.

5. DNA databases contain DNA samples from people who **have never been in prison / have been arrested**.

6. It is **easier / harder** to make mistakes with DNA testing than with other types of evidence.

4 **WORD WORK**

Find the boldfaced words in the article and guess their meaning from the context. Then match the words with the definitions.

_____ 1. explode

_____ 2. similar

_____ 3. commit

_____ 4. evidence

_____ 5. sample

_____ 6. database

_____ 7. reliable

a. almost the same

b. can be trusted or depended on

c. a large amount of data stored in a computer

d. a small amount of something

e. do something wrong or illegal

f. blow up

g. facts that prove that something is true

Show what you know! Talk about DNA evidence

GROUPS. Discuss. Do you think that DNA testing has improved the fairness of our legal system? Explain.

Listening and Speaking

1 BEFORE YOU LISTEN

A **GROUPS.** Make a list of all the traffic laws you can think of. What can happen if you break traffic laws?

B **PAIR.** Look at the words and their definitions. Which ones have you heard before?

contest (v) = to say formally that you do not think something is right or fair

fine (n) = money you have to pay as a punishment for breaking the law

be in the right = not to have broken the law or done something wrong

points on a license = penalties you receive for traffic violations. If you get too many points, you may lose your license.

run a stop sign = drive past a stop sign without stopping (a traffic violation)

ticket = a printed note saying that you must pay money because you have done something illegal while driving or parking your car

traffic school = a course in traffic safety and safe driving practices

2 LISTEN

A CD2 T57   Listen to a talk show about cars. What topic is Carl Mansfield answering questions about?

B CD2 T57   Read the statements. Then listen to the conversation again. Write *T* (true) or *F* (false). Correct the false statements.

_T_ 1. Caller 1 got a ticket because she didn't stop for a stop sign.

_____ 2. A branch was covering the stop sign.

_____ 3. Carl thinks that Caller 1 was in the right.

_____ 4. Carl thinks that if Caller 1 shows a judge a picture of the sign, she won't have to pay the fine.

_____ 5. Caller 2 wants to get the points on his license removed.

_____ 6. Carl thinks that the police will clear Caller 2's driving record if he gets a traffic-school certificate.

C **GROUPS.** Discuss. Should people be required to go to traffic school if they have committed traffic violations? Why or why not?

CD2 T58

A Listen to the sentences. Notice the weak pronunciation of the words in blue. Then listen and repeat.

Look **at** this.
Take **a** picture **of the** sign.
I got **a** ticket **for** running **a** stop sign.
How much is it **for**?

Pronunciation Watch

Words like *a, the, at, of,* and *for* are usually weak when another word comes after them. The vowel sound is quiet and short. Words like these have a stronger pronunciation at the end of a sentence.

CD2 T59

B Ana got a ticket. Listen and read.

Ana: Look at this! I got a parking ticket!

Cho: Oh, no. How much is it for?

Ana: One hundred bucks! But why did they give me a ticket? I didn't get a ticket last night even though I parked in exactly the same spot!

Cho: Look! Your car is the only one on this side of the street.

Ana: You're right!

Cho: Let's see—look at this sign. It says that the city sweeps this side of the street every Tuesday morning. That's why everyone moved their cars to the other side of the street last night—except you!

Ana: That explains why I got the ticket! My car was blocking the street sweeping truck.

4 PRACTICE

A PAIRS. Practice the conversation.

B ROLE PLAY. PAIRS. Role-play this situation.

Student A: You received a speeding ticket in the mail. A camera took a picture of you while you were speeding by a school. You don't understand why you got the ticket, because you never drive above the regular speed limit.

Student B: Tell Student A that he or she was in a school zone and got a ticket for driving too fast past the school when children were in the area. Explain the posted speed limit shown at the right.

C MAKE IT PERSONAL. GROUPS. Discuss.

1. Why are there so many traffic laws?

2. What would happen if some of these laws didn't exist?

3. Are there any traffic laws that you think should be changed? If so, which ones? Why?

Grammar

Adverb clauses of condition and contrast

Adverb clause (condition/contrast)	Main clause (result)
As long as the traffic violations **aren't** too serious,	you **can go** to traffic school.
Even if you **are** mad at another driver,	you **shouldn't honk** your horn.
Even though I **parked** in the same spot,	I **got** a ticket.

Grammar Watch

- Use *as long as* to show the conditions needed for something to happen.
- Use *even if* to show that the condition in the adverb clause does not matter; the result does not change.
- Use *even though* when there is a surprising or unexpected contrast between the information in the two clauses.
- An adverb clause can start or end a sentence. Use a comma after an adverb clause when it starts a sentence.

1 PRACTICE

Read the first statement. Write *T* (true) or *F* (false) for each of the following statements.

1. Even if the road is empty, you aren't allowed to turn left at a red light.

   _____ a. You can turn left at a red light if the road is empty.

   _____ b. You can't turn left at a red light when the road is empty.

2. As long as you have a valid driver's license, you are allowed to drive anywhere in the country.

   _____ a. You don't need a valid driver's license to drive anywhere in the country.

   _____ b. You are allowed to drive anywhere in the country if you have a valid driver's license.

3. Even though she obeyed all the traffic laws, she had an accident.

   _____ a. She obeyed all the traffic laws, but she had an accident anyway.

   _____ b. She didn't obey all the traffic laws; that's why she had an accident.

4. Even if the speed limit is high, many drivers slow down in bad weather.

   _____ a. Many drivers like to drive at a slower speed when the weather is bad.

   _____ b. Many drivers like to drive at a higher speed when the weather is bad.

A Complete the sentences with the conjunctions in the box. Use one conjunction more than once.

> even if   as long as   even though

1. _____ you obey the traffic laws in your state, you won't get a traffic ticket.

2. _____ her headlights didn't work, she drove her car at night. But then she got a ticket.

3. The police officer gave the Changs a ticket _____ they said that they would buy a car seat for their baby as soon as possible.

4. You shouldn't honk your horn in a traffic jam _____ you are really late for an appointment.

B Complete the sentences with your own ideas.

1. Even if everyone obeyed the traffic laws, _____.

2. Even if an intersection doesn't have a traffic light, _____.

3. As long as you drive carefully, _____.

4. As long as you wear your seat belt, _____.

5. Even though the light was red, _____.

Show what you know! Discuss traffic laws

GROUPS. Discuss.

1. Should drivers be required to drive at lower speeds if the weather is bad?
2. Should people below the age of 16 be permitted to drive?
3. Should older people be allowed to drive as long as they pass vision and driving tests?

Can you... discuss traffic laws? ☐

Write about different legal systems

Writing

1 BEFORE YOU WRITE

A GROUPS. Read the rights of people who are arrested in the U.S. Discuss. What does each right mean? Do people have these rights in your home country?

- The right to remain silent while you are questioned by the police.
- The right to have a lawyer present while you are questioned.
- The right to a free lawyer if you cannot pay for one yourself.
- The right to a speedy, public, and fair trial.

B Read the writing model. What is the topic of the paragraph?

The Rights of the Accused in the U.S. and My Home Country

In the U.S., a person who is accused of a crime has the right to a speedy trial. In most states, the law says that a trial must take place within a certain number of months. But in my home country, people do not have the right to a speedy trial. They often have to wait in jail for many years before they go to trial. In the U.S., people have the right to a fair trial, with independent judges and competent lawyers. In contrast, when a person who is accused of a crime in my country finally does get a trial, the trial may not be fair. The judges are not always independent. Their decisions are often influenced by the wishes of politicians. Also, in my country, competent lawyers are very expensive, and many people cannot afford to hire one. Similarly, competent lawyers are expensive in the U.S. However, if a person cannot afford to hire a lawyer, the court will provide one. These are just some of the differences in the rights of accused people in the U.S. and my home country.

C PAIRS. Answer the questions.

1. What is the writer contrasting?
2. According to the writer, what are two differences between the rights of people accused of a crime in the U.S. and his home country?
3. What similarity exists between lawyers in the U.S. and lawyers in the writer's home country? What difference exists between the rights to a lawyer in the two places?

Writing Tip
Compare and Contrast

When comparing and contrasting two things, use words such as *similar, similarly,* and *like* to signal similarities and words such as *but, in contrast,* and *however* to signal differences.

2 THINKING ON PAPER

A BRAINSTORM. **Think about your legal rights in two places: the U.S. and your home country. Compare or contrast how an accused person is treated.**

Do you have the right to remain silent if you are questioned by the police?

Do you have the right to have a lawyer with you if you are questioned by the police?

Do you have the right to a free lawyer?

Do you have the right to a speedy and public trial?

Do you have the right to a fair trial?

Do you have the right to a jury trial?

B **Use your answers to the questions in Exercise A to complete the chart.**

Citizen's Rights in the U.S.	Citizen's Rights in the _____
1.	1.
2.	2.
3.	3.
4.	4.
5.	5.
6.	6.

C **Select two rights from your chart in Exercise B to compare or contrast the U.S. and your home country.**

3 WRITE

Write a paragraph that explains similarities or differences between the legal rights of accused people in two places: the U.S. and your home country. Focus on the two points that you selected from the chart.

4 CHECK YOUR WRITING

☐ Did you focus on two specific points about legal rights in the U.S. and your home country?

☐ Did you describe how those legal rights are alike and/or different in both places?

☐ Did you use words to signal similarities and differences?

☐ Did you use correct capitalization, punctuation, and spelling in your paragraph?

1   REVIEW   For your grammar review, go to page 255.

2   ACT IT OUT   What do you say?

STEP 1. CLASS. Review the conversations on page 207 and 219 (CD2, Tracks 51 and 59).

STEP 2. ROLE PLAY. PAIRS. Role-play this situation.

Student A: You are upset. You moved yesterday, and you needed to throw out your broken air conditioner. It was too big to put in the trashcan, so you carried it out into the street and left it there. A police officer saw you and gave you a ticket for dumping trash illegally.

Student B: Student A is your friend. You tell him that large items like air conditioners cannot be left in the street. Explain that the Sanitation Department has special days and times that they make pickups.

3   READ AND REACT   Problem-solving

STEP 1. GROUPS. Read about Polly's problem.

Polly was visiting a friend and parked her car in a parking lot close to her friend's house. She didn't realize that the parking lot was part of an apartment complex. There were no signs saying that the parking lot was private property. When she came back to pick up her car, she found out it had been towed away. She had to take the bus to pick up her car, and she had to pay a big fine to get her car back. Polly thinks it was unfair to tow away her car, because there was no way for her to know that it was illegal for her to park in the parking lot.

STEP 2. **What is the problem? Discuss a solution. Describe what Polly should do.**

4   CONNECT   For your Self-Evaluation Activity, go to page 262.
For your Team Project, go to page 273.

Which goals can you check off? Go back to page 205.

 Go to the CD-ROM for more practice.

Saving and Spending

Preview

Read the title. Where are the people? What are they doing?

UNIT GOALS

- [ ] Describe bank services

- [ ] Talk about starting a business

- [ ] Prepare a monthly budget

- [ ] Interpret and complete an income tax form

- [ ] Talk about dreams for the future

- [ ] Write about giving money to a charity

Listening and Speaking

1 BEFORE YOU LISTEN

A CLASS. Discuss. How often do you go to the bank? What kinds of bank services are important to you?

B GROUPS. Look at the online advertisement for a checking account. Talk about the services. What does each statement mean? Discuss any unfamiliar vocabulary.

> *interest rate* = money that a bank pays you when you keep your money in an account

> The Federal Deposit Insurance Corporation (FDIC) protects bank customers by guaranteeing deposits up to $250,000.

http://www.apollo.com

Special Online Offer

FREE CHECKING ACCOUNT!

- No monthly maintenance fee
- No minimum balance required
- Current interest rate: 1.5%
- Free online banking service
- Overdraft protection available

Apollo Bank, N.A. Member FDIC

2 LISTEN

CD2 T60

A John Foster, a customer service officer at Apollo Bank, is talking to Ling Wu. What kind of account does Ling decide to open? Why?

CD2 T60

B Read the statements. Then listen to the conversation again. Write *T* (true) or *F* (false). Correct the false statements.

__T__ 1. The MyMoney account has a good interest rate.

_____ 2. A MyMoney account requires a minimum balance of $1,000.

_____ 3. Ling can get a free checking account, but it doesn't pay interest.

_____ 4. The interest-free checking has a maintenance fee of $30 per month.

_____ 5. If Ling gets overdraft protection, she will have to pay a fee if she uses the service.

_____ 6. Ling thinks she will make a lot of overdrafts.

C GROUPS. Would you open an account at Apollo Bank? Which kind of account would work best for you? Explain.

3 CONVERSATION

(A) Listen to the compound nouns. Notice the stress. Then listen again and repeat.

• password   • checking account   • credit card   • maintenance fee

(B) Underline the compound noun in each sentence. Put a dot over the stressed syllable. Then listen and check your answers.

1. I'm thinking about opening a savings account.
2. I looked at the website for my bank.
3. One of their accounts has an interest rate of 3%.
4. You have to pay a service fee if your balance is less than $1,000.

(C) John and Ling are finishing their conversation. Listen and read.

John: OK, you're all set! Do you have any questions?

Ling: Actually, I do. Can I pay my bills online?

John: Definitely. You can even set up automatic payments for your bills. You can also check your account balance at any time.

Ling: Really? That sounds great. But is it safe?

John: Yes. Our website is secure, and you'll create your own password, so no one else can access your account.

Ling: Great. The online option really sounds like the best one for me.

4 PRACTICE

(A) PAIRS. Practice the conversation.

(B) ROLE PLAY. PAIRS. Role-play this situation. Use the conversation as a model.

Student A: You want to open a savings account. Ask the clerk about the options for savings accounts.

Student B: You are a customer service officer. A customer wants to open a savings account. Tell the customer about two different options. The SaveMore account has a 2.25% interest rate. There is a minimum balance requirement of $500. The regular savings account offers a 1.2% interest rate. You can open an account with as little as $25. There is no minimum balance requirement.

Grammar

Articles: *a, an, the,* no article (Ø)

Indefinite articles

Singular count nouns

	Article	Noun
I'd like to open	**a**	**checking account**.
Please talk to	**an**	**assistant**.

Plural count nouns / Noncount nouns

	Article	Noun
I won't have a problem with	**Ø**	**overdrafts**.
You don't earn	**Ø**	**interest**.

Definite articles

	Article	Noun
The bank replaced		**debit card** I lost.
The assistant told me about	**the**	**accounts** this bank offers.
The assistant gave us		**information** we wanted.

······ **Grammar Watch**

- Use the indefinite article with singular count nouns that are not specific.
- Do not use an article (Ø) with plural count nouns or noncount nouns.
- Use the definite article with a noun that is specific for you and your audience.
- Use the definite article when you mention a person, place, or thing for the second time: *Please talk to an assistant. The assistant at that desk will help you.*
- Do not use an article (Ø) with possessive adjectives: *Use your debit card for smaller purchases.*

1 PRACTICE

Read the brochure about debit cards and credit cards. Circle the nouns without articles. Explain why there is no article.

interest rate = the percentage you must pay to the credit card company that loans you money

What's the difference between debit cards and credit cards?

➤ When you use a debit card, you take out money from your bank account when you buy something. When you use a credit card, you borrow the money you spend from a credit card company or bank.

➤ Debit cards are easier to get than credit cards. Nowadays, when you open an account, the credit card company gives you a debit card.

➤ Most credit cards have very high interest rates. The credit card company charges you a monthly fee, or finance charge, for any unpaid balance.

Money Tip: Use a debit card for smaller purchases, like at the supermarket. Use a credit card for bigger purchases. But whichever card you use, make sure you don't spend too much!

A Complete the advertisement. Circle the correct answer. (Ø means no article is necessary.)

So you want to start **(a)**/ **the** business. Congratulations!
But where are you going to get **the** / **Ø** money you need?
At Monrovia Bank, we can help you.

- Do you want to buy **a** / **the** car or truck for your business? Ask about our vehicle loans.

- Do you need **the** / **Ø** equipment, such as **the** / **Ø** appliances, tools, or computers? Our equipment loan may be **the** / **Ø** loan for you.

- Do you need to buy **a** / **Ø** real estate? With our real estate loans, you can build **a** / **the** new building or remodel **an** / **the** old building.

Contact our loan officers at www.monroviabank.com or call 1-800-555-3000 today!

B Complete the paragraph about home loans. Use *a, an, the,* or *Ø*. More than one answer may be possible.

___Ø___ Houses are expensive. Most people have to borrow _____ money if they want to buy _____ house. But _____ banks don't give _____ home loans to everyone. To get approved for _____ home loan, you need to show _____ bank that you have _____ job. You also need to have enough _____ savings to pay for part of _____ house. And you need _____ good credit. To check people's credit, _____ banks look at things like _____ credit card payments and bill payments. If you have a lot of _____ debt and your credit is bad, you should spend less and pay your bills on time. Try to make your credit good before you fill out _____ application for _____ loan.

Show what you know! Describe bank services

GROUPS. Discuss the bank services below. Which services are easy to get? Which ones are more difficult to get? Why? Give reasons.

business loan   checking account   debit card   mortgage   savings account

Can you… describe bank services? ☐

Reading

1　BEFORE YOU READ

CLASS.　Discuss. If you were starting a business, what type of company or service would you choose? Where would you get the money to start your business? What else would you have to do?

2　READ

CD2 T64

Read and listen. What was Jose's dream? How did he try to achieve it?

A Dream Come True

An empty storefront **sat idle** with a FOR RENT sign. The storefront was inside a strip mall with a paint store, a pizza restaurant, and a barbershop. But to Jose Tenas, the storefront represented a dream.

Tenas, who came from Guatemala, had worked for years as a cook. He was an **aspiring** entrepreneur, and his dream had always been to own a restaurant. Prince William County, Virginia, has a large community of people from Central and South America, but there was not one Guatemalan restaurant. Jose called the landlord and took over the $2,400-a-month lease. He planned to open the restaurant right away.

But he had no idea how difficult it would be to open a restaurant. First, he needed start-up money for the business, which he borrowed from friends and relatives. He also took out a loan on his house. He needed to **pass** seven inspections and get seven **permits**. To prepare for the inspections, he hired contractors to help him fix up the restaurant.

Tenas passed the gas, plumbing, mechanical, fire, and electrical inspections. But the health inspection did not go well. As the health inspector walked around the restaurant, he made notes. When the inspector left, he gave Tenas a list of twenty health code violations. On the form was a stamp: NOT APPROVED. Tenas was upset, but he didn't give up. He cleaned up the restaurant and made the necessary improvements. Then he scheduled another appointment with the inspector. This time he passed.

Tenas had won his battle to open his business. Yet his success was still not a sure thing. One out of three restaurants fails. And Tenas owes $250,000 for fixing up the restaurant. But he is confident. "I know I will have the business," he says. "I have the **clientele**. The people who live here . . . they've been waiting for a Guatemalan restaurant." And indeed the restaurant fills up every day at lunchtime and hums with business all day long.

3 CHECK YOUR UNDERSTANDING

A Read the Reading Skill. Then check (✓) the better summary of the article.

_____ Jose Tenas thought that there should be a Guatemalan restaurant in Prince William County. There were a lot of people from Central and South America in the area, but no Guatemalan restaurants. Jose started a restaurant in an empty storefront that he rented for $2,400 a month.

_____ Jose Tenas worked hard to reach his dream of owning a Guatemalan restaurant. He got loans from the bank as well as from his friends and family. It was not easy to pass the inspections and get the permits he needed, but eventually Jose succeeded.

B Read the article again. Complete the statements.

1. Jose Tenas dreamed of opening a _____ in the strip mall.

2. Jose used to be a _____.

3. Jose borrowed some of the money he needed to start his business from _____.

4. Jose failed the _____ inspection the first time.

5. In order to pass the inspection, Jose made a number of _____.

6. Jose believes his restaurant will be successful because there are many people from _____ in Prince William County, but only one Guatemalan restaurant.

4 WORD WORK

Find the boldfaced words in the article and guess their meaning from the context. Then match the words with their definitions.

1. _____ sat idle
2. _____ aspiring
3. _____ pass
4. _____ permits
5. _____ clientele

a. to be officially approved
b. people who regularly go to a store, restaurant, etc.
c. having a strong desire to achieve something
d. was not being used for any purpose
e. official written statement giving you the right to do something

Show what you know! Talk about starting a business

GROUPS. **Discuss. Do you think Jose started his business in the right way? Did he make any mistakes? What would you do differently?**

Prepare a monthly budget

Listening and Speaking

1 BEFORE YOU LISTEN

A PAIRS. Are you good at managing money? Do you know how much money you earn and spend every month?

B GROUPS. Look at the budget worksheet. It shows Angela and Ricardo's income and their expenses. What is *income*? Which expenses are *fixed*? Which are *variable*? Explain how these two kinds of expenses are different.

INCOME		EXPENSES	
		FIXED EXPENSES	
Angela's job	$800/month	Rent	$600/month
		Bus fare	$120/month
Ricardo's job	$1600/month	VARIABLE EXPENSES	
		food	$400/month
		utilities	$200/month
		clothing	$60/month

C PAIRS. Think about your own expenses or spending habits. What *fixed* and *variable* *expenses* are in your budget? Make a list.

2 LISTEN

CD2 T65

A Patricia Wong, a financial expert, is giving advice to a caller on the radio show "MoneyWise." Listen to the conversation. What is the caller's problem?

CD2 T65

B Read the statements. Then listen to the conversation again. Write *T* (true) or *F* (false). Correct the false statements.

_F_ 1. The caller wants to take out a personal loan.

_____ 2. The caller owes a total of about $20,000.

_____ 3. The interest rate on the caller's credit cards varies from just under 9 percent to 18 percent.

_____ 4. Patricia tells the caller to ask the credit card company to reduce his interest rate.

_____ 5. Patricia tells the caller to increase his monthly payment by fifty dollars.

_____ 6. Patricia tells the caller to work overtime in order to earn more money to pay off his debt.

3 CONVERSATION

CD2 T66

Pablo and his friend Luis are talking about money. Listen and read.

Luis: Pablo, do you want to go out this weekend?

Pablo: I can't. I'm trying to cut expenses.

Luis: Seriously? But you have a good job.

Pablo: True, but I have to watch my money because I have many bills to pay.

Luis: Don't you keep a budget?

Pablo: No, not really. I just try to make sure I have enough to pay the bills.

Luis: Well, if you make a list of your regular expenses, you'll know exactly how much money you have for other things.

Pablo: That makes sense. And if I know exactly how much money I have, I won't worry so much all the time.

4 PRACTICE

A PAIRS. **Practice the conversation.**

B ROLE PLAY. PAIRS. **Role-play this situation.**

Student A: You want to buy a car, but you can't save up enough money to buy one. Talk to your friend about the situation.

Student B: You think your friend should make a budget. With a budget, he/she will find out what he/she is spending money on, and it will be easier to cut back and save.

C GROUPS. **Look at the budget worksheet in Exercise 1B. Imagine that Angela and Ricardo want to save money to buy a new car. How can they cut their expenses? What can they do to have more income? Make suggestions.**

D MAKE IT PERSONAL. **Look at the budget worksheet on page 276.**

STEP 1. **Create your own budget.**

STEP 2. GROUPS. **Discuss. Have you ever made a budget? Did it help you to save money? What are the most difficult things to save money on?**

Grammar

Future real conditionals

If clause	Result clause
If you **increase** your monthly payment,	you**'ll finish** paying off the loan sooner.
If you **don't cut** your expenses,	you **won't save** enough money.

Grammar Watch

- Use future real conditional sentences to talk about what will happen if something else happens.
- Use the simple present in the *if* clause. Use the future in the result clause.
- Use a comma after the *if* clause only if it starts the sentence: *You'll know exactly how much money you have if you keep a budget.*

1 PRACTICE

A Match the *if* clauses with the correct result clauses.

___c___ 1. If you figure out how much money you need to save every month,

_____ 2. If you turn down the heat in your apartment,

_____ 3. If you save your receipts,

_____ 4. If you watch TV instead of going to the movies,

_____ 5. If you don't smoke,

_____ 6. If you can fix your own car,

a. you'll be able to keep track of your variable expenses.
b. you'll save money on entertainment.
c. it will be easier to meet your savings goals.
d. you'll be healthier and you'll save a lot of money.
e. you'll save money on repairs.
f. your utility bills will go down.

B Complete the conversations. Circle the correct words.

1. **A:** If I **don't** / **won't** go back to Colombia next summer, **I** / **I'll** miss my sister's wedding. But the airfare is so expensive.

   B: I know. But you can still go. If **you** / **you'll** save $100 every month, **you** / **you'll** have enough money to buy a ticket by next summer.

2. **A:** If **I** / **I'll** take some computer classes, **I get** / **I'll be able to get** a better job. But I don't have enough money to pay for the classes.

   B: Those classes are important. You should save up the money to pay for them. If **you** / **you'll** make a budget, **you** / **you'll** see how much you're spending and you can save more.

Complete Alicia and Oscar's conversation about their budget. Use the correct form of the verb in parentheses.

Alicia: I don't know what to do. My family in Mexico needs help, but with my salary, I don't think I can help.

Oscar: You know, I send money to my parents and sisters in Colombia. If I _____ (not / help) them, my two sisters _____ (not / be able to) go to school.

Alicia: Really? Can you show me how you do it? That is, if you _____ (not / mind).

Oscar: No, not at all. Budgeting is a lot of *ifs*. If you _____ (not / do) this, then you _____ (be able to) do that. For example, right now, you're renting a one-bedroom apartment. Here's one *if*. If you _____ (not / mind) living in a studio, then you _____ (save) a couple of hundred dollars in rent, maybe more. That's $200 that you can send to your family. Let's see you try another *if*.

Alicia: OK. I have a landline and a cell phone. If I _____ (cut) my landline, then I _____ (save) forty-nine dollars a month in phone bills!

Oscar: Yep. Let's see. How about commuting costs? Do you drive to work?

Alicia: Yeah. If I _____ (take the bus), . . .

Oscar: How much is bus fare? And how much do you spend on gas per week?

Alicia: Forty-two dollars a week in gas, and bus fare is $1.25 one way, that's $2.50 both ways. A savings of almost thirty dollars per week, for a total savings of $120 a month! Wow!

Oscar: See how your savings can mount up by cutting here and there?

Alicia: I sure do! Thanks, Oscar. I feel better now.

Show what you know! Prepare a monthly budget

Look at the budget you created on page 276.

STEP 1. Think of how you can cut back on your monthly expenses. ("If I bring my lunch to work, I'll save seventy-five dollars a month.")

STEP 2. GROUPS. Discuss ways that you can spend less and save more.

Can you...prepare a monthly budget? ☐

Life Skills

1 LEARN ABOUT TAX FORMS

Read about how income tax is handled in the U.S.

When you work in the U.S., a portion of your salary is paid to the government for taxes. At the end of the year, your employer sends you a summary of your earnings and the amount of tax that you paid. This summary is called a wage and tax statement, or W-2 form. Taxpayers must use their W-2 forms to file income tax forms each year. The federal income tax form is called the 1040 ("ten forty"). The short version of the form is called the 1040EZ.

2 PRACTICE

Read the W-2 form below. How much money did Felipe Guzman earn in 2008?

a Employee's social security number 354-00-7777	OMB No. 1545-0008	**Safe, accurate, FAST! Use** IRS e file	Visit the IRS website at www.irs.gov/efile.
b Employer identification number (EIN) 22-9006542	**1** Wages, tips, other compensation $35,470.38		**2** Federal income tax withheld $7,541.25
c Employer's name, address, and ZIP code Office World 10765 SW 6th Street Miami, FL 33174	**3** Social security wages $35,470.38		**4** Social security tax withheld $1,443.67
	5 Medicare wages and tips $35,470.38		**6** Medicare tax withheld $822.77
	7 Social security tips		**8** Allocated tips
d Control number	**9** Advance EIC payment		**10** Dependent care benefits
e Employee's first name and initial Felipe J. Last name Guzman Suff.	**11** Nonqualified plans		**12a** See instructions for box 12
	13 Statutory employee Retirement Plan Third-party sick pay		**12b**
f Employee's address, and ZIP code 32 NW 106th Ct. Miami, FL 33172	**14** Other		**12c**
			12d

15 State	Employer's state ID number 22-9006542	**16** State wages, tips, etc. $35,470.38	**17** State income tax $0	**18** Local wages, tips, etc.	**19** Local income tax	**20** Locality name

Form **W-2** Wage and Tax Statement   **2008**
Copy B—To Be Filed With Employee's FEDERAL Tax Return.
This information is being furnished to the Internal Revenue Service—Internal Revenue Service

A Write the information using the W-2 form in Exercise 2.

1. Felipe Guzman's total compensation in 2008: _____

2. Name of Felipe's employer: _____

3. Amount of federal income tax withheld from Felipe's pay: _____

4. Amount of social security tax withheld from Felipe's pay: _____

5. Amount of medicare tax withheld from Felipe's pay: _____

6. Amount of state income tax withheld from Felipe's pay: _____

B Look at these sections of the 1040EZ form. Use the information on Felipe's W-2 form to fill in lines 1, 4, 7, and 9. Line 10 is done for you.

Income **Attach** **Form)s W-2** **here.** Enclose, but do not attach, any payment.	1 Wages, salaries, and tips. This should be shown in box 1of your Form(s) W-2. Attach your Form(s) W-2.		1	
	2 Taxable interest. If the total is over $1,500, you cannot use Form 1040EZ.		2	0
	3 Unemployment compensation and Alaska Permanent Fund dividends (see page 10).		3	0
	4 Add lines 1, 2 and 3. This is your **adjusted gross income**.		4	

Payments and tax	7 Federal income tax withheld from box 2 of your Form(s) W-2.		7	
	8a **Earned income credit (EIC).**		8a	0
	b Nontaxable combat pay election	8b		
	9 Add lines 7 and 8a. These are your **total payments**. ▶		9	
	10 **Tax.** Use the amount on **line 6 above** to find your tax in the tax table on pagaes 18–26 of the booklet. Then, enter the tax from the table on this line.		10	$5,293

C CLASS. A *tax refund* is money that the government gives back to you if you have paid too much in taxes. Look at the W-2 form and the 1040 EZ form. Will Felipe get a tax refund, or does he owe additional taxes? How much?

D PAIRS. Turn to page 277 and complete the 1040 EZ form. Make up the information about your compensation.

Can you…interpret and complete an income tax form? ☐

Listening and Speaking

1 BEFORE YOU LISTEN

CLASS. Discuss. Have you ever heard stories about people who suddenly come into a lot of money? What do they usually do with the money?

2 LISTEN

CD2 T67

A Chantal and Eduardo are friends. They're talking about what they would do if they suddenly got a lot of money. Listen to the conversation. What would Chantal do?

CD2 T67

B Read the questions. Listen to the conversation again. Circle the correct answers.

1. How much money did the person who works in Eduardo's office get?
   a. $100,000
   b. $500,000
   c. $1,000,000

2. What is one thing the person did with the money?
   a. He bought a car.
   b. He bought a house.
   c. He went to medical school.

3. Why does Chantal want to go back to school?
   a. She doesn't like her current job.
   b. She's not good at her current job.
   c. She wants to become a doctor.

4. What would Chantal do after she was finished with school?
   a. set up a health clinic in the U.S.
   b. set up a health clinic in Haiti.
   c. give Americans free medical care

5. What would Eduardo do if he got a lot of money?
   a. move to Haiti
   b. stop working
   c. travel around the world

6. What would Eduardo buy if he got a lot of money?
   a. a new car
   b. a big house
   c. houses for all his friends and family

CD2 T68

A Listen to the pronunciation of *would you*. Then listen again and repeat.

What **would you** do if you had a lot of money?

Would you quit your job?

CD2 T69

B Listen to the sentences. Circle the words you hear.

1. **Will / Would** you buy a house?
2. **Will / Would** you travel a lot?
3. Where **will / would** you go?
4. **Will / Would** you go to South America?
5. What **will / would** you do there?

CD2 T70

C Omar and Linh are talking about what they would do if they had a lot of money. Listen and read.

Omar: What would you do if you had a lot of money?

Linh: I would quit my job at this convenience store and start my own business. I've always wanted to be my own boss.

Omar: That sounds like a good idea.

Linh: Why? What would *you* do if you had a lot of money?

Omar: I think I would travel for a year or two.

Linh: Where would you go?

Omar: Australia. And South America. I've always wanted to go to Argentina and Brazil.

Linh: Hmm…. Maybe I'd join you. My business can wait a year or two.

4 PRACTICE

A PAIRS. Practice the conversation.

B MAKE IT PERSONAL. GROUPS. Discuss. What would you do if you had a lot of money?

Talk about dreams for the future

Grammar

Present unreal conditionals

If clause	Result clause		
If you **had** a lot of money,	what **would** you **do**?		
If I **had** a lot of money,	I **would buy** a house. or: **I'd buy** a house.		
If that house **were** less expensive,	he	**could** **might**	**buy** it.

Grammar Watch

- Use present unreal conditional sentences to talk about things that are untrue, imagined, or impossible.
- Use the simple past in the *if* clause. Use *were* for all subjects when the verb in the *if* clause is a form of *be*.
- Use *would, could,* or *might* + the base form of the verb in the result clause. *Would* expresses desired results. *Could* and *might* express possible options.

1 PRACTICE

A Read the paragraph. Circle the *if* clauses and underline the result clauses.

> Let's face it, money is important. If I had more money, I would work less and I would have more time to do the things I want to do. If I worked less, I would spend more time with my family. And if I had more time, I might take college classes. I could get a better job if I had a college degree. There's no doubt that my life would be very different if I had more money.

B Complete the sentences. Circle the correct words. Then check the sentences that are true for you.

_____ 1. If someone **gives / gave** me a lot of money, **I / I would** start my own business.

_____ 2. If I **was / were** rich, **I'll / I'd** donate a lot of money to charity.

_____ 3. If I **had / would have** a lot of money, I **quit / might quit** my job.

_____ 4. If I **work / worked** part time, **I / I would** spend more time with my family.

_____ 5. If I **speak / spoke** better English, I **get / could get** a better job.

_____ 6. If I **have / had** health insurance, I **will / would** go to the doctor more often.

PRACTICE

Under what conditions, if any, would you do these things? Write present unreal conditional sentences. Use *would, could,* or *might* in the result clause.

1. cut back on your spending

   If I had a lot of expenses, I'd cut back on my spending.

2. loan money to a friend

   _____

3. ask a friend to loan you money

   _____

4. refuse to loan money to a family member

   _____

5. take out a loan for a large sum of money from a bank

   _____

6. quit your job

   _____

7. start your own business

   _____

Show what you know! Talk about dreams for the future

STEP 1. **Write sentences about the different things you would do if you had a lot of money/time/power. Use the topics in the box or your own ideas.**

my family   my friends   my school   my community   my country

STEP 2. GROUPS. **Compare your answers.**

STEP 3. CLASS. **Present your ideas to the class. Which ideas are the most popular? Can you think of any ways to make your "dreams" come true?**

Can you... talk about dreams for the future? ☐

Writing

1 BEFORE YOU WRITE

Ⓐ GROUPS. Read the facts about charitable giving in the U.S. Discuss. Why do people donate time or money to charitable causes?

- Americans give more money to charity than citizens of other developed countries.
- In 2006, Americans gave away almost $300 billion of their personal incomes to charity.
- On average, low-income working families give away 4.5 percent of their income compared to 2.5 percent among middle class families and 3 percent among high-income families.
- The average American household gives about $1,000 to charity a year.

Ⓑ Read the writing model. What is the writer's main point?

Doctors Without Borders

If someone gave me $1,000 and told me to give the money away, which organization would I choose? Without a doubt, it would be Doctors Without Borders. This international organization believes that every person in the world has a right to medical care. Doctors Without Borders was started by a group of French doctors in 1971. Each year, the organization sends volunteer doctors, nurses, and administrators from different parts of the world to give medical care to people in more than seventy countries. The organization provides all kinds of medical care, from surgery and nutrition programs to mental health care and doctor training. In 1999, Doctors Without Borders received the Nobel Peace Prize for its good works. Doctors Without Borders helps victims of war, sickness, hunger, and natural disasters. I think this organization needs help more than any other organization in the world, so it is the one that would receive my financial support.

Ⓒ PAIRS. Answer the questions.

1. What question does this paragraph ask and answer?
2. What facts and examples does the writer give to support her answer?
3. Why would the writer give her $1,000 to Doctors Without Borders?

Ⓓ Reread the paragraph. Underline the writer's question and answer.

Writing Tip:

One way to focus a paragraph is to ask a question and answer it. You not only give an answer. You explain your answer by giving supporting details such as facts and examples.

2 THINKING ON PAPER

A BRAINSTORM. **Look at this list of charitable causes. Which one would you support? Why?**

- disaster relief organizations
- blood banks
- environmental organizations

- soup kitchens and homeless shelters
- child and family services
- religious organizations

B Complete a question-and-answer chart.

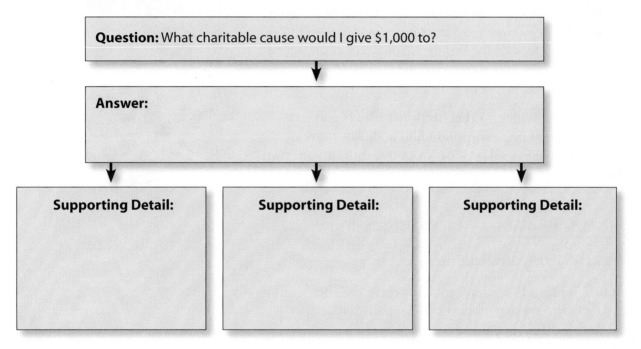

Question: What charitable cause would I give $1,000 to?

↓

Answer:

↓   ↓   ↓

Supporting Detail: **Supporting Detail:**   **Supporting Detail:**

C Circle the most convincing facts, examples, and other supporting details on your chart.

3 WRITE

Write a paragraph about a charity that you would give $1,000 to. Use the information in your chart to organize the paragraph. Begin with your question. State your answer. Then explain your answer by giving facts, examples, and other supporting details.

4 CHECK YOUR WRITING

☐ Did you ask and answer a question?

☐ Did you explain the reasons for your answer by giving supporting details?

☐ Did you use correct capitalization, punctuation, and spelling?

1 **REVIEW**   For your grammar review, go to page 256.

2 **ACT IT OUT**   What do you say?

STEP 1. CLASS. Review the conversations on pages 232 and 233 (CD2, Tracks 65 and 66).

STEP 2. ROLE PLAY. PAIRS. Role-play this situation.

> **Student A:** Talk to Student B about your dream of opening your own grocery store. You have some money saved up, but not enough to start the business. You don't know where to get the money you need to start the business.

> **Student B:** Tell Student A that his or her idea is good. Suggest ways that he or she might find additional money for his or her business. Use ideas from this unit or your own ideas.

3 **READ AND REACT**   Problem-solving

STEP 1. GROUPS. Read the problem.

Oksana and Ivan Bulov have money problems. They want to buy a house, but they can't save any money. Look at their budget:

INCOME		EXPENSES	
		FIXED EXPENSES	
Oksana's job	$1,000/month	Rent	$1,000/month
		Train fare	$200/month
Ivan's job	$1,200/month	VARIABLE EXPENSES	
		food	$400/month
		utilities	$200/month
		clothing	$300/month

STEP 2. Discuss a solution. How can Oksana and Ivan save money to buy a house? Are there any expenses they can cut back on?

4 **CONNECT**   For your Self-Efficacy Activity, go to page 262.
For your Team Project, go to page 274.

Which goals can you check off? Go back to page 221.

 Go to the CD-ROM for more practice.

Grammar Review

A Complete the conversation. Circle the simple present or the present continuous.

Patty: Hey, Chang. **Are you working / Do you work** again today?

Chang: Yes. Marty usually **is working / works** on Fridays, but today **I'm taking / I take** his shift.

Patty: Why? What **is he doing / does he do**?

Chang: **I'm not knowing / I don't know** for sure. I think his family **is visiting / visits**.

B Complete the conversation with the correct future form.

Alicia: Hey, Mom. I _____ in a few minutes.
(leave)

Mom: OK. What _____ tonight?
(you / do)

Alicia: Dania and I _____ a movie.
(be going to / see)

Mom: What time _____ home?
(you / be going to / be)

Alicia: I'm not sure. But don't worry. I _____ home too late.
(will not / get)

Mom: All right. Remember that you _____ me to work in the morning.
(take)

Alicia: Yep. I _____ ready to leave at 7:00.
(will be)

C Complete the conversations. Use the simple past or the correct form of *used to*. Sometimes more than one answer is possible.

1. **A:** My husband and I _____ into a new apartment last weekend.
(move)
   I'm glad, because our old apartment was far from my work.

   B: Really? Where _____?
(you / live)

2. **A:** I saw you driving today. I _____ you had a car.
(not know)

   B: Well, I _____ one. I _____ that one about a month ago.
(not have)   (buy)

3. **A:** How's your brother? He _____ near me, but then he
(work)
   _____ a new job.
(get)

   B: He's doing well. He _____ a manager a few months ago.
(become)

4. **A:** _____ how to cook from your mother?
(you / learn)

   B: No. My grandmother _____ me to cook.
(teach)

UNIT 2

A Complete the conversation. Use gerunds or infinitives. If possible, write two answers.

A: Olivia doesn't like _working OR to work_ at the bank anymore. She wants
     (work)

_____ a new job. Actually, she's thinking about
    (find)

_____ a career change. She's interested in
    (make)

_____ a nurse.
    (become)

B: Really? Well, she'll probably need _____ a college degree
               (get)

before she can get a nursing job. Is she planning on _____
               (go)

to school?

A: Actually, she started _____ nursing at the community
        (study)

college a few years ago. Now she wants to continue _____
               (work)

towards her degree.

B: That's great. I think Olivia will be very good at _____ care
             (take)

of people. And I think she'll enjoy _____ others.
         (help)

B Complete the conversations. Circle the simple past or the present perfect.

1. **A:** How long **have you worked / did you work** at your current job?
   B: Well, I **have started / started** last June, so I've been / was at this job for about six months.

2. **A:** I've learned / learned so much in my business class already, and the semester is only half over.
   B: Yeah, I **have taken / took** a business class last year, and I really **learned / have learned** a lot, too.

3. **A:** Adela **has been / was** a manager at Data Tech, Inc. for twelve months now. She **has accomplished/ accomplished** a lot in a very short time.
   B: She sure has. It's hard to believe that she **has taken / took** that job only a year ago.

4. **A:** Gabriel is a good employee. We **have hired / hired** him two years ago, and since then, he **has never missed / never missed** a day of work.
   B: Yeah, he **has had / had** a good reputation at his last job, too.

UNIT 3

A Complete the paragraph. Circle the correct participial adjective.

I used to be **worried / worrying** about crime in our town, and I was **frustrated / frustrating** by our litter problem. But things are changing. Community members are **interested / interesting** in making a difference. It's **satisfied / satisfying** to see people working to improve the community, and it's **encouraged / encouraging** to see them working together. The community is making some **excited / exciting** changes, and I'm **amazed / amazing** at our progress.

B Read the first sentence in each item. Then complete the second sentence to express a wish for the opposite.

1. There aren't a lot of restaurants in our neighborhood. We wish that
   ____*there were*____ more restaurants in our neighborhood.

2. Richard doesn't have time to go to the movies very often. He wishes that _____
   time to go to the movies more often.

3. Mrs. Salas worries a lot. Her children wish that she _____ so much.

4. The school can't get a computer for every student. Everyone wishes that _____
   a computer for every student.

5. The bus is always late. I wish that _____ always late.

C Read the first sentence in each item. Then complete the second sentence. Include an object + infinitive.

1. The residents of our community don't participate in community events.
   We should encourage _____ in community events.

2. I parked in my neighbor's parking spot last night. She reminded _____ there.

3. Several people in our neighborhood were robbed last week because they opened the door
   for strangers. The police warned _____ the door for strangers.

4. We are all invited to attend meetings of the City Council. The City Council president urges
   _____ its meetings.

5. The streets in our neighborhood are dirty because people constantly litter. They just pay no
   attention to the signs that tell _____

A Complete the conversations. Put the words in parentheses in the correct order. If more than one answer is possible, write both answers.

1. Would you please _turn off the light OR turn the light off_?
   (turn / off / the light)

2. Can you look at this with me? I'm having a problem, and I can't quite

   _____.
   (figure / out / it)

3. If you ever need help, you know you can always _____.
   (count / on / me)

4. Do you have a moment? I'd like to _____ with you.
   (talk / over / these plans)

5. She was really hurt by her co-worker's remark. It won't be easy for her to

   _____.
   (get / over / it)

B Read Person B's response. Then write a negative question that Person A could have asked.

1. **A:** _Shouldn't I take_ my break soon?

   B: Yes, you should. You should take it when Dina finishes her break.

2. **A:** _____ about the schedule change?

   B: No, I didn't. I didn't hear anything about it.

3. **A:** _____ the equipment yet?

   B: No, they haven't. They haven't cleaned it because they've been doing other work.

4. **A:** _____ questions if she doesn't understand something?

   B: Yes, she should. She should ask questions any time she's not sure.

5. **A:** _____ the report tomorrow?

   B: No, we can't. We can't finish it tomorrow because Mr. Luna needs it today.

C Read the first statement in each item. Then complete the second sentence to make an indirect instruction or request with the same meaning.

1. My co-worker to me: "Wear comfortable shoes." My co-worker advised _____
   comfortable shoes.

2. The supervisor to us: "Check the new schedule." The supervisor reminded _____
   the new schedule.

3. Anita to Sarah: "Don't be late for work." Anita warned _____ late for work.

4. Shen to Franco: "Work carefully." Shen told _____ carefully.

A Combine the two clauses to make a conditional sentence. Keep the clauses in the same order and add *if* to one clause. Include a comma if necessary.

1. a person is badly injured / don't move him or her

   If a person is badly injured, don't move him or her.

2. you don't have a smoke detector / you need to get one

   _____

3. get under a piece of furniture / there's an earthquake

   _____

4. you are prepared for a fire / you have a better chance of surviving it

   _____

5. call 911 / there's an emergency

   _____

B Complete the sentences. Circle the correct adverb.

1. You should check the weather frequently **until / when** there's a severe weather watch.
2. **Until / As soon as** we felt the earth shake, we got under the table.
3. They didn't know about the hurricane **as soon as / before** they saw the weather report.
4. **After / Before** the storm started, everyone stayed inside.
5. Stay on the phone with the 911 operator **until / after** he tells you to hang up.

C Complete the sentences. Circle the correct answer.

1. I see smoke. There _____ be a fire somewhere.
   a. may   b. must   c. can't
2. In an emergency, some people _____ be very nervous.
   a. couldn't   b. might   c. must not
3. It _____ rain today. I didn't see the weather report, so I'm not sure.
   a. could   b. must   c. couldn't
4. Jane is allergic to milk, but she didn't have an allergic reaction after she ate that cookie. The cookie _____ have milk in it.
   a. may not   b. might not   c. must not
5. There's a hurricane watch for this area. The storm _____ affect us.
   a. may   b. must not   c. couldn't

A Complete the sentences with the correct form of the verb. Make the sentence negative if necessary.

1. Tenants _____ to have pets. It's against the rules.
   (allow)
2. Visitors _____ to park in this lot. It's for tenants only.
   (permit)
3. Please don't throw away those soda cans. We _____ to recycle them.
   (suppose)
4. The landlord must put a smoke alarm in your apartment. He _____ to do it.
   (require)
5. The laundry room is open from 6:00 AM–9:00 PM. Tenants _____ to use the
   (allow)
   laundry room during these hours only.

B Complete the sentences with tag questions.

1. You moved recently, _____
2. We don't have to pay the rent yet, _____
3. The tenants pay for electricity, _____
4. The landlord didn't call back, _____
5. The lock isn't broken, _____
6. The windows are closed, _____

C Read the first statement in each item. Then complete the second sentence with reported speech. Use formal English.

1. Tom told Beth: "I like my new neighbors."

   Tom told _Beth (that) he liked his new neighbors._

2. My landlord said, "Your dogs are too noisy."

   My landlord said _____

3. The tenant told his landlord, "I'll read the lease and return it to you on Friday."

   The tenant told _____

4. Kim-Ly told the building manager, "Our lobby needs a new carpet."

   Kim-Ly told _____

5. Lucy told Mike, "My neighbor plays his TV really loudly."

   Lucy told _____

UNIT 7

A Complete the conversations. Use the words in the box.

get	than	rather	would you rather
to	buying	prefer	would you prefer

1. **A:** Would you _____ take your car to a mechanic or do repairs yourself?

   B: I'd _____ having a professional take care of any problems.

2. **A:** Would Theo prefer _____ a new car _____ a used car?

   B: Well, he would rather _____ a new car _____ a used one.

   But he doesn't want to spend a lot either.

3. **A:** _____ a compact car or something larger?

   B: I'm not sure. What about you? _____ drive a big car or a small one?

B Complete the conversations. Change the direct questions to embedded questions.

1. **A:** I wonder *if you can take a look at my car's tires.*
      (Can you take a look at my car's tires?)
   B: Sure. Can you tell me _____
      (What is the problem?)
   A: Well, the treads are really worn. I wonder _____
      (Do I need new tires?)

2. **A:** I just put new windshield wipers on my car, but they're not very good. I don't know

   _____
      (Why don't they work?)
   B: Hmmm. I wonder _____
      (Did you get the wrong size?)
   A: That might be it. I wasn't sure _____
      (What size should I get?)

C Complete the conversations. Use the correct form of the past perfect.

1. **A:** My wife _____ a hybrid for a long time, so we finally bought one.
      (want)
   B: I think you'll be happy with it. We _____ to get a more fuel-efficient car
      (decide)
   a long time ago. So when the hybrid cars came out, we bought one right away.

2. **A:** After she _____ for about a year, Maritza got a new car.
      (save)
   B: Oh yeah? _____ at a lot of cars before she made her choice?
      (she/look)
   A: Yes, she _____. She _____ to several dealers.
      (go)

A Complete the conversation. Use the correct form of the present perfect continuous.

Dr. Pratt: Hello, Mrs. Lee. _____ you _____ long?
(wait)

Mrs. Lee: No, I haven't, thank you.

Dr. Pratt: Good. So, how _____ you _____ since your last
(feel)

appointment?

Mrs. Lee: I _____ better every day. I _____ well at night, and I
(get)   (sleep)

_____ naps during the day.
(not take)

Dr. Pratt: That's great. And _____ you _____ your medication?
(take)

Mrs. Lee: Yes, I have. My husband _____ me every night.
(remind)

Dr. Pratt: Good. And _____ you _____?
(exercise)

Mrs. Lee: Well, my daughter and I _____ together every day.
(walking)

Dr. Pratt: Very good. You _____ everything right!
(do)

B Complete the conversation. Circle the correct words.

Malena: Hey, you look great! What have you been doing?

Susana: Nothing special—just following my doctor's advice. She said I **better / 'd better** make some lifestyle changes to stay in good health.

Malena: Oh, yeah? What kinds of changes? Maybe I should make some changes, too.

Susana: Well, she said I **ought to / ought** get more exercise. She thinks I **should to / should** do some moderate exercise at least three times a week.

Malena: But I already have **so many / so much** things to do. I'm **so / such** busy that I don't have time!

Susana: Well, you can start by doing small things like taking the stairs instead of the elevator. It can make **so / such** a difference that you'll be amazed. Listen, we **had better / ought to** take a walk a few days a week at lunchtime. Do you want to go with me today?

Malena: Sure. Let's meet downstairs at 12:00, OK?

Susana: OK. And you **had better / have better** be there! Remember, your health is **such / so** important that you must **making / make** time to take care of yourself!

A Read the statements. Combine the sentences using either *because* or *since*. Don't change the order of the clauses.

1. <u>Since Lucia is having trouble with math, I want to talk to her teacher. OR:</u>

   <u>Because Lucia is having trouble with math, I want to talk to her teacher.</u>

2. Our son really likes to play sports. We encourage him to read books about them.

   _____

3. Parents and teachers should communicate. It helps students do better in school.

   _____

4. David's grades have improved. He started getting extra help after school.

   _____

B Complete the conversations. Circle the correct words.

1. **Eliana:** I sent Manolo's teacher a note **because / to** I want to set up a meeting with her. But she hasn't called or written me back.

   Victor: She **might not have / must have** gotten the note. She doesn't seem like the kind of person **which / who** ignores messages. When did you send it?

   Eliana: Last week. I put it in Manolo's backpack **so that / to** he could give it to her.

   Victor: You should check. Manolo **could have / must not have** forgotten about it.

2. **Janet:** Did you go to the PTO meeting last night?

   Mi-Cha: No. I didn't go **because / so that** I don't really know what the group does.

   Janet: Well, PTO stands for Parent Teacher Organization. It's a group **who / that** works to improve both the school and students' learning.

   Mi-Cha: It sounds like a good organization. I **should have / must have** gone to the meeting.

   Janet: Don't worry. You can go to the next one **to / so that** learn more about it.

3. **Farah:** Ugh—that test was so hard! Even Luisa said it was hard, and she's someone **that / which** always gets good grades.

   Laila: I know. The people **I talked to / which I talked to** all thought they got a bad grade. I **shouldn't have / can't have** done well on it.

   Farah: Me neither. I **should have / may have** studied more.

4. **Mai:** Some schools are trying **to / so that** help parents get involved. Many teachers meet with parents in the evenings. That's a big help for parents **who work / work** during the day.

   Tien: Yeah, at my son's school there are translators **that can / can** help parents **who / which** are still learning English. A translator helped me last year, and she was great. Without her, I **may have been / might not have been** so involved in my son's education.

UNIT 10

A Complete the sentences. Use the words in the box.

> have   makes   lets   get   made   had

1. They didn't want to work late, but the supervisor _____ them stay until 9:00.

2. Please find Mr. Jones and _____ him sign this. Then give it back to me.

3. The company _____ employees leave early the day before some holidays.

4. Can you _____ someone to take your shift? Ask your co-workers.

5. The store was so busy yesterday! My boss _____ me work on the cash register, and I usually don't do that.

6. Our company _____ us clock in and out for every shift.

B Complete the sentences with the correct reflexive pronouns.

1. Don't lift heavy objects by _____. Get someone to help you.

2. I finished all the work _____. No one helped me.

3. Mrs. Yang burned _____ while cooking dinner.

4. Workers need to use caution with that machine. They could hurt _____.

5. You and John can't do this project by _____. You'll need some help.

6. We're really proud of _____. We worked hard, and we got the job done.

C Complete the conversations. Use the words in the box.

> Why don't you
> Would you mind
> Could I
> Why don't I

1. **A:** _____ borrow your pen for a minute?

   B: Sure. Here you go.

2. **A:** I can't go to lunch with you today because I forgot my wallet.

   B: _____ lend you some money? You can pay me back tomorrow.

3. **A:** _____ driving me home after work today?

   B: No, it's no problem at all.

4. **A:** _____ talk to our supervisor about your problem?

   B: That's a good idea. I'll talk to her today after my shift ends.

UNIT 11

A Complete the sentences. Use the simple past or the past continuous.

1. While the defense attorney _____ for the trial, the police
   (prepare)
   _____ new evidence.
   (discover)

2. I _____ at a red light when an SUV _____ my car.
   (wait)   (hit)

3. When his wife _____ home, Walter _____ courtroom TV.
   (get)   (watch)

4. The witness _____ when the attorney _____ him.
   (talk)   (interrupt)

5. Paula _____ a car accident while she _____ at the bus stop.
   (see)   (stand)

B Read the active sentences. Complete the passive sentences so they have the same meaning.

1. Attorneys on both sides of a case choose juries.

   Juries _____ by attorneys on both sides of a case.

2. They sent the criminal to jail for 10 years.

   The criminal _____ to jail for 10 years.

3. The government calls most U.S. citizens to jury duty sometime in their lives.

   Most U.S. citizens _____ to jury duty sometime in their lives.

4. Lawyers explained the details of the case to the jury.

   The details of the case _____ to the jury.

5. After hearing the facts, jurors discuss the case.

   After hearing the facts, the case _____ by the jurors.

C Complete the sentences. Use the subordinating conjunctions in the box. You may use each conjunction more than once.

> even if
> as long as
> even though

1. Don't speed, _____ you're in a hurry.

2. You won't get a ticket _____ you follow the traffic laws.

3. _____ I was really late for my appointment yesterday, I didn't speed.

4. _____ there aren't other cars around you, you should still use your turn signals. It's a good habit to get into.

5. _____ you study, you'll pass your driver's license test.

6. I always drive with my headlights on, _____ it's not dark.

A Complete the paragraph. Use *a, an, the,* or Ø.

    With _____ credit card, you can buy things now and pay for them later. This can

be useful, but it can also be expensive. That's because _____ credit card companies charge

_____ interest on the amount you owe them. _____ debit card is different—it's linked

to _____ bank account. When you pay for something with _____ debit card, the money

comes out of _____ account it's linked to.

    If you have _____ credit card, use it carefully. And make sure you always pay _____

full amount of the bill as soon as you can. Try not to have _____ unpaid balance so you

don't have to pay _____ interest charges.

B Complete the sentences so that they make future real conditional statements.

1. If I _____ a bank account, the bank _____ me a debit card.
         (open)   (give)
2. We _____ go on vacation, if we _____ our money.
        (be able to)   (save)
3. If she _____ a loan, she _____ pay interest.
        (get)   (have to)
4. It _____ easier to save money, if you _____ a budget.
        (be)   (make)

C Complete the sentences so that they make present unreal conditional statements.

1. They _____ their own business if they _____ enough money.
        (start)   (have)
2. We _____ money if we _____ the bus instead of driving.
        (save)   (take)
3. If I _____ out so much, I _____ a lot less on food.
        (not eat)   (spend)
4. If you _____ a Mexican restaurant, people _____.
        (open)   (come)

D Complete the sentences. Use the correct form of the verb.

1. If you suddenly _____ a lot of money, would you quit your job?
          (get)
2. If she _____ money, I'll lend it to her.
       (need)
3. I wouldn't do that if I _____ you.
         (be)
4. If we stop buying coffee at the coffee shop, we _____ about $20 a week.
              (save)

Persistence Activities

Unit 1   Find Someone Who

A Write the names of classmates who can answer "yes" to these questions. Then ask the follow-up questions.

> Follow-up questions are questions that ask for more detail or additional information related to a previously asked question.

Find someone who . . .

1. has visited another city in the United States. _____
   Which city? _____

2. went to see a movie in the last month. _____
   Which movie? _____

3. knows how to play a musical instrument. _____
   What instrument? _____

4. did something fun or exciting last weekend. _____
   What did you do? _____

B PAIRS. Compare your answers. What did you learn that was interesting?

C After class, talk to a classmate who gave an answer you found interesting. Ask your own follow-up questions to get to know this classmate better.

Unit 2   Characteristics of a Good Learner

A Make a chart like the one below. Include ten rows.

B BRAINSTORM. GROUPS. What are the characteristics of a good learner? Record each idea in the first column.

Characteristic of a good learner	I do this.	I don't do this.	I want to work on this.
Plans a specific time to study	✓	✗	✓✓
Asks questions when he or she doesn't understand			

C Look at the learner characteristics in your chart. Put a check (✓) next to the ones you already do, an X next to the ones you don't do, and two checks (✓✓) next to the ones you want to work on.

D PAIRS. Share your charts. Look at the items with two checks (✓✓). Discuss ways you can help each other develop these learner characteristics.

Unit 3   Favorite Celebrations

A   Think of your favorite holiday or celebration in your country or in the United States.

B   Prepare to talk about this holiday or celebration with a partner. Use the following questions to help you remember and organize details.

> With whom do you spend the holiday or event?
>
> Where do you celebrate?
>
> What special things do you see?
>
> What sounds do you hear?
>
> What kinds of things do you smell?
>
> What foods do you eat?
>
> What special activities do you do?

C   PAIRS.   Tell your partner about your favorite holiday or celebration.

Unit 4   What Is Your Work Style?

A   Look at the list of different work styles. Check (✓) the styles that are true for you. Put an X next to the styles that aren't true for you.

Work style preference	Yes	No
I like to work alone.		
I like to work in groups or teams.		
I like to have deadlines.*		
I like to get detailed instructions from my boss.		
I like to work with my hands.		
I like to solve problems.		
I like to work in an office.		
I like to create things.		
I like to do a lot of writing.		
I like to work with different people.		
I like to work within a definite schedule. No overtime!		

*Deadlines are specific times or dates when a task has to be completed.

B   Look at the items you checked. Do your preferences match the job that you have now? How can knowing your work style preferences help you choose your job?

C   PAIRS.   Share your answers to Exercises A and B. Can you think of other jobs that might match your or your partner's preferences? Explain.

Unit 5 Snow Days

A Create a word web for the topic: "Reasons for school closings and class cancellations." Write those words in the center of a page. Draw a line out from the center and label it: "Weather-related reasons."

Reasons for school closings and class cancellations

Weather-related reasons
_____
_____
_____

B BRAINSTORM. Think about class cancellations.

1. What are the common weather-related reasons for school closings and class cancellations? List those specific examples below "Weather-related reasons."

2. What other reasons for class cancellations do you know? Add another line and label it. List specific examples for that reason.

C PAIRS. Discuss. How can you take advantage of school closings to learn English? Create a word web similar to the one in Exercise A to record your ideas.

Unit 6 How Far Have You Come?

A Think about what have learned in this English class. Leaf through your textbook, your workbook, and any written work.

B Make a chart like the one below. Include at least 10 rows. In the first column, list all the things that you have learned.

Things I have learned	Situations where I can apply what I have learned

C Look at the items you listed. How and where in your daily life can you apply each one? Write specific examples in the second column.

D PAIRS. Share your charts. Is there anything in your partner's list that is not in yours? Can it help you in your every day life? If so, add it to your chart.

Unit 7   Looking Forward

A What are you looking forward to studying in English class? Think about your goals
and any daily activities or situations when you need to use English. Then look at
the units in this book that you haven't studied yet. Identify at least five topics,
grammar points, readings, vocabulary, or life skills that might help you in your
daily life. Make a list.

1. _____
2. _____
3. _____
4. _____
5. _____

B GROUPS. Talk about each item on your list. Explain why it is important
to you. Compare your lists. Talk about the similarities and differences.
Agree on five things that are important to the whole group. Make a list.

C CLASS. Present your common list to the class.

Unit 8   Advertising English!

A PAIRS. Discuss. What is your favorite advertisement? Where
are these advertisements—on billboards, television, radio,
magazine, newspapers, brochures? What do you like about that
advertisement? Does it have a slogan?

> Billboards are large outdoor
> signs for advertising.
> A slogan is a short, easily
> remembered phrase used in
> advertising, politics, etc.

B GROUPS. Describe your favorite advertisement. Talk about what
makes an advertisement successful and memorable. Take notes.

C GROUPS. Discuss. Why is English important in your life? How can knowing
how to speak, read, and write in English help you? What would happen if you
didn't learn English? Take notes.

D GROUPS. Now create a poster advertising the importance of English in daily
life. Think of a slogan for your advertisement. What colors will you use?
Will you use pictures? How will you make your advertisement memorable?

E CLASS. Present your group's poster to the class. Display the posters in your
classroom and, with your principal's permission, in your school to inspire
others to learn English!

Unit 9   Then and Now

A Think about how a pre-school child learns to speak a language, whether it is English or a native language. Then think of how you, as an adult, are learning English. Complete the chart below.

	Learning as a child	Learning as an adult
What strategies do children or adults use to learn a language? By imitating? By listening to an audio? By reading?		
Where do children or adults learn a language? At home? At school? In the playground?		
What do children or adults learn when learning a language? Vocabulary? Conversation? Grammar?		
From your observation, who is the faster learner, a child or an adult?		
In your opinion, what is the best way for children or adults to learn a language?		

B PAIRS. Share your answers to Exercise A. How do you feel about learning English as an adult?

Unit 10   How Students Learn Best

A Think of how you've been learning English. Check (✓) five types of activities you liked best.

- ☐ working alone
- ☐ working in pairs
- ☐ working in groups
- ☐ reading activities
- ☐ conversations
- ☐ grammar activities
- ☐ listening activities
- ☐ writing activities
- ☐ vocabulary activities
- ☐ using life skills materials (maps, graphs, forms, etc.)
- ☐ Other: _____

B Look at the activities you checked. What did you like about them? How did they help you learn English?

C PAIRS. Talk about other activities in the book. Which activities didn't you like? Why?

D GROUPS. Compare your answers to Exercises A, B, and C. What are some similarities in the ways you prefer to learn English? Make a list of activities that help students learn effectively.

E CLASS. Present your list to the class. Explain why these activities help students learn. Also discuss the activities that you didn't include. Why do you think those activities aren't as effective?

Unit 11 My Writing Checklist

A Look back at the checklists in Check Your Writing for each unit. Did those checklists help you write better paragraphs?

B Now look again at the paragraphs you wrote for this class. What common mistakes did you make? For example,

- Did you forget to use punctuation?
- Did you use capital letters correctly?
- Were there any misspellings?
- Did you make mistakes in subject-verb agreement?
- Did you forget to provide details to support a statement?

Create your own checklist for editing your writing. Include anything that will help you review, correct, and improve your writing.

C PAIRS. Compare your checklists. Explain why you included the items you did. Which items from your partner's checklist would you add to your checklist?

Unit 12 The Door of Opportunity

A Staple two pieces of paper together. On the first page, draw a picture of a door. You can make the door simple or elaborate. On the second page, make a chart like the one below.

What I will remember about English class	Where I will go from here

B Imagine yourself walking through a door and leaving your English class. What will you remember about the class? Who will you remember? What lessons and new knowledge will you take with you? Record these ideas in the first column.

C In the second column, write about where you want to go after this English class. Do you want to take more classes? Do you want to look for a new job? What are your plans now that English class is finished?

D CLASS. Share your door with the class. Describe one thing that you will remember about English class. Describe something that you will do now that you've finished class.

Team Projects

Unit 1   Routines   <u>MAKE A POSTER</u>

Materials
- large paper
- markers
- camera (optional)

TEAMS OF 2   Captain, Spokesperson

GET READY   **Captain:** Ask your teammate about his or her current and past routines.
Find out how your routines are similar and different. Keep time. You have ten minutes.
Assistant: Take notes in the chart.

Name	Current routines	Past routines

CREATE   **Captain:** Get the materials. Then keep time. You have ten minutes.
Team: Create a poster about your routines. Use the information from your chart to make a Venn diagram. Label each of the circles with a team member's name. Write the routines that are the same for team members in the center. Write the routines that are different in the outer circles. If you can, take photos of the teammates and place them by the appropriate circles.

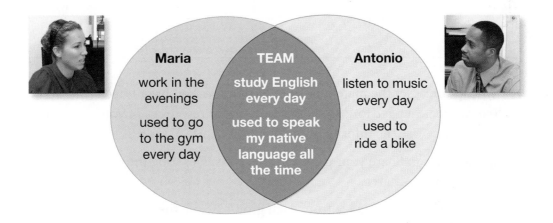

REPORT   **Spokesperson:** Share your poster with the class. Describe your team's routines.

Unit 2　Job-Search Resources　<u>MAKE A BOOKLET</u>

TEAMS OF 4　Captain, Co-captain, Assistant, Spokesperson

GET READY　**Captain:** Ask your teammates about resources in your community where you can find information about job openings and careers. Ask what kind of information you can find from each resource.
Co-captain: Keep time. You have ten minutes.
Assistant: Take notes in the chart.

Materials
- 1 piece of white paper
- pens or markers
- stapler and staples

Resources	Services provided

CREATE　**Co-captain:**　Get the materials. Then keep time. You have fifteen minutes.
Team: Create a page for a booklet about career resources in your community. Use the information from your chart. Add art if you want.

REPORT　**Spokesperson:** Share your page with the class. Describe the career resources in your area.

COLLECT　**Captains:** Collect the page from each group. Staple the pages together to make a booklet about career resources in your community.

Unit 3 Community Services MAKE A POSTER

TEAMS OF 4 Captain, Co-captain, Assistant, Spokesperson

GET READY **Captain:** Ask your teammates about community services in your area. Ask them where the places are and how to get there.
Co-captain: Keep time. You have ten minutes.
Assistant: Take notes in the chart.

Materials
- large paper
- markers
- rulers
- bus and street maps of your city (optional)

Place name	Location	How to get there

CREATE **Co-captain:** Get the materials. Then keep time. You have fifteen minutes.
Team: Choose one of the places you talked about. Use the information from your chart to create a poster about that place. Write directions to get there. Include a map if you want.

REPORT **Spokesperson:** Share your poster with the class. Describe the community service and how to get there.

Unit 4　Team Players　<u>MAKE AN OUTLINE</u>

Materials
- 1 piece of white paper
- pens or markers
- stapler and staples

TEAMS OF 4　Captain, Co-captain, Assistant, Spokesperson

GET READY　**Captain:** Ask your teammates how to be a successful team player. Ask what you should and shouldn't do at work to get along well with your co-workers.
Co-captain: Keep time. You have ten minutes.
Assistant: Take notes in the chart.

How to be a successful team player	
You should . . .	**You shouldn't . . .**

CREATE　**Co-captain:** Get the materials. Then keep time. You have fifteen minutes.
Team: Imagine you will be giving a presentation to employees about how to be successful team players. Create an outline for your presentation. Include the information from your chart.

REPORT　**Spokesperson:** Share your presentation outline with the class. Describe three ways to be a successful team player.

COLLECT　**Captains:** Collect the outline from each group. Staple the pages together to make a booklet about how to be a team player.

Unit 5 Be Prepared <u>MAKE A POSTER</u>

Materials
- large paper
- markers

TEAMS OF 4 Captain, Co-captain, Assistant, Spokesperson

GET READY **Captain:** Ask your teammates to name disasters that could happen where you live. Ask what supplies you need to prepare and what you need to do before a disaster strikes.
Co-captain: Keep time. You have ten minutes.
Assistant: Take notes in the chart.

Type of disaster: _____	
Supplies needed	**Things to do**

CREATE **Co-captain:** Get the materials. Then keep track of the time. You have fifteen minutes.
Team: Create a poster about how to prepare for a disaster. Use the information from your chart. Add art if you want.

REPORT **Spokesperson:** Share your poster with the class. Describe three ways to prepare for a disaster.

Unit 6 Website Design <u>MAKE A BOOKLET</u>

Materials
- 1 piece of white paper
- pens or markers
- stapler and staples

TEAMS OF 4 Captain, Co-captain, Assistant, Spokesperson

GET READY **Team:** Imagine you are on a website design team. The website is for newcomers to the United States. It is your job to design a page about renting an apartment. Suggest information for the website page.
Captain: Keep time. You have ten minutes.
Assistant: Take notes below.

_____

_____

_____

_____

_____

_____

_____

CREATE **Co-captain:** Get the materials. Then keep time. You have fifteen minutes.
Team: Create a website page about renting an apartment. Use the information from your notes. Add art if you want.

REPORT **Spokesperson:** Share your website page with the class. Describe your website.

COLLECT **Captains:** Collect the website design from each group. Staple the pages together to make a booklet about renting an apartment.

Unit 7   Used Car for Sale   DESIGN AN INTERNET AD

Materials
- large paper
- markers
- magazine or Internet car advertisements (optional)

TEAMS OF 4   Captain, Co-captain, Assistant, Spokesperson

GET READY   **Team:** Imagine you have a used car that you want to sell.
Captain: Ask your teammates to describe the car you're selling.
Co-captain: Keep time. You have ten minutes.
Assistant: Take notes in the chart.

Make and model	
Year	
Mileage	
Options	
Other information	

CREATE   **Co-captain:** Get the materials. Then keep time. You have fifteen minutes.
Team: Create an Internet ad for your car. Use the information from your chart. Add art if you want.

REPORT   **Spokesperson:** Share your ad with the class. Describe the car you want to sell.

Unit 8   How to Reduce Stress <u>MAKE A BOOKLET</u>

Materials
- 1 piece of white paper
- pens or markers
- stapler and staples

TEAMS OF 4 Captain, Co-captain, Assistant, Spokesperson

GET READY **Team:** Many people have a hard time staying relaxed with their busy and changing lives. This can cause stress. According to health experts, stress can affect our health in many ways. Discuss the health issues that can result from stress.
Captain: Ask your teammates to make suggestions for ways to reduce stress.
Co-captain: Keep time. You have ten minutes.
Assistant: Take notes below.

_____

_____

_____

_____

_____

_____

_____

CREATE **Co-captain:** Get the materials. Then keep time. You have fifteen minutes.
Team: Create a page for a booklet about reducing stress. Use the information from your notes. Include a paragraph about ways to reduce stress.

REPORT **Spokesperson:** Share your page with the class. Tell the class your suggestions.

COLLECT **Captains:** Collect the page from each group. Staple the pages together to make a booklet of suggestions on reducing stress.

Unit 9 After-School Programs <u>MAKE A BOOKLET</u>

Materials
- 4 pieces of white paper
- pens or markers

TEAMS OF 4 Captain, Co-captain, Assistant, Spokesperson

GET READY **Team:** Imagine you are on a parent committee at your child's school. It is your job to design an after-school program for elementary students.
Captain: Ask your teammates to suggest eight after-school activities—for example, chess, sports, art, language.
Co-captain: Keep time. You have ten minutes.
Assistant: Take notes below.

_____

_____

_____

_____

_____

_____

CREATE **Captain:** Get the materials. Then keep time. You have fifteen minutes.
Team: Create a booklet about the after-school program. Include a sentence or two about each activity. Add art if you want. (Each student writes about two activities.)

REPORT **Spokesperson:** Share your booklet with the class. Describe your after-school program.

COLLECT **Captains:** Collect the booklet from each group. Staple the pages together to make a booklet of after-school programs.

Unit 10   Problem at Work   WRITE AN ADVICE COLUMN

Materials
- 1 piece of white paper
- pens or markers
- stapler and staples

TEAMS OF 4   Captain, Co-captain, Assistant, Spokesperson

GET READY   **Team:** Discuss issues you or someone you know has had at work. What was the problem? What happened? How was the problem solved?

Captain: Ask your teammates to choose one of the issues that you discussed.

Co-captain: Keep time. You have ten minutes.

Assistant: Take notes below.

_____

_____

_____

_____

_____

_____

CREATE   **Co-captain:** Get the materials. Then keep time. You have twenty minutes.
Team: Write a short letter to an advice columnist about the work issue you chose. (Each student writes for three minutes. Then check and correct your work.)

CREATE MORE   **Team:** Exchange letters with another team. Imagine you are advice columnists. Write a short response to the other team's issue.

REPORT   **Spokesperson:** Show the other team's letter and your response to the class. Describe the issue and your team's advice.

COLLECT   **Captains:** Collect the letter and response from each group. Staple the letters together to make a booklet of advice on work problems.

Unit 11 Rights and Responsibilities MAKE A POSTER

TEAMS OF 4 Captain, Co-captain, Assistant, Spokesperson

GET READY **Team:** In this unit, you learned about people's rights when they are arrested for a crime in the United States. Discuss. What other *rights* do people living in the U.S. have? What *responsibilities* do they have?

Captain: Ask your teammates to list both rights and responsibilities in the United States.

Co-captain: Keep time. You have ten minutes.

Assistant: Take notes in the chart.

Materials
- large paper
- markers

Rights	Responsibilities

CREATE **Co-captain:** Get the materials. Then keep time. You have twenty minutes.
Team: Create a poster about rights and responsibilities in the United States. Use the information from your chart. Add art if you want.

REPORT **Spokesperson:** Share your poster with the class. Describe the rights and responsibilities you thought of.

Unit 12 A New Business <u>MAKE A POSTER</u>

TEAMS OF 4 Captain, Co-captain, Assistant, Spokesperson

GET READY **Team:** Imagine you are going to start your own business.
What are some kinds of businesses you might start?
Captain: Ask your teammates to decide on the kind of business
you are going to start. Have the team choose a name for the business
and think of the products or services you will offer.
Co-captain: Keep time. You have ten minutes.
Assistant: Take notes below.

_____

_____

_____

_____

_____

_____

Co-captain: Get the materials. Then keep time. You have fifteen minutes.
Team: Create a poster about your business. Use the information from your
notes. Add art if you want.

REPORT **Spokesperson:** Share your poster with the class. Describe your team's
business. Be enthusiastic!

Materials
• large paper
• markers

Employee's Report of Work-related Injury

To be completed immediately after the accident and submitted to your supervisor

Employee Name: _____ ID Number: _____

Male ☐ Female ☐ Date of Birth: _____ Marital Status: _____

Home Address: _____
                  Street   City   ZIP Code

Home Phone No. _____ Cell Phone No. _____

Job Title: _____

Employment Start Date: _____

Date of Accident: _____

Location of Accident: _____

Describe in detail how the accident occurred:

```



```

(describe the work you were engaged in, describe how the injury occurred, and explain the cause)

Part of body injured: _____
(be specific - example: right middle finger, left ankle, upper back)

Type of injury: _____
(example: sprain, burn and degree of burn, contusion, sutured)

Was medical treatment sought? If so: _____ _____
                        Name and address of medical provider   Phone Number

No. of days missed from work: _____

Return to work date (as stated by physician): _____

Type of leave used: _____

No. of days worked with restrictions: _____

Name of witness (es): _____ Phone No. _____

Was safety equipment provided? Yes ☐ No ☐

Was safety equipment used? Yes ☐ No ☐

Signature of employee: _____ Date: _____

Questions? Call 650-555-9827

MONTHLY BUDGET		
INCOME	EXPENSES	MONTHLY AMOUNT
Wages or Salary:	FIXED EXPENSES	
Other:	Mortgage or Rent:	
	Car	
	Loan Payments:	
	Insurance:	
	Other Insurance:	
	Home:	
	Life:	
	VARIABLE EXPENSES	
	Utilities	
	Electric:	
	Gas:	
	Water:	
	Telephone:	
	Cable or Satellite TV:	
	Internet Access:	
	Car Expenses	
	Gasoline:	
	Maintenance:	
	Medical Expenses	
	Medical Bills	
	Prescription Drugs	
	Other Transportation:	
	Food & Groceries:	
	Toiletries	
	School Supplies:	
	Entertainment:	
	Meals Out	
	Newspapers, Magazines:	
	Gifts:	
	Charity:	
	Other:	
TOTAL INCOME:	TOTAL EXPENSES:	

Form
1040EZ

Department of the Treasury—Internal Revenue Service
**Income Tax Return for Single and
Joint Filers With No Dependents**

2010

Label Use the IRS label. Otherwise please print or type.	L A B E L H E R E	Your first name and initial	Last name		Your social security number
		If a joint return, spouse's first name and initial	Last name		Spouse's social security number
		Home address (number and street).		Apt. no.	▲ You **must** enter your SSN(s) above.
		City, town or post office, state, and ZIP code.			

Presidential Election Campaign ▶   Check here if you, or your spouse if a joint return, want $3 to go to this fund . . . . ▶ ☐ You   ☐ Spouse

Income

Attach Form(s) W-2 here.
Enclose, but do not attach, any payment.

1	Wages, salaries, and tips. This should be shown in box 1 of your Form(s) W-2. Attach your Form(s) W-2.	1	
2	Taxable interest. If the total is over $1,500, you cannot use Form 1040EZ.	2	
3	Unemployment compensation and Alaska Permanent Fund dividends.	3	
4	Add lines 1, 2 and 3. This is your **adjusted gross income**.	4	
5	If someone can claim you (or your spouse if a joint return) as a dependent, check the applicable box(es) below and enter the amount from the worksheet on back. ☐ You ☐ Spouse If no one can claim you (or your spouse if a joint return), enter $8,750 if **single**; $17,500 if **married filing jointly**. See back for explanation.	5	
6	Subtract line 5 from line 4. If line 5 is larger than line 4, enter -0-. This is your **taxable income**. ▶	6	

Payments and tax

7	Federal income tax withheld from box 2 of your Form(s) W-2.	7	
8a	**Earned income credit (EIC).**	8a	
b	Nontaxable combat pay election 8b		
9	Add lines 7 and 8a. These are your **total payments**. ▶	9	
10	**Tax.** Use the amount on **line 6 above** to find your tax in the tax table on pages 18–26 of the booklet. Then, enter the tax from the table on this line.	10	

Refund
Have it directly deposited!

11a	If line 9 is larger than line 10, subtract line 10 from line 9. This is your refund.	11a	
▶b	Routing number		
▶			▶ c Type: ☐ Checking ☐ Savings
▶d	Account number		

Amount you owe

12	If line 10 is larger than line 9, subtract line 9 from line 10. This is the **amount you owe.** ▶	12	

Third party designee

Do you want to allow another person to discuss this return with the IRS? ☐ **Yes.** Complete the following. ☐ **No.**

Designee's name ▶   Phone no. ▶ ( )   Personal identification number (PIN) ▶ ☐☐☐☐☐

Sign here
Keep a copy for your records.

Under penalties of perjury, I declare that I have examined this return, and to the best of my knowledge and belief, it is true, correct, and accurately lists all amounts and sources of income I received during the tax year. Declaration of preparer (other than the taxpayer) is based on all information of which the preparer has any knowledge.

Your signature ▶	Date	Your occupation	Daytime phone number ( )
Spouse's signature. If a joint return, **both** must sign. ▶	Date	Spouse's occupation	

Paid preparer's use only

Preparer's signature ▶		Date	Check if self-employed ☐	Preparer's SSN or PTIN
Firm's name (or yours if self-employed), address, and ZIP code ▶		EIN		Phone no. ( )

Form **1040EZ** (2010)

Grammar Reference

UNIT 1, Lesson 2, page 8

Stative (non-action) verbs

Emotions
admire
adore
appreciate
care
dislike
doubt
fear
hate
like
love
regret
respect
trust

Possession and relationship
belong
contain
have
own
possess

Mental states
agree
assume
believe
consider
disagree
expect
guess
hope
imagine
know
mean
mind
realize
recognize
remember
see (understand)
suppose
think (believe)
understand
wonder

Wants and preferences
hope
need
prefer
want
wish

The senses
feel
hear
notice
see
smell
sound
taste

Appearance and value
appear
be
cost
equal
look (seem)
matter
represent
resemble
seem
weigh

Irregular verbs

Base form	Simple past	Past participle	Base form	Simple past	Past participle
awake	awoke	awoken	keep	kept	kept
be	was/were	been	know	knew	known
beat	beat	beaten	lead	led	led
become	became	become	leave	left	left
begin	began	begun	lend	lent	lent
bite	bit	bitten	let	let	let
blow	blew	blown	lose	lost	lost
break	broke	broken	make	made	made
build	built	built	mean	meant	meant
buy	bought	bought	meet	met	met
catch	caught	caught	pay	paid	paid
choose	chose	chosen	put	put	put
come	came	come	quit	quit	quit
cost	cost	cost	read	read	read
cut	cut	cut	ride	rode	ridden
dig	dug	dug	ring	rang	rung
do	did	done	run	ran	run
draw	drew	drawn	say	said	said
drink	drank	drunk	see	saw	seen
drive	drove	driven	sell	sold	sold
eat	ate	eaten	send	sent	sent
fall	fell	fallen	shake	shook	shaken
feed	fed	fed	sing	sang	sung
feel	felt	felt	sit	sat	sat
fight	fought	fought	sleep	slept	slept
find	found	found	speak	spoke	spoken
fly	flew	flown	spend	spent	spent
forget	forgot	forgotten	stand	stood	stood
forgive	forgave	forgiven	steal	stole	stolen
get	got	gotten	swim	wam	swum
give	gave	given	take	took	taken
go	went	gone	teach	taught	taught
grow	grew	grown	think	thought	thought
hang	hung	hung	throw	threw	thrown
have	had	had	understand	understood	understood
hear	heard	heard	upset	upset	upset
hide	hid	hidden	wake	woke	woken
hit	hit	hit	wear	wore	worn
hold	held	held	win	won	won
hur	hurt	hurt	write	wrote	written

Infinitives and Gerunds

Verbs followed by the infinitive (*to* + base form of verb)

agree	decide	mean	refuse
appear	deserve	need	request
arrange	expect	offer	seem
ask	fail	pay	volunteer
attempt	help	plan	wait
can('t) afford	hope	prepare	want
can('t) wait	learn	pretend	wish
choose	manage	promise	would like

Verbs followed by the gerund (base form of verb + *-ing*)

admit	escape	postpone
advise	explain	practice
appreciate	feel like	prohibit
avoid	finish	quit
can't help	forgive	recommend
consider	give up (stop)	regret
delay	imagine	report
deny	keep (continue)	risk
discuss	mention	suggest
dislike	mind	tolerate
enjoy	miss	understand

Verbs followed by the infinitive or the gerund

begin	hate	remember
can't stand	like	start
continue	love	stop
forget	prefer	try

UNIT 2, Lesson 5, page 34

Gerunds as Objects of Prepositions

Verb + Preposition

admit to	complain about	insist on	rely on
advise against	count on	keep on	resort to
apologize for	deal with	look forward to	succeed in
approve of	dream about/of	object to	talk about
believe in	feel like/about	pay for	think about
choose between/among	go along with	plan on	wonder about

Adjective + Preposition

afraid of	careful of	good at	satisfied with
amazed at/by	concerned about	happy about	shocked at/by
angry at	curious about	interested in	sick of
ashamed of	different from	nervous about	sorry for/about
aware of	excited about	opposed to	surprised at/about/by
awful at	famous for	ready for	terrible at
bad at	fed up with	responsible for	tired of
bored with/by	fond of	sad about	used to
capable of	glad about	safe from	worried about

UNIT 3, Lesson 2, page 48

Participial adjectives

-ed	-ing	-ed	-ing	-ed	-ing
alarmed	alarming	embarrassed	embarrassing	overwhelmed	overwhelming
amazed	amazing	encouraged	encouraging	pleased	pleasing
amused	amusing	excited	exciting	relaxed	relaxing
annoyed	annoying	exhausted	exhausting	satisfied	satisfying
bored	boring	fascinated	fascinating	shocked	shocking
confused	confusing	frightened	frightening	surprised	surprising
depressed	depressing	horrified	horrifying	terrified	terrifying
disappointed	disappointing	humiliated	humiliating	thrilled	thrilling
disgusted	disgusting	interested	interesting	tired	tiring
disturbed	disturbing	irritated	irritating	touched	touching

-ed Adjective + Preposition

alarmed at/by	disgusted with/by/at	frightened of/by	surprised at/about/by
amazed at/by	disturbed by	horrified at/by	terrified at/by
amused at/by	embarrassed by	interested in	thrilled at/with/by
bored with/by	encouraged by	irritated with/by	tired of
confused about/by	excited about	pleased with	touched at/by
depressed about	exhausted by	satisfied with	worried about
disappointed in/with	fascinated with/by	shocked at/by	

Phrasal verbs: Separable transitive

Phrasal verb	Meaning	Phrasal verb	Meaning
bring … up	*raise (children)*	look … up	*try to find (in a book, etc.)*
bring … up	*call attention to*	make … up	*invent*
call … back	*return a phone call*	pass … up	*decide not to use*
call … off	*cancel*	pay … back	*repay*
check … out	*examine*	pick … out	*choose*
cheer … up	*cause to feel happier*	pick … up	*lift; stop to get*
clean … up	*clean completely*	point … out	*indicate*
clear … up	*explain*	put … away	*put in an appropriate place*
close … down	*close by force*	put … back	*return to its original place*
cover … up	*cover completely*	put … off	*delay*
cross … out	*draw a line through*	put … together	*assemble*
cut … up	*cut into small pieces*	set … up	*prepare for use*
do … over	*do again*	shut … off	*stop (a machine, etc.)*
figure … out	*understand*	sign … up	*register*
fill … in	*complete with information*	start … over	*start again*
fill … out	*complete (a form)*	take … back	*return*
fill … up	*fill completely*	talk … into	*persuade*
find … out	*learn information*	talk … over	*discuss*
give … back	*return*	tear … down	*destroy*
give … up	*quit, abandon*	think … over	*consider*
hand … in	*submit*	throw … away	*put in the trash*
hand … out	*distribute*	turn … down	*lower the volume; reject*
help … out	*assist*	turn … off	*stop (a machine, etc.)*
leave … out	*omit*	turn … on	*start (a machine, etc.)*
let … down	*disappoint*	turn … up	*make louder*
look … over	*examine*	write … down	*write on a piece of paper*

Phrasal verbs: Inseparable transitive

Phrasal verb	Meaning	Phrasal verb	Meaning
count on	*depend on*	get over	*feel better after something bad*
fall for	*feel romantic love for*	look after	*take care of*
get off	*leave (a bus, train, etc.)*	look into	*investigate*
get on	*board (a bus, train, etc.)*	run into	*meet accidentally*
get through	*finish*	stick with	*not quit, not leave*

Phrasal verbs: Intransitive

Phrasal verb	Meaning	Phrasal verb	Meaning
act up	cause problems	go on	continue
break down	stop working (a machine)	go out	leave
catch on	become popular	grow up	become an adult
catch on	learn, understand	hang up	end a phone call
close down	stop operating	hold on	wait
come back	return	keep on	continue
come in	enter	keep up	go as fast as
dress up	wear special clothes	lie down	recline
drop in	visit by surprise	look out	be careful
drop out	quit	pay off	be worthwhile
eat out	eat in a restaurant	run out	not have enough of
end up	reach a final place or condition	show up	appear
find out	learn information	sign up	register
get ahead	make progress, succeed	sit down	take a seat
get along	have a good relationship	stand up	rise
get back	return	start over	start again
get off	leave (a bus, train, etc.)	stay up	remain awake
get on	board (a bus, train, etc.)	take off	depart (a plane)
get together	meet	turn out	have a particular result
get up	rise from bed	wake up	stop sleeping
give up	quit	watch out	be careful
go away	leave a place or person	work out	be resolved
go back	return	work out	exercise

UNIT 6, Lesson 8, p. 120

Reported speech: Changes to preserve meaning

Direct speech	Reported Speech
Lidia said, "**My** apartment **is** near the stairs."	Lidia said (that) **her** apartment **was** near the stairs.
The landlord told **us**, "**They didn't pay** last month's rent.	Tim's landlord told **us** (that) **they hadn't paid** last month's rent.
The building manager said, "**I've called** the plumber about the leak in **your** bathroom."	The building manager said (that) **he had called** the plumber about the leak in **my** bathroom.
The building manager told **me**, "The plumber **is fixing** the leak."	The building manager told me (that) the plumber **was fixing** the leak.
He explained, "**My** neighbor's dog **was barking** all night."	He explained (that) his neighbor's dog **had been barking** all night.
The tenants said, "**We've called** the landlord about that problem."	The tenants said (that) **they had called** the landlord about that problem.
The landlord replied, "**I'll call your** neighbor about the situation."	The landlord replied (that) **he would call our** neighbor about the situation.
My neighbor told **me**, "**You should send** a letter of complaint to the landlord!"	My neighbor told **me** (that) **I should send** a letter of complaint to the landlord.*

* Note: Do not change the modals *should, could, might,* and *ought to* when changing direct to reported speech.

UNIT 8, Lesson 5, page 154

Non-count nouns

Drinks	Food		Abstract ideas	School subjects	Other
coffee	beef	pasta	advice	art	furniture
juice	bread	pepper	beauty	ESL	homework
milk	broccoli	pie	fear	geography	information
soda	butter	rice	happiness	history	jewelry
tea	cereal	salad	help	language arts	mail
water	cheese	salt	love	math	medicine
	chicken	soup	luck	music	money
Community	chocolate	spinach	time	physical education	paper
problems	fish	sugar		science	
crime	fruit	yogurt		social studies	
garbage	ice cream			technology	
graffiti	jam/jelly			world languages	
noise	lettuce				
traffic	mayonnaise				
trash	meat				

UNIT 10, Lesson 5, page 194

Verbs and expressions used reflexively

allow oneself	be proud of oneself	help oneself	see oneself
amuse oneself	behave oneself	hurt oneself	take care of oneself
ask oneself	believe in oneself	introduce oneself	talk to oneself
be angry at oneself	cut oneself	keep oneself (busy)	teach oneself
be hard on oneself	dry oneself	look at oneself	tell oneself
be oneself	enjoy oneself	prepare oneself	treat oneself
be pleased with oneself	feel sorry for oneself	remind oneself	

Audio Script

UNIT 1

Page 6, Listen, Exercises A and C

Brenda: I need a burger, fries, and a garden salad.

Arturo: At 10:00 in the morning? I'm just making breakfast now. It's too early for lunch.

Brenda: Look, I agree, but that's what the customer wants. Can you do it?

Arturo: What the customer wants, the customer gets. Hey, I know you. You're Brenda. Brenda Kraig, right?

Brenda: Yes.

Arturo: I'm Arturo Pérez. My family lived next door to you on Juniper Street. Do you remember me?

Brenda: Arturo, hi. How are you? When did you start working at the Royale?

Arturo: About a year ago, but I usually work later. I'm a line cook six nights a week.

Brenda: So what are you doing here now? Where's Manny?

Arturo: Manny isn't working today. He's taking the day off to take care of some personal things.

Brenda: I hope nothing's wrong. But, hey, we can talk more during our break. Right now, my customer is waiting. I need the burger, fries, and salad.

Arturo: Coming right up.

Page 12, Listen, Exercises A and B

Brenda: Arturo, what are you reading?

Arturo: Some information I got from the Helman Culinary School. I'm starting cooking classes there next month.

Brenda: Why are you going to take cooking classes? You're already a cook.

Arturo: But I don't want to be a line cook forever. I want to become a sous-chef.

Brenda: A sous-chef? What's that?

Arturo: A sous-chef oversees just about everything that goes on in the kitchen and supervises the staff. That would be great preparation for what I'd really like to do.

Brenda: Which is what?

Arturo: Go out on my own! Ten years from now, I'd like to have my own restaurant.

Brenda: Wow! That's really ambitious. Are you going to quit your job at the Royale?

Arturo: No way! I have to keep my job.

Brenda: Hmmm … It won't be easy to work full time and go to school.

Arturo: I know, but I'll have bills to pay. Besides, I'll get a lot of great hands-on experience here.

Brenda: How long will it take to finish the culinary program?

Arturo: Two years. I'll take daytime classes and work in the evening.

Brenda: So you and I aren't going to have the same schedule anymore.

Arturo: Unfortunately, no. Manny will be back on his regular schedule next week, and I'll go back to my regular schedule after that.

Page 18, Listen, Exercises A and B

Hello, everyone. Welcome to "Real-Life Entrepreneurs." I'm your host, Holly Maxwell. This week, our show focuses on entrepreneurs in California.

Our guest today is Nadia Gorsky, founder of Grandma's Natural Frozen Soups. Nadia grew up in a three-generation household in northern California. When she was a child, her parents would go to work early in the morning, and Nadia's grandmother would watch her. Nadia used to help her grandmother around the house. In particular, Nadia used to help her grandmother make soup from her home country of Russia. One dish she often made was borscht, a beet soup usually served with sour cream.

Nadia's parents weren't able to finish high school, but they made sure that Nadia got a good education. They used to tell her that she could be anything she wanted to be. She received both a bachelor's and a master's degree in biology. Nadia's career goal was to be a nutritionist, and when she graduated, she got a job as a nutritionist at the local hospital planning healthy meals for the patients. But after a few years, Nadia realized that she wasn't satisfied. She began to dream about owning her own business.

In 2000, Nadia started Grandma's Natural Frozen Soups. The company makes and sells soups using all natural ingredients. Grandma's made almost a million dollars last year.

UNIT 2

Page 26, Listen, Exercises A and C

Catherine: Good afternoon. I'm Catherine Tote. I'm an employment specialist here at Sun County Career Center.

Nedim: Hello. I'm Nedim Buric. It's nice to meet you.

Catherine: People in Sun County come to our Career Center for many reasons—to learn English, to take training classes, to use our computer center. What brings you here today?

Nedim: I want to find a job as soon as possible.

Catherine: We can help you with that, Mr. Buric. But before we can start looking at available positions, there are several things we need to talk about.

Nedim: I'm sure you'd like to know about my work experience. I'm not employed at the moment. I came to the U.S. just last month. Before that, I was a university student in my home country, Bosnia.

Catherine: Do you have *any* job experience?

Nedim: Yes. My uncle is a lawyer. I worked in his office part time while I was in school.

Catherine: Do you have good computer skills?

Nedim: Yes. I've always been a fast learner when it comes to computers. I'm also a very organized person. I'm very careful with details, and I'm an excellent problem solver.

Catherine: I see. Did you finish school?

Nedim: Not yet. I studied for two years in Bosnia. But then I decided to come to the U.S. with my family. I expect to complete my degree in a year or so, in night school.

Page 32, Listen, Exercises A and B

Lisa: When I moved to the U.S. from Hong Kong twenty years ago, I didn't know anyone, and it was difficult for me to find a job. I tried looking in the newspaper, but there weren't a lot of things that I was capable of doing. I was really worried about not having enough money to live on when I finally saw a "Help Wanted" sign in the window of a flower shop. I went in and talked to the store manager, filled out an application, and started working the next day. I was lucky to get hired. It was difficult at that time to find out where the job openings were. Today, you have more ways to find a job. Just think about it … You can go online to look for work, and there are several job placement agencies in our neighborhood. But in my opinion, networking is the best thing you can do. You have family, and we have friends and neighbors who might be able to help you. You should think about talking to everyone you know to get information about possible jobs.

Page 38, Listen, Exercises A and B

Mr. Lee: Tell me a little about yourself, Mr. Santos. How long have you been a driver?

Mr. Santos: Ten years. I've worked for Trends Supermarkets since 2006. Before that, I was with Grand Supermarkets.

Mr. Lee: OK. I see from your application that you have a commercial driver's license and you've driven a number of different kinds of trucks.

Mr. Santos: That's right. And I've never had an accident.

Mr. Lee: That's excellent. So, if you don't mind my asking, why are you thinking about leaving your current employer-- Trends?

Mr. Santos: A couple of reasons. First of all, I want to work days. Most of the driving I do now is at night. Also, I think there will be more opportunities for me in a company like yours. I'm interested in working as a dispatcher someday.

Mr. Lee: So, in other words, you'd like to work in the office some day?

Mr. Santos: Yes. I think it would present a new and different kind of challenge. I think I'd be good as a dispatcher because I've had so much experience as a driver and I would understand the big picture. Plus I'm good with technology and I like to problem-solve.

UNIT 3

Page 46, Listen, Exercises A and B

Mali: Hi, Eric. I'm going to the Thai Festival this weekend. Do you want to come? My friends and I go every year.

Eric: The Thai Festival? What's that, Mali?

Mali: It's a celebration of the Thai New Year. It's on the first Sunday in April. Come on. You'll have fun.

Eric: Do you think so?

Mali: Definitely. It's really fun. There's traditional dancing and music. They have kick boxing demonstrations. There are stands with traditional Thai crafts.

Eric: Well, it sounds interesting…

Mali: Oh, and the food! The food is amazing! All the restaurants are open, but there are also stands with food.

Eric: Hmm. I love Thai food. It's really hot!

Mali: Oh, one thing. Kids might throw water at you. Don't be surprised.

Eric: You're kidding, right?

Mali: No! It's part of the tradition. People have water guns or containers of water and throw it at each other.

Eric: Wow. OK. So what time do you want to go?

Page 50, Listen, Exercises A and B

Jenna: Hello, Mrs. Suarez. This is Jenna Smith from the Hanson Park Community Center. I'm returning your call about our after-school program.

Raquel: Oh, hello! Thank you for getting back to me.

Jenna: Your message said you were looking for art classes and tutoring in reading for your daughter who is in the 7th grade.

Raquel: Yes. My daughter loves art but could also use help with her reading.

Jenna: We actually have reading tutors at the center every day. Many children need extra help with reading.

Raquel: That's great. What about art classes?

Jenna: Unfortunately, we don't have art classes right now.

Raquel: Too bad. Do you have other kinds of classes?

Jenna: Yes, we have a lot of sports activities because we're located inside Hanson Park. We offer gymnastics, swimming lessons, basketball, and tennis.

Raquel: Those sound great!

Jenna: Do you think your daughter would like to be involved in sports?

Raquel: I think she'd like tennis, but I'll ask her.

Jenna: OK. Do you have any other questions?

Raquel: Yes. Um, what are your hours?

Jenna: We start classes right after school—at 3:00—and the last class ends at 7 P.M.

Raquel: So, my daughter could take classes from 3:00 to 7:00.

Jenna: Yes, that's right.

Raquel: What do I have to do to enroll her?

Jenna: You have to come to the center and fill out an application.

Raquel: Are there any fees?

Jenna: Our center is a partnership with the public school system, so no, there are no fees. All our classes are free.

Raquel: That's wonderful!

Page 51, Listen, Exercise B

Raquel: I'd like to come to the center after work today to fill out an application.

Jenna: Sure.

Raquel: Can you give me directions to the center?

Jenna: Yes. Where are you coming from?

Raquel: From work . . . 82 Vine Street . . . near the water.

Jenna: You're pretty close to us. First, you need to drive north on Vine Street.

Raquel: OK.

Jenna: Then you'll make a right on Route 10 and travel east.

Raquel: Uh-huh.

Jenna: Then you're going to make a left on Hanson Park Drive and travel two miles north. We're at 1200 Hanson Park Drive.

Raquel: What is your nearest cross-street?

Jenna: Our nearest cross-street is Memorial Boulevard.

Raquel: Great. Thank you. I'll see you around 6:30.

Jenna: I look forward to meeting you.

Page 52, Listen, Exercises A and B

Jamil: I wish the city would do something about cleaning up the park in our neighborhood. There's trash everywhere, and there's graffiti on all the benches.

Linlin: You know, when I go downtown, everything is nice and clean. I wish the Streets and Sanitation Department didn't spend all of their time downtown. I wish they would come to our neighborhood once in a while.

Jamil: They want things to look good downtown for the businesses and tourists, but you have a point. What about us? We pay taxes, too.

Linlin: And it's not just the streets and parks. I wish I had better garbage pick-up at my house. I'm never sure which day of the week the garbage truck is going to come, and last week they never came at all.

Jamil: Did you complain?

Linlin: I had no choice. But there was still no garbage pick-up until yesterday.

Jamil: We have the same problem. I keep calling to complain about it and about the vacant lot on the corner of Lawrence Avenue and River Street.

Linlin: The amount of trash in that vacant lot is horrible. It's a health hazard. Where does it all come from?

Jamil: Hmm, I think a lot of it is from the fast-food restaurants on Lawrence. The teenagers who go there eat their burgers and fries and throw the empty containers in the vacant lot.

Linlin: What are they doing hanging out by the vacant lot? They should be in school.

Jamil: And after school, they should be going to the community center. I just wish there were more after-school programs in the community.

Page 58, Listen, Exercises A and B

Clara Ramos: Thank you for coming here to meet with me this evening. As your City Council representative, it's my job to listen to the concerns of the community.

Hugo Lopez: Most of us in the neighborhood want to have better services. We don't want the city to take away services that we already have.

Clara Ramos: Exactly what services are you talking about, sir?

Hugo Lopez: The last time we met with you, we asked you to increase the number of police officers at the Southland District Police Station. Instead, the station is closing. Do you expect us to be happy with that decision?

Clara Ramos: Please, sir. I urge you not to believe everything you hear. The police station isn't closing. I spoke with the mayor and the chief of police. I couldn't convince them to provide more patrol officers, but don't worry. We have a plan.

Hugo Lopez: Let's hear it. We'd like you to explain how we can reduce the crime in this area.

Clara Ramos: The idea is to expand our community-policing program in the Southland District.

Hugo Lopez: Do you mean that we do the work instead of the police?

Clara Ramos: No, of course not. The program encourages neighborhood residents to work *with* the police to identify problems and find solutions. The police will still investigate specific incidents, but with community policing, they expect to see fewer crimes.

Hugo Lopez: I see. Because we can help the police identify problems before the crimes occur?

Clara Ramos: Exactly. The first meeting of the Southland Community Policing Program will take place next week. How many people in this room plan to attend?

UNIT 4

Page 66, Listen, Exercises A, B, and C

Robert: Welcome to People's Bank. I'm sure you'll like working here. Are you ready to get started?

Sandra: Yes. I'll just be observing you today, right?

Robert: That's right. For the first week, you'll be observing. By the end of the week, you should be ready to take over some duties and handle some customer needs on your own.

Sandra: Great. It'll be helpful to see the bank's procedures firsthand.

Robert: That's the idea. Let's start with deposits. This will be for a personal, not a business, account.

Sandra: Do many customers deposit cash?

Robert: No. Most deposits are checks, so let's talk about that. Make sure the customer endorses each check and fills out the deposit slip completely.

Sandra: With their name and address, right?

Robert: Yes, but pay special attention to the money amount on the deposit slip. It must be the same as the amount of the check. Then look for the customer's bank-account number and ask whether it's a savings or a checking account.

Sandra: And how do I print a receipt?

Robert: After you enter the amount of the deposit into the computer, put both the check and the deposit slip through this machine. It'll automatically print a receipt.

Sandra: Got it!

Robert: Well, it's almost one o'clock. We can pick up after lunch. How does this all seem to you so far?

Sandra: OK … I'm a little nervous, but I'll get over it.

Page 72, Listen, Exercises A, B, and C

Conversation 1

Doctor: So, how is Mr. Cordova doing today?

Resident: He's doing well. Let me take a look at his chart. Carolina, could you please give me Mr. Cordova's chart?

Carolina: Here it is.

Resident: Thank you. Hmm. I don't see any recent vital signs. Carolina, didn't someone take Mr. Cordova's vital signs this morning?

Carolina: Mercedes was the nursing assistant on duty this morning. I thought she did but you're right, they're not here. Maybe she forgot to record them. I'll take Mr. Cordova's vitals right now.

Resident: Thanks, Carolina.

Conversation 2

Doctor: How is Mrs. Worth doing?

Resident: She's coming along. Carolina, how many times has Mrs. Worth been out of bed since her gall bladder operation?

Carolina: She got up once and sat in the chair for an hour.

Resident: She had the procedure yesterday. She needs to start walking. Haven't any of the nurses tried to take her down the hall?

Carolina: There aren't a lot of nurses on the floor right now, but I'll walk with her down the hall as soon as I finish my rounds.

Resident: OK, good. Thank you.

Page 78, Listen, Exercises A and B

Dennis: Hi, Helena. How are you today?

Helena: Just fine, thanks. I'm a little nervous, though.

Dennis: Oh, you don't need to be nervous. The performance review is a conversation, really.

Helena: OK.

Dennis: First of all, I want you to know that we're happy in general with your work.

Helena: Oh, thank you!

Dennis: Yes, the quality of your work is very good. You're meeting your quotas, which is really important. I gave you a "3" in both categories.

Helena: Thank you. I understand how important it is to get all the packages out on time.

Dennis: Exactly. And you're good at following instructions. I gave you a "3" there, too.

Helena: Sometimes I have to ask for clarification…

Dennis: That's great. You should always ask if you're not sure. It's better to ask than to do the wrong thing.

Helena: OK. Good.

Dennis: I know you also have a positive attitude. That's really important.

Helena: Thanks. I agree. It makes things more pleasant when people are positive.

Dennis: I really appreciate that you work well with your co-workers. I've noticed that you often volunteer to help them if you finish your work early. You deserve the "4" I gave you for teamwork.

Helena: I enjoy working with everyone. I like being part of a team.

Dennis: Well, it shows. So I think the only thing that we need to talk about is the issue of clothing, well, jewelry and shoes, really. I had to give you a "2" in safety procedures. Employees are supposed to leave earrings and rings at home and not wear jewelry on the job. Yesterday you were wearing a long necklace that could have gotten caught in the machinery. And the other day, you were wearing sandals. You know that company policy requires all employees to wear shoes that will protect their feet and prevent them from slipping and falling if the floors are wet.

Helena: I'm so sorry. I stopped wearing my earrings and rings, but I didn't realize that I couldn't wear a necklace. It won't happen again. And I know about the shoes. I just forgot. I understand. Safety is very important.

UNIT 5

Page 86, Listen, Exercises A and B

Thank you all for being here this evening. I'm happy to see that so many people are concerned about fire safety. Tonight's class will focus on what you can do to prevent a fire in your home. Let's begin with a room that's very important in many homes—the kitchen.

Cooking is the number-one cause of house fires in the U.S. When you're in the kitchen, pay attention to what you're doing. Keep hair and clothing away from fire, and keep your cooking areas clean. If a pan of food catches fire, immediately put a lid over it and turn the stove off. Also remember to turn off the stove and oven when you finish preparing your food. And never leave the kitchen while food is still cooking on the stove. Remember that it takes only a few seconds for a fire to start.

If you have children, you should be extra careful. They're curious, so they'll want to know what's going on in the kitchen. Teach children not to touch anything on the stove.

Now, are there any questions before I go on?

Page 92, Listen, Exercises A, B, and C

Henry Ponce: Today we're discussing hurricanes with meteorologist Dr. Kay Wilkins. Dr. Wilkins, welcome.

Dr. Wilkins: Thank you, Henry. It's a pleasure to be here.

Henry Ponce: Let's begin with the basics. I know that hurricane season in the U.S. is during the summer months.

Dr. Wilkins: You're right, Henry, but not completely. Officially, hurricane season in the Atlantic Ocean is from June 1 through November 30. Most hurricanes will occur during these six months, but there have also been bad storms in May and December.

Henry Ponce: Tell me, Dr. Wilkins. What's the most important thing that everyone should know about hurricanes?

Dr. Wilkins: To take them seriously. Some people refuse to leave their homes during a hurricane. When the National Weather Service orders an evacuation, pay attention. Follow the evacuation order and go to a safe location.

Henry Ponce: Um hmm. There are very powerful winds and heavy rain during a hurricane. What are some of the other dangers?

Dr. Wilkins: Flooding is a major concern. In addition to the heavy rains, people who live along the coast should be prepared for high waves.

Henry Ponce: What about people who live inland? Do they have to worry about hurricanes?

Dr. Wilkins: Hurricanes get their power over water, so coastal areas are usually the hardest hit. After they hit land, hurricanes lose strength. But they can also cause damage in inland areas.

Henry Ponce: Can you explain the difference between a hurricane watch and a hurricane warning for our listeners?

Dr. Wilkins: I get that question a lot. The National Weather Service issues a hurricane watch when there is the possibility of a hurricane within the next 36 hours. The watch means that you should pay attention and begin to prepare for the severe weather.

Henry Ponce: Um hmm. I see. And a hurricane warning?

Dr. Wilkins: A hurricane warning means that you can expect a hurricane to arrive in your area within 24 hours. As soon as you hear the warning, make sure that your emergency preparations are complete.

Page 98, Listen, Exercises A and B

Hello. I'm emergency medical technician Iris Chen, and I want to remind you about Emergency Medical Services Week—EMS Week. During this week, please take time to honor 911 operators, EMTs, and other emergency personnel who provide our city with lifesaving services. Also use EMS Week as an opportunity to make sure that everyone in your family, including young children, knows how to make a 911 call.

In an emergency, some people may not think clearly, so be prepared. Put the 911 number and your own number next to every phone in your home. Then practice. With your phone turned off, show your family how to dial 911, and demonstrate what to do during the call. Stay calm and speak slowly. Explain what the emergency is in as few words as possible. Give information about whether there is anyone who is bleeding, unconscious, or not breathing. Give the location of the emergency. Listen carefully, and answer the operator's questions. Finally, don't hang up until the operator tells you to hang up.

Help us help you. A 911 call could save the life of someone you love.

UNIT 6

Page 106, Listen, Exercises A, B, C, and D

Mother: So, tell me about the apartment. It has three bedrooms?
Jessica: Yes. They're small, but that's OK.
Mother: You said the rent is $1200? Are utilities included?
Jessica: Water is included. So we just have to pay for gas and electricity.
Mother: How much was the security deposit?
Jessica: One month's rent--$1200. Between the three of us, we'll manage it. It'll be only $400 apiece.
Mother: All right. I might be able to help you a little with that.
Jessica: That'd be a big help, Mom.
Mother: So, remember, keep everything nice and clean. Be sure not to damage anything.
Jessica: Damage anything? Mom, don't worry. We won't damage anything.
Mother: Well, not on purpose you wouldn't. But you could by accident. And then, when you move out, the landlord will keep your security deposit.
Jessica: Oh Mom, stop worrying, we'll be careful.
Mother: I hope you have quiet neighbors.
Jessica: I know. Me, too. Well, at least there won't be any barking dogs. Tenants aren't allowed to have pets.
Mother: That's good. Now, what else can I worry about?

Page 112, Listen, Exercises A and B

Henry: Welcome to This Week. I'm your host Henry Sullivan. Our guest today is Manuel Rodriguez, a tenant rights lawyer. Today Manuel is going to answer questions on tenant law in Texas. Manuel, it's nice to have you back on our show.
Manuel: Thanks, Henry. Glad to be here.

Henry: Listeners, do you have problems with your landlord? If you do, give us a call. The number is 1-800-555-3333. ...Ah, I see we have our first caller. Armando from Dallas, you're on the air.
Caller 1: Hi, Manuel. The smoke alarms in my apartment don't work anymore. I called the landlord several times but he never called me back. He has to replace the smoke detectors, doesn't he?
Manuel: Yes, in Texas, the landlord is required to put a working smoke detector outside each bedroom. But if the smoke detectors stop working, you have to notify the landlord in writing. Send your landlord a letter explaining the problem. Make sure to keep a copy of the letter.
Caller 1: I'll do that. Thank you, Manuel!

Page 112, Listen, Exercise C

Henry: Now for our next caller. Carla in San Antonio, you're on the air.
Caller 2: Hi, Manuel. My landlord is going to raise my rent to $700 a month. I can't afford to pay that much, and I'll have to move. Is he allowed to do that?
Manuel: How much time is left on your lease?
Caller 2: Six months. It's a one-year lease and it'll be up on September 1st.
Manuel: And have you ever paid your rent late or damaged the apartment?
Caller 2: No, I haven't. I'm a good tenant.
Manuel: It sounds like your lease is still in effect. That means the landlord is *not* allowed to raise your rent until after September 1st. But after that date, you'll have to sign a new lease, and he can raise the rent.
Caller 2: Oh well. At least I have six months to find a new apartment! Thanks, Manuel!

Page 118, Listen, Exercises A and B

Oscar: What's that noise? It's so loud.
Marta: The neighbors are watching TV.
Oscar: Which neighbors? The ones in 2A?
Marta: No, 2C.
Oscar: What's their name?
Marta: I don't remember. I've only seen them in the hallway.
Oscar: Well, I'm going over there and telling them they have to turn down the TV. We just got the baby to sleep.
Marta: I already went over there.
Oscar: You did?
Marta: Yes, I told them the baby was sleeping and I asked them if they could be quieter.
Oscar: What did they say?
Marta: They didn't say anything. They slammed the door in my face.
Oscar: What! I'm going over there right now!
Marta: Oscar, don't lose your temper. Yelling at them won't do any good. Let me call the building manager.
Oscar: What can he do?
Marta: He can call them and remind them about the building rules—no loud TV or music after 10 P.M. They might listen to him. He also said we could call the police if there's noise after 10 P.M.

Oscar: I'm not calling the police about noise. I'll go over there and settle it myself.

Marta: OK, fine, but let me call the building manager first. It's better if we let him handle it.

UNIT 7

Page 126, Listen, Exercises A and B

Eva: Mark, did you have a chance to look at the auto section this morning? Some of the ads looked interesting.

Mark: Yeah, … but some of the new cars are really expensive. I'm looking at these used-car ads from Tri-State Motors now.

Eva: Oh! I was looking at the used-car ads, too. There were some from dealers and others from private owners. Who would you rather buy from, a dealer or a private owner?

Mark: A dealer. We can get a warranty from a dealership but not from an individual seller.

Eva: You're right—good point. Does Tri-State have any of the models we're looking for—a compact that gets good gas mileage?

Mark: As a matter of fact they do. There are a few here with the features we want: four-doors with power steering, CD player, and air-conditioning. We can live without a sunroof, but air-conditioning is a must.

Eva: Don't forget about the safety features. We've got to have airbags.

Mark: Absolutely. With the newer cars, front airbags are standard, but we should look for a car that has side airbags—and antilock brakes, too.

Eva: I agree.

Mark: I just realized that we've never talked about color. Would you rather have a light color or a dark color—like black, maybe?

Eva: Hmm … Well, now that I think about it, I've always wanted to drive a *red* car.

Mark: Red, huh? I read somewhere that red cars get more speeding tickets.

Eva: Really? Hmm. How about this … Let's start looking and we'll see what's out there and what kind of deal we can get. Then we'll worry about the color.

Page 131, Practice, Exercise A

Amy: I'm thinking of buying a car.

Tom: Congratulations! Will it be your first car?

Amy: Yes, it will—well, at least in this country. I know you have to have insurance here when you own a car, but I really have no idea how to go about getting it. What did you do?

Tom: When I was shopping for my car, a friend of mine gave me the name and number of a good car insurance company. You can try them. I use All Country.

Amy: OK. I'll check them out. And I'm sure I can find information about other insurance companies on the Internet.

Tom: Good idea! You could also look through the yellow pages of the phone book.

Amy: Great. Thanks for the help.

Page 131, Practice, Exercises C and D

Amy: I'm ready to call and get a quote for car insurance.

Tom: Good. Are you ready for all the questions they'll ask?

Amy: I thought I would be asking most of the questions.

Tom: Actually, your premium will depend on how you answer some of their questions.

Amy: Really? What kinds of things will they ask?

Tom: They'll want to know what kind of car you drive. If you own a sports car, for example, the premium is usually higher.

Amy: OK. What else will they ask? How about safety features? A salesperson at the used-car lot told me that having lots of safety features would probably help keep my premium low.

Tom: Yes. That's true. And they'll want to know how many miles you expect to drive each year.

Amy: How can I predict how many miles I'll drive?

Tom: It's just a guess. Premiums are usually higher for people who drive a lot.

Amy: OK. Is there anything else I should know?

Tom: They'll probably ask you if you're single or married and also your age.

Amy: Why do my marital status and my age make a difference?

Tom: I think there are statistics that show that older, married people have fewer accidents.

Page 132, Listen, Exercises A and B

This is Jake Alexander, and you're listening to *All Things Auto*. It's time for our Car Care Question of the Week. I have an e-mail here from Nicole. Nicole writes, "Can you tell me what your number-one car-care tip is?" Well, listeners, when it comes to car maintenance, there's one thing you should always remember, and that is "Don't delay. Do it today." Of course, you should change the oil regularly. For most cars, that's every three months or every 3,000 miles. But there are other things that you should do regularly, too. Your car's tires are very important for your safety, so inspect them once a month. Check the tread, and check the air pressure. If you don't know how much air your tires should have, look in your owner's manual. Finally, check for leaks once a week. Look under the hood and under your car. And look for color. For example, transmission fluid is red. Engine coolant is bright green or yellow, and oil is light brown. If you see a problem, take your car to a good mechanic right away. Fix small problems before they become serious. It's impossible to say exactly how many years this will add to the life of your car, but you'll definitely save money and you'll have a vehicle that's safer and easier to drive. Remember, listeners—"Don't delay. Do it today!"

Page 138, Listen, Exercises A, B, and C

Nora: Are you OK? You aren't hurt, are you?

Frank: No, I'm fine. Are you all right?

Nora: Yes, but I can't say the same for my car. The right headlight is out, and there are huge dents in the hood and fender.

Frank: I don't know what happened. I'd already started moving into the right lane when I saw you. By that time, there was nothing I could do. I remember putting on my turn signal and looking for cars coming from the opposite direction, but I didn't see any cars.

Nora: I didn't see you either—until the very last minute. I had just slowed down because of the rain, but there still wasn't enough time for me to stop. You know, we should pull the cars to the side of the road. Now, where's my cell phone?

Frank: Are you going to call the police? I think we should do that.

Nora: Yes. We have to report the accident. It's the law. Besides, our insurance companies will definitely want a police report. You have insurance, don't you?

Frank: Of course. My insurance card and my driver's license and vehicle registration are in the car. I'll get them.

Nora: I'll get mine, too. Oh, by any chance, do you have a camera?

Frank: Why do we need a camera?

Nora: Well, my insurance agent told me to take pictures if I were ever involved in an accident.

Frank: That's a good idea. Actually, my cell phone has a camera. I'll get it.

UNIT 8

Page 146, Listen, Exercises A and C

Dr. Kim: Good morning, Mrs. Garcia. What brings you here today?

Irma Garcia: To tell you the truth, Doctor, I haven't been feeling well for the past couple of weeks.

Dr. Kim: What seems to be the problem?

Irma Garcia: For one thing, I can't sleep at night. I have a lot of congestion, so I can't breathe.

Dr. Kim: Anything else?

Irma Garcia: Yes. I feel achy. My whole body hurts! Oh, and I've been sneezing a lot lately.

Dr. Kim: Hmm … And you say this has been going on for about two weeks?

Irma Garcia: Right. At first, I thought I had a cold, but now I'm worried that it's something more serious.

Dr. Kim: I think you might have an allergy. The question is what's causing it. Is there anything different about where you live or work?

Irma Garcia: No, my husband and I live in the same house, and I still work in our family business.

Dr. Kim: OK. What about your diet? Have you been eating any new kinds of food?

Irma Garcia: Well, I eat the same food as always, but I've been cooking a lot more since my daughter came home from college a few weeks ago.

Dr. Kim: Aha! That could be the answer.

Irma Garcia: What? You think I'm allergic to my daughter?

Dr. Kim: No, Mrs. Garcia. Not your daughter, but maybe something your daughter brought into the house, such as perfume or a houseplant. We'll do a few tests to find out for sure.

Page 152, Listen, Exercises A and B

Operator: 911, what is your emergency?

Caller: I need an ambulance here.

Operator: OK. Where are you located?

Caller: 136 Elm Street.

Operator: OK. The paramedics are on their way. Can you tell me what's going on?

Caller: It's my husband and he's … I don't know, he's having chest pain. And he's sweating, really badly.

Operator: Is he conscious or unconscious?

Caller: He's conscious . . but he's having so much chest pain it's hard for him to breathe.

Operator: Try to stay calm. You need to help him until the paramedics get there. How old is your husband?

Caller: 58.

Operator: Does he have any ongoing medical problems?

Caller: Yes, he has diabetes.

Operator: Is he taking medication for that?

Caller: Yes.

Operator: Is he on any other medication?

Caller: No, I don't think so. Are the paramedics almost here?

Operator: Yes, help is on the way. You're doing great. Just continue to watch him. Call again if anything changes before the paramedics get there.

Page 158, Listen, Exercises A and B

The end of summer is almost here, and that means more than getting notebooks, pencils, and clothing for the new school year. School officials say that parents should not wait until the last minute to get their children the immunizations they'll need. State law requires specific vaccinations for all students entering school for the first time and for students in pre-school programs, kindergarten, grade 5, and grade 9. This is a reminder that student immunization records must be updated no later than September 15. Parents ought to have their children immunized now to avoid the early September rush. It's very important to make the September 15th deadline.

As part of a back-to-school effort, health clinics around the city will be offering free vaccination services. In addition, the annual Health for Life Fair will take place this weekend. Among the many activities at the health fair will be free medical check-ups for children ages 5 through 12 and free immunizations. All events and services will be in the Downtown Civic Center from 10:00 AM until 6:00 PM on Saturday and from noon until 6:00 PM on Sunday. For more information, look in the health news section of your local newspaper, or visit the Radio WDKM website at www.wdkm.com.

UNIT 9

Page 166, Listen, Exercises A and C

Mr. Bowman: Thanks for coming to my office today, Mrs. Adamski. I know you took time off from work to meet with me. I want to talk to you about your daughter.

Mrs. Adamski: Monika? Oh, Monika is a good student. My son has some problems with his grades, but not Monika.

Mr. Bowman: Oh, yes. Your daughter is an excellent student! And that's exactly why I want to talk with you. Since Monika will start high school next fall, it's time to start thinking about college.

Mrs. Adamski: College? Uh, Monika is only 13 years old. College is a long way off.

Mr. Bowman: Well, yes and no.

Mrs. Adamski: What do you mean, "Yes and no"?

Mr. Bowman: It's never too early to start thinking about college. I'd like Monika to have as many opportunities as possible, because she is one of our best students.

Mrs. Adamski: Thank you.

Mr. Bowman: But when I talk to Monika about college, she isn't interested, because she thinks she can't afford it.

Mrs. Adamski: Well, my husband and I can take care of our family, but we don't make a lot of money.

Mr. Bowman: Many schools offer scholarships and financial aid to help students pay for their education.

Mrs. Adamski: Oh, really? How can we make sure Monika gets a scholarship?

Mr. Bowman: Well, there are no guarantees. But the first thing to do is talk to Monika about classes that will prepare her for college.

Mrs. Adamski: OK, and I'd like to make another appointment with you. Next time I'll bring my husband so that we can both talk to you about scholarships and financial aid.

Page 172, Listen, Exercises A, B, and C

Secretary: Good morning. How can I help you?

Mr. Lopez: Hello. I'm Pablo Lopez, and this is my daughter, Marta. I need to enroll Marta in school. We just moved here.

Secretary: Oh, yes. You're the one I spoke with on the phone last week. Marta finished first grade at Newtown Elementary, right?

Mr. Lopez: Yes, that's right. She's ready for second grade.

Secretary: OK, I can help you get her enrolled. Do you have proof that you live in School District 15? For example, can you show me the lease for your new apartment?

Mr. Lopez: I don't have a lease, but I brought an electric bill that has my name and address on it.

Secretary: Perfect. Now, I'll need a few other things from you. Do you have Marta's school records from Newtown?

Mr. Lopez: Yes. I also brought her birth certificate and her medical and dental records.

Secretary: Excellent. I'll also need a phone number that we can call if there's an emergency. Here's a form you can fill out with that information.

Mr. Lopez: OK.

Secretary: And here's a list of school supplies—pencils, notebooks, and folders—which your daughter has to bring with her to class.

Mr. Lopez: Thank you.

Secretary: You're welcome. Let me know if you have any questions.

Page 178. Listen, Exercises A and B

I want to welcome you to the first meeting of this advisory committee. Before we do anything else, I'd like to explain the purpose of the committee.

Because he has talked about it so many times, you must have heard about the mayor's plan to improve school safety. He could not have come up with this plan without the support of parents' advisory committees all over the city. The plan requires all schools to identify five improvements to keep students safe and to create a better atmosphere for learning. I am asking you as advisory committee members to assist me in preparing a school safety plan for West Apollo Elementary School.

Every person in this room has something to contribute to our plan. Some of you are parents, and your children might have talked to you about problems at school. Some of you live near here, so you are familiar with problems in the neighborhood. The teachers in this group are familiar with how students behave in classrooms, in the cafeteria, and on the playground. Any one of you may have thought about changes that we should make in our procedures and school buildings. I hope all of you will contribute your ideas to our safety plan.

UNIT 10

Page 186, Listen, Exercises A and B

Sam: Oleg, have you finished the cabinets yet?

Oleg: I'm sorry, Sam. The supplier was out of the wood. It just came in yesterday.

Sam: Then we're a week behind schedule! Why didn't you tell me there was a problem with the supplier?

Oleg: I did. I called your office and left a message on your machine.

Sam: Why didn't you call the cell phone?

Oleg: I did. I called three times, but no one picked up. I even had Boris call you from the van.

Sam: Never mind . . . Now listen. You've got to finish the cabinets. How soon do you think you'll be done?

Oleg: Two weeks.

Sam: Come on. Can't you do it in a week and a half?

Oleg: Well, I need two weeks to make quality cabinets. You want me to do a good job, don't you?

Sam: OK, you're right. Two weeks. In the meantime, you need to let the counter guy measure space for the counter.

Oleg: Oh, sure. No problem.

Page 192, Listen, Exercises A, B, and C

Asad: Wait, Claudia! Don't turn on the press yet!

Claudia: What's the matter?

Asad: You can't wear a bracelet when you're operating the press. . . . See those moving rollers? Your bracelet could get caught in the roller. You could hurt yourself very badly.

Claudia: Oh. I'll take it off right now.

Asad: Didn't you go to the safety training?

Claudia: I did. But I thought they just said no loose clothing.

Asad: Or jewelry, like bracelets and necklaces. These machines are dangerous. Did you read the safety manual yet?

Claudia: Yes, of course, but I don't remember everything it said.

Asad: I see. OK. Let's do a safety check. I always do a safety check before I start. First, make sure the guards are all on the machine. Make sure you're not wearing long sleeves or jewelry. Keep your hands a safe distance from the rollers. OK, now it looks like you're ready to start. I'm going to watch you work for a while to make sure you're working safely.

Claudia: Thanks so much, Asad!

Asad: You're welcome.

Page 198, Listen, Exercises A and B

Don: Hi, Lisa. Could I talk to you for a minute?

Lisa: Oh, sure. Umm, is everything OK?

Don: Yes! Here, have a seat. I want to talk to you about your future with Parcel Movers.

Lisa: Oh, thanks! That's great.

Don: You've been doing an excellent job. Let's see. You started out with us six months ago as a sorter… You're very efficient. I can see you're moving 400 packages in an hour.

Lisa: Thank you.

Don: And you're accurate. I see you've made mistakes with only three packages in three months.

Lisa: I try my best.

Don: Also, when your co-workers need help, you try to help them.

Lisa: Well, thanks. I guess we're all part of a team.

Don: The other thing that's important is safety practices. You follow the safety practices you learned in the safety training course.

Lisa: Well, safety is important. I don't want to get hurt!

Don: Right, everyone wants to be safe. But you're especially conscientious. Vikram told me that you saw him lifting the wrong way and warned him . . .that's the kind of thing we like to see in a supervisor. So . . . I'm promoting you to the position of training supervisor.

Lisa: . . .Oh, wow! That's great . . .

Don: You'll be responsible for seven employees, starting on the 12th. Why don't you come to my office tomorrow morning—let's say at 10:15?—and I'll give you more details.

Lisa: Thank you, Don. I'm really excited to have this opportunity.

Don: You're welcome. You earned it.

UNIT 11

Page 206, Listen, Exercises A and B

Solange: David, what's the matter? You don't look so good.

David: I'm all right . . .but something happened last night that shook me up a little. While I was watching the 10 o'clock news, I got a call on my cell. When I picked up, I thought it would be Caroline telling me she was on her way home. But it was the police.

Solange: The police?

David: Yes, they had Caroline at the police station!

Solange: The police picked up *Caroline*?

David: It-it was OK. You know, when they first told me she was there I panicked—what was wrong—what might have happened—but she was fine, and she hadn't done anything wrong. —She'd just been out a little too late. There's a curfew for teenagers now in the city. After 10 PM, no kids below the age of 18 are allowed downtown. It was around 10:15 . . . Caroline and her friends had just been to the movies and were on their way home. An officer came by and picked them up for violating a city ordinance.

Solange: I didn't know there was a curfew.

David: Neither did I. But when I got to the station, the cops were very nice. While I was waiting, they explained the reasons for the ordinance.

Solange: Like what?

David: There have been some incidents downtown after dark. Someone got robbed. The curfew is meant to keep kids from being victims of crime.

Solange: I had no idea. I'd better tell Fabiola about the curfew. I don't want her getting into trouble or getting robbed.

David: Yeah. I told Caroline she has to be home by 10 PM in the future.

Page 212, Listen, Exercises A and B

Lisa: Alex! Don't tell me you're watching that program again.

Alex: What do you mean? What's wrong with this program?

Lisa: It's garbage.

Alex: How can you call it garbage? This program is watched by millions of people all over the country. It shows how the law works.

Lisa: Oh, do you really believe that? There's no real law on that show, just people complaining about their relationships.

Alex: Oh, come on, Lisa.

Lisa: Those aren't real cases at all—those stories are all made up. And they certainly aren't heard by real judges. They're all actors …

Alex: Ah ah ah not true—some of the shows are real cases. Or they're based on real ones.

Lisa: Oh, brother.

Alex: Listen to this case that was just on. It's really interesting. There were two roommates. One roommate was behind on his car payments, and the bank was going to repossess his car. So he got his roommate to lend him $2,000 for the car payment.

Lisa: Uh—not a good idea.

Alex: Uh, yeah! You're right about that! The roommates got into a big fight and moved out. And the guy with the car didn't pay back the $2,000 he owed his roommate. So they went to court, and the case was decided by a judge. He said to the guy who loaned his friend the money, "Well, your friend has to pay you the money back, but here's some advice. Never lend money to your friends."

Lisa: Hmm. That reminds me. . .

Alex: What?

Lisa: You owe me 50 bucks.

Page 218, Listen, Exercises A and B

Host: Welcome back to Car Chat! I'm your host Frank Evans, and I'm here with former traffic court judge Carl Mansfield. He's here to answer your questions about traffic violations. … Caller 1, you're on the air.

Caller 1: Hi, Carl. A police officer recently gave me a ticket for running a stop sign. But I couldn't see the sign because a tree branch was hanging over it. Do I really have to pay the fine?

Carl: It sounds like you're in the right. I advise you to ask for a trial to contest the ticket. But first go back to the stop sign and take a picture of it. Then you can show the picture to a judge in traffic court. He or she will probably dismiss the ticket.

Caller 1: Thanks, Carl.

Carl: You're welcome. Caller 2? How can I help you?

Caller 2: I've gotten a few traffic tickets, so I have some points on my license. I heard that if I go to traffic school, I can get the points on my license erased. Is that true?

Carl: Well, that depends on the state where you live. In this state, as long as your traffic violations aren't too serious, you can go to traffic school to get the points erased from your license. What kind of tickets are they?

Caller 2: Oh, they're mostly parking tickets. But I did get one ticket for speeding. How do I sign up for traffic school?

Carl: Well, it's easy. You can sign up online. After you complete the course, they'll give you a certificate. As soon as you show the certificate to the police, your driving record will be clean again.

Caller 2: Great! Thanks for the information!

UNIT 12

Page 226, Listen, Exercises A and B

John: Hello. What can I do for you?

Ling: Hi. I'd like to open a checking account.

John: OK. We have several options. Our MyMoney account is very popular. There's no monthly maintenance fee, and it has a pretty good interest rate.

Ling: That sounds good.

John: It requires a minimum balance of $1,500, though.

Ling: Uh … What happens if I go below fifteen hundred?

John: Well, you'll be charged a monthly maintenance fee.

Ling: I see. You know, a lot of banks offer free checking. Don't you have something like that?

John: Sure we do. You want an interest-free checking account then. There's no minimum balance requirement.

Ling: Yeah, interest-free checking—that's what I want. Are there any fees I should know about?

John: Well, the usual—you pay an overdraft fee if you write a check or make an automatic bill payment for more than the amount in your checking account. If you're interested, the bank offers overdraft protection for a monthly flat fee.

Ling: And how much is that?

John: $30.

Ling: No, thanks. I'll just have to keep an eye on my account balance.

John: OK … Interest-free checking then. Let me get your information …

Page 232, Listen, Exercises A and B

Host: Welcome back to MoneyWise. I'm Helen Duncan. We're here today with financial expert Patricia Wong. Patricia is taking questions from our listeners now. Here's our first caller.

Rafael: Hi, Patricia, I'm Rafael. Thanks for taking my call.

Patricia: No problem. I'm here to help you with your money questions. Go ahead.

Rafael: I have a lot of debt, and I'm having a hard time paying all my bills each month.

Patricia: What kind of debt, Rafael?

Rafael: Credit card and some personal loans.

Patricia: How much in personal loans and credit card debt are we talking about?

Rafael: Uh, I borrowed $5,000 from my credit union and I have about $20,000 in credit card debt.

Patricia: I see. That's $25,000 more or less. How old are you and what do you do?

Rafael: 27. I work in a hospital—I'm a technician.

Patricia: And what's the interest rate on your credit cards?

Rafael: They vary—from 9.99% to 18%.

Patricia: Whoa! What happened? Why 18%?

Rafael: Well, I missed a payment on one of my credit card bills.

Patricia: That's what usually happens. Well, your situation isn't hopeless, Rafael. The first thing that you should do is talk to the credit card companies. Try to get the rate lowered on the card with the 18% interest rate. If they lower the rate by just a point or two, it will make a big difference in your monthly payment.

Rafael: OK. I'll try.

Patricia: Next, if you can, pay off the cards with the highest interest rate by increasing your monthly payment. Let's say you're paying $50 a month now on a balance of $1000. If you increase your monthly payment to $75, you'll finish paying the loan seven months sooner.

Rafael: That sounds like something I can do. It's just $25 a month more than I'm paying now.

Patricia: Here's one more idea for you: try to get a second job and use your second income to pay off your debt. If you follow just one or two of those suggestions, you'll start reducing your debt in no time. Good luck.

Rafael: Thanks so much, Patricia. Those are all good suggestions.

Page 238. Listen, Exercises A and B

Eduardo: Hey, what would you do if you suddenly inherited a lot of money?

Chantal: I'd be quiet about it, and I'd keep working for a while. Why?

Eduardo: This guy in my office—turns out he had a rich uncle. Well, the uncle died and left him half a million!

Chantal: Really? What's he going to do with the money?

Eduardo: He already spent it! He bought a really expensive sports car and a motorcycle! Then he quit his job. And now he's traveling around the world.

Chantal: That's crazy. That money will disappear quickly. If I came into a lot of money, I would do something more useful with it.

Eduardo: Like what?

Chantal: I'd go to medical school. I've always dreamed of becoming a doctor.

Eduardo: You don't like being a nurse?

Chantal: I do, but I'd rather be a doctor.

Eduardo: Then you'd still work here?

Chantal: No, I'd go back home—to Haiti. I'd build a clinic in my village, and I'd give the people in my village free medical care.

Eduardo: You have such a good heart! As for me, if I found myself with a lot of money, I'd probably spend it on myself!

Chantal: What would you do?

Eduardo: I'd quit my job for sure. I don't like my job. Then I'd pay off all my debts. Finally, I'd buy a big house on the beach.

Chantal: But wouldn't you get lonely in that big house all by yourself?

Eduardo: Oh, no! I wouldn't live there by myself. I'd invite my parents, my brothers and sisters, cousins, even my closest friends to live with me.

Chantal: Whoa! That would be an entire village!

Eduardo: Exactly. Imagine what fun that would be. Of course, I'd invite you to come and visit me.

Chantal: It's a deal!

Index

Credits

Photo credits

All original photography by Richard Hutchings/Digital Light Source. Page 4 (top) Shutterstock, (bottom) Shutterstock; 5 Jack Hollingsworth/Corbis; 10 Devorah Hernandez; 18 Design Pics Inc./Alamy; 25 Blend Images/Alamy; 38 Michael Newman/PhotoEdit; 45 Ambient Images Inc./Alamy; 46 (top) David Young Wolff/PhotoEdit; 52 Michael Newman/PhotoEdit; 56 Rudi Von Briel/PhotoEdit; 58 (bottom) Kayte M. Deioma/PhotoEdit; 59 Michelle D. Bridwell/PhotoEdit; 65 Jupiterimages/Pixland/Alamy; 76 Image Source/Getty Images; 85 Visions of America, LLC/Alamy; 90 Roger Ressmeyer/Corbis; 92 Stockbyte Platinum/Getty Images; 93 Salina Journal/Jeff Cooper/Associated Press/PA Photos; 98 Blend Images/Alamy; 99 iStockphoto.com; 105 Stockbyte/Getty Images; 106 Robert Brenner/PhotoEdit; 112 Roger McClean/iStockphoto.com; 116 Shutterstock; 125 Bob Daemmrich/PhotoEdit; 126 Blend Images/Alamy; 133 William Casey/Alamy; 145 Image Source Black/Alamy; 146 Jose Luis Pelaez Inc./Photolibrary; 152 Joan Slatkin/Omni-Photo Communications; 165 Blend Images/Getty Images; 176 Shutterstock; 185 Jeff Greenberg/PhotoEdit; 188 Andersen Ross/Getty Images; 190 (top left) Ian McDonnell/iStockphoto.com; (middle left) Bill Varie/Corbis, (top right) Shutterstock, (bottom) Brown Brothers/WPA/Franklin D. Roosevelt Presidential Library; 192 (top) David R. Frazier Photolibrary, Inc./Alamy, (bottom) Kim Steele/Photolibrary; 198 Jupiterimages/Photos.com; 205 Ron Chapple/Getty Images; 206 (left) Jeffrey Coolidge/Getty Images, (middle) iStockphoto.com; (right) Rob Walls/Alamy; 212 Bubbles Photolibrary/Alamy; 216 Mario Villafuerte/Getty Images; 219 Shutterstock; 225 Helene Rogers/Alamy; 230 Mia Song/Star Ledger/Corbis; 238 Heide Benser/zefa/Corbis.

Illustration Credits

Luis Briseño pp. 52, 87, 107, 127, 132; Laurie Conley pp. 124, 144, 164, 184, 204, 210, 224, 244; Deborah Crowle p. 97; Brian Hughes p. 51; Stephen MacEachern pp. 58, 61; Luis Montiel pp. 24, 44, 64, 84, 138, 158-159; Allan Moon pp. 136, 156; Fred Willingham pp. 128, 178, 186;